Reviews Of THE HOMOPOLAR HANDBOOK by Thomas Valone

1 of 1 people found the following review helpful:
Good approach for understanding it, September 23, 2001
Reviewer: Marco Antonio de la Cuadra from Santiago de Chile
The Valone book is a good compilation of Valone's work and homopolar phenomena. If you want to build some weird machine, you can start by reading it but don't believe here is the clue. For this, better read Mr. Bruce de Palma and others.

9 of 9 people found the following review helpful:
Review of Thomas Valone's work in homopolar R&D, April 6, 2000
Reviewer: **David B. Hamilton** from USA Tom has done a good job in providing a text that is a recording of historical events and his own experiences homopolar research and development with a very detailed appendix. Although the homopolar motor is a bit of an anomaly in traditional electromagnetics, Tom provides a reasonable explanation for the experimental results and other developments. The discussion of relativistic effects of rotating systems is quite insightful and would indicate that classical Electromagnetic theory needs an update!

Review of The Homopolar Handbook , J. of New Energy, Feb 1995
Reviewer: **Hal Fox, PhD** from USA (excerpt) In the 1980s, Valone became very interested in the homopolar motor, first discovered by Faraday in 1831. The result has been both experimental and investigative research…In between, Valone has written forthrightly and without the flurry of emotion that often attends discussion of past relics and future promises… For anyone who would be involved in the development of financing of homopolar motors or generators, this book should be carefully studied. Valone does not predict that this type of machine will provide over-unity energy, nor does he deny future developments. He does note that no one, to his knowledge, has proven that such a device can generate more energy than used to drive the device. … [It is an] excellent contribution [that] Valone makes to the subject.

Also by the author and most available from Integrity Research Institute (see website)

BOOKS:
Electrogravitics Systems: A New Propulsion Methodology, 1994,
Proceedings of the Conference on Future Energy (COFE1), 1999
Zero Point Energy: The Fuel of the Future, 2007
Harnessing the Wheelwork of Nature: Tesla's Science of Energy, 2003
Electrogravitics II: Validating Reports on a New Propulsion Methodology, 2004
Proceedings of COFE2, 2006 – Proceedings of COFE3, 2009 – Proc. of SPESIF 2012

REPORTS & BOOKLETS (expanded reprints of published articles)
Energy Policy Recommendations, 69 pages, online at IRI website, 2009
Energy Crisis, Comprehensive National Energy Strategy Evaluation, 2000
Electromagnetic Fields and Life Processes
Inertial Propulsion: Concept and Experiment (Parts I & II)
Scalar Potentials, Fields, and Waves
T.T. Brown's Electrogravitics Research
Tesla Technology Research Report
The Origin of Life Experiments of Andrija Puharich, MD, LLD
Non-Conventional Energy and Propulsion Database
The Implications of the Backster Effect: An Appeal to the Scientific Community

ARTICLES
Spiral Magnetic Motor – Electrokinetics – Zero Bias Diode, journal peer-reviewed papers online at IRI website
How Energy Medicine Will Save Healthcare, *Superconsciousness,* Issue 4, Vol. 4, 2011
Celebrating Nikola Tesla, *Infinite Energy,* Guest Editor for Issue 89, 2010
Zero Point Energy is the Fuel of the Future, *Explore for the Professional,* V. 18, No. 6, 2009
Energy of the Future, *Superconsciousness,* Issue 4, Vol. 2, 2008
Energy Challenges: the Next Thousand Years, *Humanity Three Thousand,* Foundation for the Future, 2007
Raising Questions: Reopening the File on Electrogravitics, *Atlantis Rising,* Number 24, 2000, p.39
Future Energy Technologies, *Proc. of the World Future Society Confer.,* 2000
New Physics Patents, *Science,* Vol. 284, June 18, 1999, p. 1929
Electrogravitics Research of T. Townsend Brown, *Exotic Research,* Vol. 2, No. 12, 1999
Inside Zero Point Energy, *Infinite Energy,* Vol. 5, No. 25, 1999, p.53
Air Purification, Using Tesla's Ionizer and Ozonator, *TESLA: A Jour. Of Mod. Sci.,* 1st Qtr.,1997
The Real Story of the N-Machine, *Extraordinary Science,* 1996
Fresh Air Curative Effect, Related to Ions and Traces of Ozone, *Explore More,* Nov 16, 1996, 21
Tesla Technology Research Results, *Proceedings of the Int. Tesla Symp.,* 1992
Inertial Propulsion: Concept and Experiment (Parts I & II), *Proc. of the IECEC,* 1991, 1992
Nonconventional Energy and Propulsion Methods, *Proceedings of the Int. Tesla Symp.,* 1990
Tesla's History in Western New York, *Proc. of ITS,* 1986
The Homopolar Generator, Tesla's Contribution, *Proc. of ITS,* 1986
The One-Piece Faraday Generator, *Proc. of the 1st Inter. Symp. on Nonconventional Energy,* 1981

THE HOMOPOLAR HANDBOOK
A Definitive Guide to Faraday Disk and N-Machine Technologies

A scientific investigation into an alleged UFO energy source

Thomas Valone, Ph.D., P.E.
Foreword by Gary L. Johnson, Ph.D.

Integrity Research Institute

Cover Photo: FARA-DRUM 10, courtesy of Parker-Kinetic Design, Inc.

Figure 1 from The Electrical Experimenter, Sept. 2, 1891
Figure 2 courtesy of J. Wiley & Sons, New York
Figure 7 courtesy of American Assoc. of Physics Teachers ,
Figure 9 courtesy of CBS College Publishing
"Parameter Selection" article reprinted by permission of Taylor & Francis, owners of Hemisphere Pub.

"Swoosh! It's a Railgun" article reprinted by permission of TIME magazine.
"Origin of the Force on a Current-Carrying Conductor" reprinted by permission of American Association of Physics Teachers.
"Real Story of the N-Machine" and "Homopolar Generator, Tesla's Contribution" reproduced with permission of the International Tesla Society.
"Investigation of the N-Effect" reprinted by permission of Tim Wilhelm
"Critique of Trombly-Kahn N-Machine" reprinted by permission of Bruce DePalma
"Researchers See Long Life..." reprinted courtesy of Phillips Publishing.
Proposal to Dart Industries reprinted courtesy of Edgar Mitchell
Excerpt of Dr. D.C. White's Report reprinted courtesy of Dr. White
"Interview with a Physicist" reprinted courtesy of Awe Gusts
"Roller Magnet Experiments" courtesy of Electric Spacecraft Journal, Leicester, NC
"New Paradigm and N-Machine" courtesy of Dr. S. Inomata

The Homopolar Handbook:
A Definitive Guide to Faraday Disk and N-Machine Technologies

First Edition, October, 1994
Second Edition October 1998
Third Edition, October 2001
Fourth Edition, August 2012

ISBN 978-0964107014

Published by:
Integrity Research Institute 5020 Sunnyside Avenue, Suite 209, Beltsville MD 20705, Phone: 301-220-0440, 800-295-7674

Visit our Website at: www.IntegrityResearchInstitute.org

ACKNOWLEDGEMENTS

The subtitle word "N-Machine" comes from Bruce DePalma of Santa Barbara, DePalma Institute. Acknowledgement and credit is given to him for assigning it to the one-piece Faraday generator when it is attached to a Faraday disk motor, as illustrated in one of his drawings in the Appendix.

For their help, support, encouragement, and intellectual aid, I would like to acknowledge the following people, each unique in their own way and invaluable: Bruce DePalma, Dr. George Land, Adam Trombly, Dan Winter, Tim Wilhelm, Dr. Hans Nieper, Dr. Dollinger, Dr. Jonathan Reichert, Joe Beldon, Norman Paulsen, the late C. Bernard, Astronaut Edgar Mitchell, Dr. Dimock, Ed Furlani, George Hathaway, Pat Kujawa, Dave Alexander, Dr. Pat Flanagan, Ken MacNeil, and Lynn Surgalla. Also, I wish to acknowledge the SUNYAB Physics Machine Shop which provided excellent service, as well as Erie Community College which was very accommodating to allow my generator to occupy laboratory space for an extended period of time.

My special thanks to Rita Fryer without whose help this book might have been delayed indefinitely.

My special, special thanks to my wife Jackie, who patiently scanned the camera ready version of this book and made this electronic version available for publication. Her support and patience in all my projects for many years has been invaluable and cannot be expressed in words.

COVER PHOTOS: The FARA-DRUM 10 Homopolar Generator. Photo of Edgar Mitchell at Bruce DePalma's workshop in 1980 courtesy of George A. Land

This machine operates at 10 megajoules and 1.5 megamperes output (see specification sheets on P. 45 & 46). The FARA-DRUM 10 is the only commercially available homopolar generator in the world at the time of this printing. It sports the highest energy density (1000 Jzkg) and the highest current density output of any homopolar generator ever manufactured. Thanks to Clif Drummond, President of Parker Kinetic Designs, Inc., Austin, Texas, for permission to use photo and data sheets in this handbook.

Previously published under the title:

The One-Piece Faraday Generator: Theory and Experiment

FOREWORD

While teaching the first electromagnetics course at Kansas State University, I would usually take in demonstrations to illustrate some of the theoretical concepts. For Faraday's Law I would take in a permanent magnet, a coil of wire, and an analog voltmeter, and show deflection of the meter when the magnet was moved with respect to the coil, and the same deflection when the coil was moved with respect to the magnet. I would comment about the inability of the meter to tell which was moving, the coil or the magnet, and that this was consistent with Special Relativity.

About a decade ago, I read some papers on Faraday disk generators, or the homopolar generator, that indicated the results were different when rotary motion was involved rather than linear motion. The meter would deflect only when the disk moved, *but not when the magnet moved*. This struck me as unexpected, so I decided to build my own classroom demonstrator. I took a disk of 16 oz. copper flashing, purchased from the local plumbing shop, and mounted it on a small DC motor. A large disk magnet from a loudspeaker was mounted on another DC motor. Copper cups were made to hold mercury for a low impedance brush contact. A second, smaller copper disk was mounted concentric with the larger disk, and another mercury was attached to it to form the second contact. Both shafts were horizontal.

The main problem was my inability to get this mercury to uniformly wet the copper. Part of the perimeter of the disk was nicely coated with mercury, while the remainder was reasonably clean copper. The wetting effect would cause mercury in the cup to flow up on the disk during part of the rotation, and away from the disk for the non-wetted portion. This movement would cause the mercury to splash out of the cups if the rotation speed was very high. After reading safety bulletins on mercury poisoning, I kept the disk speed rather low, but still adequate to deflect the meter.

I would take the homopolar generator into class, rotate the disk with the magnet fixed, and observe the meter deflection. Then, I would ask the class to predict what would happen if the disk were fixed and the magnet rotated. After the demonstration of the linear motion case and the discussion on relative motion, most of the class would predict the same deflection. They would then feel stupid when the magnet was rotated, even at much higher speeds than the disk, and there was *no deflection* of the meter. I would also show them that the meter deflection remained the same for a given rotational speed of the disk, whether the magnet was rotated at the same speed in the same direction, in the opposite direction, or faster or slower. After a comment about Special Relativity only applying to linear motion, we would move on to other considerations or Faraday's Law.

Like these students, I find the homopolar generator to be frustrating. It still seems to me that if the magnetic field is made of lines of flux produced by spinning electrons around iron atoms, then when the iron is rotated, the lines should rotate also. Another way of saying this is to note that Faraday's Law has two quite different explanations: flux cutting and flux linking. Transformers are explained in terms of flux linking since there is no relative motion, but systems with relative motion can usually be explained both ways. It is quite instructive to derive the voltage of the homopolar generator both ways for the disk rotating and the magnet fixed. In the case of the disk fixed and the magnet rotating, flux linkage explains the result correctly while flux cutting does not (assuming that individual spinning electrons produce individual flux lines). If a student would ask how one knows which explanation to use when they disagree, my response, stripped of all elegant double-talk, would be: "I am the professor, trust me. Someone has determined which explanation works in each pathological case, and the student needs to memorize which explanation is accepted for each case." Needless to say, I always hoped no one would ask this question.

The homopolar generator dates back to 1831 but has not had significant commercial success because it is inherently a low voltage, high current machine. A 10 kW generator might be rated at 2 volts and 5000 amps. Such voltages and currents are extremely difficult to convert to 120 VAC in an efficient manner. Construction of the generator is non-trivial, so costs tend to be high. There are perhaps three possible benefits of research and development of the homopolar generator:

1) The first is for those niche markets which need a low voltage, high current machine, such as for pulsed welding, high current switch testing, billet heating, pulsed power experiments, and military railguns. This book will be very helpful to those doing such research.

2) Another possible benefit, alluded to in the book, is a combined homopolar generator/homopolar motor on the same shaft, which can extract energy from the surrounding space in an over-unity fashion such that mechanical power can be utilized to drive a conventional synchronous generator. This book carefully documents that such over-unity operation has not yet been demonstrated, at least not to everyone's satisfaction.

3) A third possible benefit would be to lead one of us to think new thoughts about the world around us. Suppose, for example, we model a magnet as a waveguide or conduit for virtual photons from the vacuum. Ferromagnetic materials might be said to make better waveguides than nonferromagnetic materials for reasons different from our old model of spinning electrons. Magnets would be similar to diodes in this line of thought, in that they allow only one way passage of an energy packet from the surrounding space. Then all we need to do is to complete the circuit in order to extract energy from the vacuum. This may or may not be a better explanation than what we have been taught. In fact, a more productive or more realistic explanation is likely to be fat different from this one. The point is that we need some different explanations of this experimental observation. If thinking about the homopolar generator causes someone to develop a concept to tap into a new energy source, all this work will have been worthwhile.

This book contains the references for homopolar generator papers that would be available in a good research library. Also, copies of hard-to-find papers are reprinted in the Appendix. It is a good contribution to the technical literature on a most interesting subject.

Dr. Gary L. Johnson
Professor Emeritus
Department of Electrical and Computer Engineering
Kansas State University
Manhattan, KS 66506

PREFACE

Before going into the main part of this book which details the formal report. I would like to put down on record the series of events which led me to pursue this research, with high hopes.

I started in 1980 with a book by Norman Paulsen, entitled, *Sunburst, Return of the Ancients* (now in its 2nd edition, retitled as *The Christ Consciousness*, published by the Solar Logos Foundation but it is now missing the rotating disk information reprinted in the Appendix of this book, probably for the reason that Paulsen shared with me: humankind may not be ready for this information and might use it for destructive purposes). It seemed like a very interesting autobiography with some unusual UFO stories associated with George Van Tassel. One such experience included a trip on a saucer which was very large. Part of the experience also involved seeing the "engine room" and receiving a description of its operation. There were two disks rotating in opposite directions, either one of which provided electrical power for the ship. Mr. Paulsen has since described these disks to me as non-conducting disks with magnets that had radial, instead of axial, magnetic orientation. The homopolar generator has axial magnets because of the north/south direction of the magnetic field which is along the axis. However, Mr. Paulsen did not override the Sunburst Community's interest in the DePalma generator, even though he recognized that it was substantially different than the one he experienced.

That summer, as I planned a trip to California, I contacted the community and arranged to visit them. Upon arriving, I found that it took about three days to win their confidence before I was permitted to see the $25,000 investment they had made, with the help of Mr. Bruce DePalma, formerly of 1055 Channel Drive, Santa Barbara, CA, to try and produce a generator similar to that which Norman Paulsen had seen on the ship. Bruce calls it the "N -Machine", having "N" number of applications.

What I found also, which I have included a sample of in the Appendix, was the laboratory notebook of a certain Charya Bernard who worked on several designs of magnetic disk configurations, before Bruce DePalma came onto the scene (Bernard's lab notebook excerpt is reproduced courtesy of The Builders, now renamed as the Solar Logos Foundation). These designs try to reproduce what Norman saw on his trip but without the specifications that he mentioned to me. (Mr. Paulsen was not very free with the information for he was told at the time of his trip that the world was not ready for the information). However, the story is that most of the designs that were built and tested did not work (note the circuitous conductor paths that are included in the drawing.) Unfortunately, Bernard passed away in 1979, so I didn't have a chance to talk to him. I am now taking steps to continue my research in the direction of electrostatic generators instead of unipolar or homopolar magnets.

After I left California in 1980, I began having conversations with Bruce and corresponded through the mail. Bruce DePalma was a great help in describing in detail what had happened in all of his experiments and was very willing to supply any information that I requested.

At the time I became involved in the project, Bruce was working for a famous eye doctor named Morgan Raiford. After receiving a batch of material from Bruce (including the Santa Barbara News-Press article reproduced in the Appendix), I informed my friend, Dr. George Ainsworth-Land, author of *Grow or Die*, (Dell Pub., 1973) about DePalma's ideas. George, being a scientist, was interested in the simplicity of the concept and began to research Faraday's writings to learn more. After doing some experiments of his own, he decided the generator was worth investigating. He then informed his friend, astronaut Edgar Mitchell, about Bruce DePalma, and together they took a trip to Santa Barbara to visit him (see picture in the Appendix).

About the same time, I decided to attend the Gravity- Field Energy Conference being sponsored by Dr. Hans Nieper, in West Germany, during November of 1980 (see Appendix). Dr. Nieper's last book, *Revolution in Technology, Medicine, and Science*, is available from the A. Keith Brewer Science Library, Richland Center, WI 53581. Bruce had sent me information about the conference since he was invited to speak at the conference, but he was advised not to attend because of the patent application that he was filing. When he told me that, I felt that my presence there would be of benefit to gain information and to represent Bruce by possibly giving a talk in his place.

At this point, I had already decided to build a generator of my own (as do most people who learn of this strange method of generating electricity). Also, since I needed a project to finish my Master's Degree in Physics at SUNY, I was planning to work with a good professor that I knew, Dr. Jonathan Reichert, to do it for credit Therefore, when I arrived in Germany, I was equipped with drawings and transparencies of designs that I had developed.

My experience of the conference is reproduced courtesy of Energy Unlimited magazine for the reader's benefit in the Appendix. It was certainly an exciting adventure. Areal plus was getting time to talk with Adam Trombly who was building a very expensive model of the one-piece homopolar generator with liquid Sodium-Potassium brushes. We found a lot to talk about since Adam knew Bruce very well and also had several investors in his company called "Acme Energy Research" which had an operating budget of a few hundred thousand dollars. (Adam says that ACME is an acronym for Acyclic Closed Magnetic Experiment.)

Following the conference, I also contacted Mr. Tim Wilhelm, whose organization, The Stelle Group (Stelle, IL 60919), was represented in Germany as well. Tim was also working on a large one-piece Faraday Homopolar generator, using mercury brushes, with the funding of the Stelle Group (see Appendix for pictures and drawing of Tim and his machine). He subsequently found and measured a predicted amount of back torque which confirmed classical physics and obtained no extra free energy output

THOMAS VALONE

DAS UNIPOLARHANDBUCH

EIN GRUNDLAGENWERK DER FREIEN ENERGIE:
FARADAY-SCHEIBE UND N-TECHNOLOGIEN

German edition of this book

After the Mitchell and Ainsworth-Land journey to DePalma's garage, Dart Industries was contacted for possible funding of an expanded project to prove the principle that the back torque, or drag of the generator when power is drawn from it, could be significantly lessened with the correct design (this is called the "N-effect" by Bruce). As one can see from the Mitchell letter to Dart Industries in the Appendix dated Feb., 1981, the project was thorough and steps for review and verification were built into the plan. Immediately, Dr. D.C. White from MIT''s Energy Lab was called in to see the video tape that Bruce had of the Sunburst Machine and to evaluate the validity of his claims. An excerpt from his written report is included in the Appendix.

At this point, two major stumbling blocks occurred: 1) Dr. D.C. White's report was like throwing water onto a fire, effectively casting doubts into the minds of everyone involved, except for Bruce; 2) Bruce decided to sign a contract with Dr. Morgan Raiford instead of Mitchell and Ainsworth-Land. Dr. White's findings were not unexpected based on the unavailability of the Sunburst Machine and the poor quality of the video presentation. However, it was still a letdown to learn of the withdrawal of the Mitchell/Ainsworth-Land/Dart team from the research. For those interested in the details, you may buy a copy of Bruce DePalma's 1984 USPA conference presentation, which included a showing of the Sunburst video, for $23 postpaid from the U.S. Psychotronics Association, www.psychotronics.org.

In previous editions of this book, I have usually emphasized at this point in the story the important points that Adam Trombly and Bruce DePalma make concerning the optimum design of an N-Machine homopolar generator. First, the brush resistance should be very small, on the order of a couple of microhms, in order to increase the output power capability. Secondly, the idea of "completing the magnetic circuit" through an outer steel shell is included in the Trombly device (Acme Energy Research) and is endorsed by DePalma (see *Energy Unlimited*, Summer 1984). In both regards, as can be seen from my equivalent circuits and diagrams, my Faraday generator did not meet these specifications.

However, with Trombly's consulting services, Paramahansa Tewari has designed an N-Machine motor/generator combination with both conditions built into it, in 1993. Unfortunately, his machine also suffers from a large back torque, despite his claims to the contrary. My analysis of his 1993 paper to the Inter. Assoc. for New Science Conference in Denver is included in the Appendix.

Adam Trombly, a few years after the Raiford funding of DePalma's project, described his final experiments to me, the Acme generator before the machine broke its axle sometime in 1982. The machine suffered what one scientist called "parasitic uniaxle breakdown". The iron core of the generator was powdered after this breakdown. How that could have happened is not well understood. An analysis showed a "flash process disaggregation along grain boundaries" which he feels any good metallurgist could correct by carefully regulating the amount of silicon iron. Adam claims that the efficiency was close to 250% when the device self-destructed, well below the rated level of output. Knowing how careful Adam had been in all of our conversations with calculations and instrumentation, I feel that he may have taken precise measurements. (Even power factor meters were used to determine the effective power output) Whether or not the machine could actually power itself, which is what Adam bought a $10,000 DC to AC inverter for, is anyone's guess. For those interested, Bruce DePalma's "Critique of the N-Machine Constructed by Trombly and Kahn" 10/15/85, including a complete copy of the international PCT application, is included in the Appendix, with permission of the DePalma Institute.

Adam's Acme generator has been kept from public scrutiny ever since it was built and even the lab notes and records have never been published. Years later, everyone wonders if Trombly really built and tested an N-Machine! Trombly told me that his brush design was modified after the patent was issued, for the U.S. patent application. Interestingly, the U.S. Patent Office rejected the Acme Patent application the first time, on the grounds that the electrical generation method was impossible (homopolar generators usually have that effect on scientists). They even gave Adam the comment "No way will it work". Then, upon reapplying, the Patent Office rejected it a second time, claiming "prior art", even though the brush design was novel. (The electrical generation method has been in the public domain since Faraday's time so the brush may have been the only patentable part of the machine.)

Unfortunately, the Office of Naval Intelligence stepped in shortly afterwards (since all of the U.S. military agencies review all relevant patent applications before the patent examiners have a look at them) and stamped Trombly's brush design "CLASSIFIED". He is now prohibited to talk about the NaK brush design to anyone. If he does, he has to report the name of that person to the Office of Naval Intelligence. Adam feels that the project was a success. However, he doesn't think that all of the expensive design work the generator required was balanced by the reliability that he had hoped for. He feels that there are other generators, such as the Gray Motor which offer high reliability along with over-unity performance. A copy of his presentation to the Second International Symposium of Non-Conventional Energy (1983) is available from the Planetary Assoc. for Clean Energy (100 Bronson Ave., Suite 1001, Ottawa, Ontario K1R 6G8 Canada).

The first few years of the 1980's were very exciting to me. As our collective knowledge continues to grow, stretching the boundaries of science and awareness, the future has to improve.

Thomas Valone
Washington, DC.
1994 (updated in 2012)

The DePalma N-1 Machine which used liquid mercury wetted contacts and 7000 gauss magnets producing 800 amperes of DC current at 1.2 volts per 1000 rpm or about 3.1 VDC at 800 amperes which is about 2.4 kW with about 5 kW input into the motor. DePalma however indicated that the efficiency estimate of the motor was the key to arguing for an over-unity condition. (ref.: Magnets in Your Future magazine, AZ Industries publishers, August, 1988, p. 4-7)

TABLE OF CONTENTS

INTRODUCTION

The combination of cylindrical magnet and disk, rotating together, has been the center of controversy that still rages to this day. In this investigation, the history is traced, theories proposed, and a single prototype is experimentally analyzed. Many literary confusions have been omitted for the sake of continuity.

The one-piece Faraday generator is a special case of the general homopolar generator which is illustrated in Figure 1. Several terms are used to describe this electrical generator in the literature, e.g. unipolar, homopolar, acyclic, and Faraday disk dynamo. However, all of them signify a Faraday generator without distinguishing between a stationary and rotating magnet. The IEEE Standard Dictionary of Electrical and Electronic Terms (IEEE, New York, NY, 2nd ed.), defines "acyclic machine" as "a direct-current machine in which the voltage generated in the active conductors maintains the same direction with respect to those conductors." This is also regarded as the preferred term because the generator's electric field is acyclic or irrotational since its curl is equal to zero.

As Technology Illustrated points out, "the homopolar generator is unique in that no other rotary electric machine can produce DC without using rectifiers or commutators" [1]. The article also describes a machine developed at the Center for Electromagnetics of the University of Texas at Austin that can generate up to 100 megawatts with currents as high as one million amperes. Though such machines have many industrial uses because of their 95% efficiency, this one was designed with quick braking for military railgun applications (see Appendix). As we shall see, "back torque" or "armature reaction" is developed even in the one-piece generators when current is produced. However, we can work the opposite way to produce a high current burst by applying a tremendous torque.

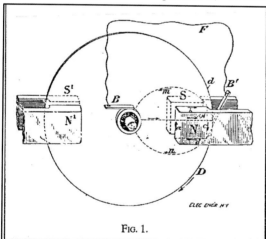

FIG. 1.

One of the largest homopolar generators in the world has been developed by the Northern Engineering Industries in England. It is estimated that the output of the machine is capable of producing 1300 megawatts continuously with the help of superconducting magnets [2].

The concept of a self-excited generator is used in some applications (see Sears Patent #3,185,877) when an electromagnet is used. In Figure 2, we see that this method involves using some of the current output of the generator to excite the field windings of the magnet [3]. The interesting part about this is that two homopolar machines may be connected in such a way as to achieve two-phase AC power generation through self-limited oscillation of the magnetic field polarities [4]. It is pointed out that a similar process may be occurring within the earth, which would help explain the periodic reversals in earth's magnetic field.

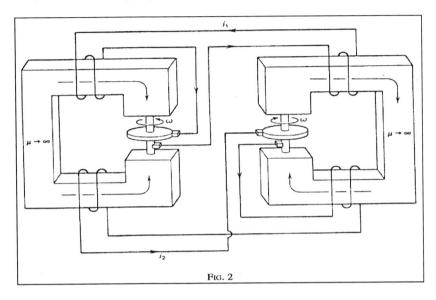

FIG. 2

HISTORICAL DEVELOPMENT OF THE FIELD ROTATION PARADOX

Now that a brief overview of acyclic generators has been provided, it can be seen that more often the field coils or the permanent magnets are left stationary. Then, the disk simply rotates between them. In my design however, the magnets are rotated with the disk (co-rotational) making the generator a "one-piece" like the earth itself. Thus, there is no stator with the one-piece Faraday generator. It seems to be equivalent, in term of electrical and mechanical behavior, to the case where the magnets are stationary. However, this paradox has resulted in an historical debate concerning the possible rotation of the magnetic field with the magnet. Even in the most recent journal publications, we see references to the unresolved physics involved.

With the very first experiments done by Michael Faraday recorded in his lab notebook [5] and also in his diary [6], using a cylindrical magnet and rotating conductor, he noted a peculiar property of the generator. Even when the conductor and the magnet were rotated together in unison, still the same voltages were developed. From 1831 onward, when Faraday first did these experiments, we see in the literature a recurring debate about the nature of a cylindrically symmetric rotating magnetic field, Faraday first published his results in the Philosophical Transactions of the Royal Society in 1832 stating the paradox:

Another point which I endeavored to ascertain, was, whether it was essential or not that the moving part of the wire would, in cutting the magnetic curves, pass into positions of greater or lesser magnetic force; or whether, always intersecting curves of equal magnetic intensity, the mere motion was sufficient for he production of current. That the latter is true, has been proved already in several of the experiments ... To prove the point with an ordinary magnet, a copper disc was cemented upon the end of a cylinder magnet... rotated together. The galvanometer needle moved as in former cases ... Hence, rotating the magnet causes no difference in the results; for a rotatory and a stationary magnet produce the same effect upon the moving copper [7].

One of the earliest articles on the subject that I could find is Professor W. Weber's "The Unipolar Induction" published in 1841. He refers to Ampere's explanation of the effect as applying "only ... to the rotation of the conductor about the magnet, discovered by Faraday, and not at all to the rotation of the magnet on its axis ... " [8]. However, Ampere considered it to be due to the same cause. We find S. Tolver Preston, in 1885, referring to Weber's ideas, as in agreement with his own and Ampere's, but opposite to Faraday's. He says, "the lines of force, or field of force, about a magnet must be considered in that sense fixed or dependent on the magnet, that this field of force rotates when the magnet rotates on its axis ... in the same sense as it would do if the magnet were bodily translated" [9]. He boasts at the end that in a recent letter, Lord Raleigh spoke favorably of his view.

Another interesting author is Plucker who, in 1852, performed a few experiments and concluded, " ... the lines of force emitted by a given portion of a magnetic surface must be considered as partaking of the motion of that portion of the surface ... " [10]. His strong conviction in the "lines of force" is typical of that period. Today we know that such a concept cannot be taken literally but we can loosely interpret the lines as a field concept.

It is humorous to see that by 1891, S. Tolver Preston has compromised and proposes, "It may be, of course, that the magnetic field partly partakes of the motion of the revolving magnet, or that something between the two hypotheses is true" [11].

In 1900, Poincare put forth the idea that even observations on open circuits cannot disprove the moving-line theory [12]. Then in 1917, we find a presumptuous title by Dr. E.H. Kennard, "On Unipolar Induction: Another Experiment and Its Significance as Evidence for the Existence of the Aether" in which he concludes at the end, "The disproof of the moving-line theory is thus completed" [13].

Other debaters of that period include: S.J. Barnett [14], S. Valentiner [15], C. Hering [16], and G.B. Pegram [17], just to mention a few. Whether or not the understanding of the unipolar induction grew with the number of authors contributing to the field is a matter of conjecture.

Another aspect of the field rotation paradox was Faraday's conclusion that since a rotating magnet produced a static charge, so must the earth produce a voltage between the equator and the poles. He records experiments in which he went out to rivers and streams to try and measure voltages across them. Though he failed, being a part of the moving body, he was still convinced that atmospheric disturbances such as the aurora borealis were due to the earth being a giant unipolar generator.

This problem has been taken up by many authors since then. Recently, J. Djuric even calculated how many thousands of volts were present between the equator and the poles, agreeing with Faraday [18]. However, in 1978, F. Lowes wrote a short article using a rigorous mathematical modeling of the earth and reached the conclusion that the voltage would only be present in the conducting part of the earth and would not be appreciably felt in the upper atmosphere. Also, he makes the point that only a non-rotating part of the atmosphere would experience such a voltage and much of the lower atmosphere rotates with the earth [19]. Also applying the unipolar mechanism to the cosmos, the August, 1983 issue of Scientific American (p. 44) does use it to explain how the magnetic fields of stars and planets may be amplified and maintained.

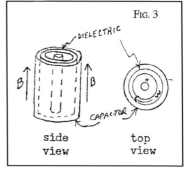

FIG. 3

side view   top view

In an experiment which shows a voltage effect across space, H.A. Wilson performed what is referred to as a "kind of inversion of Roentgen's experiment" [20]. (Remember that W.C. Roentgen rotated a dielectric between charged capacitor plates and found that it developed a magnetic field [21].) Wilson inserted a hollow, cylindrical dielectric into a stationary, uncharged cylindrical capacitor. With a uniform magnetic field along its axis, the stationary capacitor became charged when the dielectric was rotated [22]. This experiment, which is basically a homopolar effect, shows the effect of the static charge that is developed in the rotating dielectric (Fig. 3). G. Pegram also experimented with a coaxial capacitor and an electromagnet in 1917, though his results are debated [23].

To summarize, it may be mentioned that Pegram, Barnett, Kennard, and also Sir Joseph Larmor, did agree that in unipolar induction, the "seat of the electromotive force" is in the conductor [24][25]. However, there was no consensus as to the nature of a rotating magnetic field. Today, theorists agree that in principle, it is impossible to experimentally distinguish between a rotating and nonrotating magnetic field such as in the one-piece Faraday generator [26][27]. Yet, the generator continues to puzzle scientists, causing repeats of Faraday's experiments and the publication of results [28][29].

A quote from a paper by Moon and Spencer illustrates the problem beautifully:

> The subject has been discussed ever since the time of Faraday. For instance an extensive study was made by Lecher [30] in 1895. Some paradoxes were presented by Hering [31] in 1908. Blondel [32] and others argued about the subject in 1915. Another discussion occurred in the Jour. I.E. [33] in 1936. Cohn, Bewley, and Slepiam [34] exchanged some rapier thrusts in Electrical Engineering, 1949 and 1950. Various other studies have been made by physicists [35]. In each case interest seems to rise anew to a sharp peak, after which it gradually declines, leaving the subject much as it was before [36].

HISTORY OF THE TORQUE CONTROVERSY

Only in this century do there appear to be articles published dealing specifically with the torque developed in a homopolar motor or the relationship between the current into it and the magnetic field. This is of interest because of the back torque (armature reaction) that is developed in a homopolar generator when current is drawn from it. The electrons are being pushed away from their radial path by the magnetic field and interacting with the atomic lattice to produce a force or torque. (McKinnon, et.al. explains the microscopic origin of the $F=L(i \times B)$ force in AIP 49(5), 1981, p.493, as due to the transverse Hall field EH and an extra force F' caused by the positive ions.)

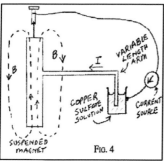

Fig. 4

In 1915, G.W.O. Howe thought that the torque was due to a reaction between the external flux of the magnet and the circuit external to the disk [37]. In 1924, Zelany and Page made a test of the torque on a homopolar motor. They attached "the external circuit" to the magnet by means of a radial arm (see Fig. 4) [38]. The radial arm was exposed to the returning magnetic field of the magnet and therefore caused a torque in the opposite direction to that within the magnet. Showing the extent of the magnetic field, it wasn't until the radial arm reached thirty times the radius of the magnet that the opposing torque went to zero. This showed that it is possible for the external circuit (radial arm) to experience a torque due to (1) the current passing through it and (2) the external magnetic field of the magnet. It does not prove that the torque within the magnet is related to the torque outside it as these early homopolar pioneers would lead you to believe. This experiment was also repeated by A.L. Kimball in 1926 [39].

What Howe and Kimball as well as others have sought to explain is the **Number One Homopolar Mystery**: *the torque is created within the conducting magnet without an apparent equal and opposite reaction!* In a famous 1936 experiment performed by Cramp and Norgrove (Fig. 5), the mystery was plainly illustrated with a disk rotated below a cylindrical magnet, current drawn from it and its back torque calculated. "Assuming the electromagnetic torque to react upon the magnet" [40], they then looked for any slight movement of the suspended magnet with the help of a mirror mounted on the top of it and a beam of light

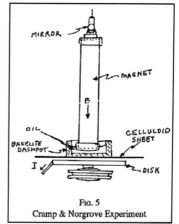

Fig. 5
Cramp & Norgrove Experiment

No movement of the magnet was detected at any speed of the disk. A similar experiment was performed in 1963 by A.K. Das Gupta when he mounted a disk and magnet freely and then passed current into the disk. With the idea that me adjacent magnet might react to the torque developed in the disk, he looked for, but could not detect, any movement of the magnet. In this case a disk magnet was used which more surface area had exposed to the current in the disk [41].

Though Howe, Kimball, and even Das Gupta demonstrate that the external circuit can react to the presence of the magnetic field (Das Gupta mentions that his wires moved a bit), it still does not resolve the *angular momentum question* that becomes apparent when one studies the lack of its conservation in the above experiments.

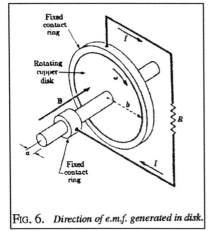

FIG. 6. *Direction of e.m.f. generated in disk.*

Richard Feynman also proposed a similar paradox in his Feynman Lectures on Physics [42]. In his example, charged metallic spheres mounted on a plastic disk cause the disk to rotate when a coaxial electromagnet on the disk suddenly interrupts its current and thus, its magnetic field. Its resolution, as well as the resolution of the torque controversy, was made clear in an article by G. Lombardi [43] as well as in a textbook by Landau and Lifshitz [44]. Lombardi points out that *static electromagnetic fields have angular momentum* and that this must be considered when computing the total conserved quantity. The angular momentum of the fields is the volume integral of r ×(E×B) from the text. In a book by Lorrain and Corson, an explanation is attempted but is not based on such a rigorous approach. They simply state, based upon relativistic transformations, that "Forces that are equal and opposite in one frame are not necessarily so in another frame. They remain equal and opposite only if their points of application have equal velocities" [45]

CLASSICAL THEORY OF THE FARADAY DISK DYNAMO

There are many approaches to analyzing the production of electromotive force in the Faraday generator. They range from the simple to the complex in their attempt to apply various physical theories to its operation. In Fig. 6 we see the basic parameters [46]. The simplest treatment starts with the Lorentz force equation,

$$\mathbf{E} = \mathbf{v} \times \mathbf{B} \qquad (1)$$

which is then put into the equation defining electromotive force:

$$\mathbf{V} = \int \mathbf{E} \cdot \mathbf{dl} \qquad (2)$$

Using v = ω r, where ω is the angular velocity, we find Eq. 2 becomes,

$$\mathbf{V} = \omega \, \mathbf{B} \int_{a}^{b} \mathbf{r} \, \mathbf{dr} \qquad (3)$$

and finally,

$$V = \omega B (b^2 - a^2) / 2 \qquad (4)$$

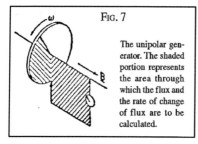

FIG. 7

The unipolar generator. The shaded portion represents the area through which the flux and the rate of change of flux are to be calculated.

where a is the radius of shaft and b is the radius of the disk. Historically, Eq. 4 was used by Lorentz along with the Faraday disk, in 1873, to give an absolute determination of the ohm, a fundamental unit of resistance [46].

However this treatment is not as fundamentally derived as most physicists would prefer. A different attempt is made in the approach used by D.R. Corson who starts with Faraday's Law and applies Stokes' Theorem. The emf is then the negative of the change in flux:

$$\oint \mathbf{E} \cdot \mathbf{dl} = -d/dt \int \mathbf{B} \cdot \mathbf{ds} \tag{5}$$

Then as noted in Fig.7, he applies the divergence theorem "to the volume swept out by the surface in a time dt" [47]. Corson then obtains,

$$\mathbf{curl\ E} = -\mathbf{dB/dt} + \mathbf{curl\ (v \times B)} \tag{6}$$

which yields $\mathbf{E} = \mathbf{v} \times \mathbf{B}$ for constant $\mathbf{B}$ and Eq. 4 can be derived as before.

It is well to insert Corson's comment also, that centrifugal forces or Coriolis forces on the electron can be shown to be negligible when dealing with homopolar generation. By taking the ratio of the Lorentz force to centrifugal force for an electron in a disk rotating with angular velocity (J) and magnetic flux density B, we find:

$$F_L/F_C = eB/(m_e \omega) \tag{7}$$

Thus, for a disk rotating at 2000 rpm in a field of 1 Tesla (10,000 Gauss), this ratio is about 10^9 because of the large charge to mass ratio. However, at this point, it must be explained that E in the above equations is really F_B/q from:

$$F_B = q\ \mathbf{v} \times \mathbf{B} \tag{8}$$

Therefore, it is called by a few authors the "effective electric field". It is created from the Lorentz force on the charges in the disk. We know however, that curl $E = 0$ because B is not changing in time and if there is an electric field, it must be irrotational, i.e. electrostatic [48]. This fact is explained by the "observed external electrostatic field" which is created as the charges build up in response to the Lorentz force [49][50]. This is shown in Fig. 8, which is from a transparency used to explain this phenomena at my lectures on this subject. These electrostatic charges accumulate until they are in equilibrium with and exactly cancel the effective electric field. This is why many investigators talk about the electric field inside the disk as being described by $\mathbf{E} = \mathbf{B} \times \mathbf{v}$ or $E = -vH/c$.

This electrostatic field, say E_s' together with the effective electric field, create a neutral environment on the rotating disk, so that as noted in the Experimental Results Section, I was unable to detect any voltage with a meter rotating on the disk. This can also be understood by putting oneself in the rotating frame of the disk and mentally watching the world spinning around it. The magnet, disk, and meter are all at rest in that frame (see next section for more details). However, the peculiarity is that one can be generating voltage, current, and power in the laboratory frame of reference but the meter on the rotating disk will still register zero volts!

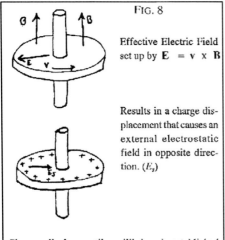

FIG. 8

Effective Electric Field set up by $E = v \times B$

Results in a charge displacement that causes an external electrostatic field in opposite direction. (E_s)

Charges displace until equilibrium is established. Fields cancel within a disk. This explains why a constant voltage will be maintained across the disk even during high current output.

Unfortunately, Dr. Corson says in his article that there are electrostatic fields given by the gradient of a scalar potential in the system where the curl of a vector is zero but "about which we are not concerned here" [51]. In his textbook, he and coauthor, Lorrain, do not mention this at all (Appendix C). The penalty for this oversight is that he then believes that the observer on the disk of a homopolar generator will report that there is an electromotive force "because of the magnetic force on the moving charges of the portion of the circuit external to the disk" [52]. Physically, we know that the magnetic field is nearly zero outside the magnet. If one uses a long solenoid instead, the above statement can be seen to be untenable. (I tried to correspond with Dr. Corson about this point and even meet with him at an American Physical Society gathering but he said that he was unprepared to discuss these details since too many years had transpired since its printing.) My "meter-on-the-disk" experiment is discussed in the Experimental Results Section. It is still a conclusive proof of the neutral electrical environment in the rotating reference frame of a homopolar generator, in opposition to the theoretical speculation of Corson.

UNIPOLAR INDUCTION IS FUNDAMENTALLY A RELATIVISTIC EFFECT

Developing the transformation equations for moments from the covariant form of the electromagnetic transformations, Panofsky and Phillips write, for components perpendicular to the direction of propagation:

$$P'\perp = \gamma (P\perp - (v \times M\perp)/c^2) \qquad (9)$$

$$M'\perp = \gamma (M\perp + v \times P\perp) \qquad (10)$$

These equations are used to explain the Wilson-type experiments with relative motion of two bodies (the Greek letter gamma "γ" is used for the relativistic transformation coefficient). The parallel components are simply $P'\| = P\|$ and $M'\| = M\|$, thus transforming without any change.

In the Faraday generator, we can look at equation (9) and set $y = 1$ and $P\perp = 0$, for the magnet rotating at low velocities compared to the speed of light. Then, we find that an equivalent electric moment arises from the motion of the magnetic moment. Panofsky and Phillips point out that equation (9) *has no nonrelativistic counterpart*, being based on the relativistic definition of simultaneity. Thus, they emphasize that "unipolar induction is fundamentally a relativistic effect" [53]. We could elaborate upon the significance of this statement made by two famous physicists known for their expertise in electromagnetics. Suffice it to say that this may be the most important quotation cited in my book, giving us an insight for transferring energy between relative frames of reference. Richard Becker, in his book, says the same words and adds, "we need the concept of the Lorentz force which is foreign to the Maxwell theory but is derivable by relativity theory" [54].

At this point in the derivation, Panofsky and Phillips point out that the unipolar generator is an accelerated frame and that they have been dealing with inertial frames where special relativity is valid (which is sort of a contradiction). They go on to say that the effective electric field (from $E = B\omega r$) has a *nonvanishing divergence* which leads to a volume charge for the generator! Being at variance with the transformation laws for linear motion, this is "an indication that the 'absolute' rotational motion of the disk (i.e., the motion relative to an inertial frame) can in principle be determined" [55]. This is quite a startling claim which is at odds with relativity theory (special or general).

However, M.G. Trocheris agrees and furthermore states that "an absolute rotation with respect to the stars can be detected" [56]. He cites Sagnac's experiment [57] and Schiff's experiment [58] both of which show the distinction between linear motion and rotation. Dr. Stefan Marinov, famous in non-conventional energy arenas, goes the furthest and uses a rotating disk experiment to measure "for the first time ... the Earth's absolute velocity" [59].

This simply prepares us, when dealing with the homopolar generator, for Sommerfeld's conclusion after calculating the same volume charge density mentioned above: "Minkowski's theory (i.e., Special Relativity) .. .is not directly applicable to problems involving rotation" [60].

GENERAL RELATIVISTIC APPROACH

Einstein points out in his book, The Meaning of Relativity, that problems involving differences in reference frames can be overcome by using General Relativity. He says, "We shall be true to the principle of relativity in its broadest sense if we give such a form to the laws that they are valid in every such four-dimensional system of coordinates, that is, if the equations expressing the laws are co-variant with respect to arbitrary transformations" [61]. With a sense of inspiration for the correct treatment of a non-inertial reference frame, I attempted to follow the work of Kerr and Thirring who developed metries for dealing with rotating bodies. The Thirring metric in particular, described in Adler, Bazin, and Schiffer's (A,B&S) text [62], is valid for low rates of spin and weak fields, though designed for a sphere. However, in working with the metric, a few terms showed that they are designed just for large masses compared to a laboratory generator. One of the terms in particular has the angular momentum divided by the cube of the speed of light. My calculation yielded about 10^{-13}.

Even in spite of a quantity of mass in the system that is lighter than a star's mass, such as a homopolar, generally covariant or completely covariant Maxwell equations can be written once the metric is found. So advised Dr. J. Dimock of SUNYAB's Mathematics Department, who also gave these guidelines for a solution: 1) Find the metric for the rotating system; 2) Compute the Christoffel symbols for the system; 3) Find the covariant derivatives; 4) Write Maxwell's equations.

I did succeed with the metric (p. 122 of the A,B&S text) and struggled to calculate the metric tensor $g_{\mu\nu}$. Afterwards, a few Christoffel symbols were nonzero so A,B&S advises that one does need the covariant derivatives. However, I did come across an excellent article, just in time, that does all of the mathematical work. "Vacuum Electrodynamics on a Merry-Go-Round" by Ise and Uretsky [63] is the great reference article for the small laboratory experiments such as mine. They note that the curvature tensor $R_{\mu\nu\lambda\tau}$ vanishes so that space may be considered to be flat and therefore admits a Lorentz metric (Cartesian coordinate system). The A,B&S text agrees (p. 149) and the work is simplified to ordinary derivatives and the tensor form of Maxwell's equations. Ise and Uretsky come up with the final form for the Lorentz force equation as $\mathbf{E} = (\boldsymbol{\omega} \times \mathbf{r}) \times \mathbf{B}$ which is the same as Eq. (1) with $\mathbf{v} = \boldsymbol{\omega} \times \mathbf{r}$.

Another article that attempts to use General Relativity is "Schiff's Charges and Currents in Rotating Matter" [64]. He uses Schiff's article [58] and adapts Schiff's solution of Maxwell's equations to a rotating magnet. He then fmds apparent of "fictitious" charge and current densities present in the rotating frame. The surface charge density seems to be independent of any conservation law because of its reliance on the angular velocity ω. Lastly, Webster claims that the charge extends throughout the volume of the magnet and into the space beyond its ends as well [65], while the fictitious current density is negligible of a permanent magnet. This is interesting because it gives researchers new tools for analyzing the homopolar generator.

A different approach to using the transformed field equations for a rotating reference frame is given by Trocheris [66]. He applies the results to a rotating solenoid as well as to a rotating magnet and claims, however, that both will be charged. Apparently he was not aware of the experiments by Kennard [13] and Barnett [14] which showed that a rotating solenoid does not develop a voltage.

A lot of information on 1) rotating magnets, conducting or non-conducting and 2) rotating dielectrics, magnetized or non-magnetized, is to be found in a text by E.G. Cullwick entitled, Electromagnetism and Relativity [49]. He states what we can adopt the viewpoint that inside the magnet, the flux rotates with the magnet. "Outside the magnet the concept of rotating flux is valid only for the calculation of the line-integral of the electric field intensity between two points on the magnet" [67].

From the textbook by Adler, Bazin and Schiffer (A,B&S) we find a fascinating description of the general relativistic viewpoint for a rotating body:

> A very interesting physical effect results from the rotational nature of the Kerr solution; a body in geodesic motion experiences a force proportional to the parameter "a" reminiscent of a Coriolis force. Loosely speaking, we may think of the rotating source as "dragging" space around with it; in a Machian sense the source "competes" with the Lorentzian boundary conditions at infinity in the establishment of a local inertial frame [68].

With this relativity quotation, this section on theory is concluded, with an eye for the future avenue of analysis.

THE THEORY OF ARMATURE REACTION AND RESULTING BACK TORQUE

In the classical treatment of torque (which is basically force times distance), for a homopolar motor, most of the textbooks take the equation for the force on a current loop in a magnetic field,

$$\mathbf{F} = i\,\mathbf{l} \times \mathbf{B} \tag{11}$$

where i is the current and l, the radial vector. This equation is then substituted into the definition for torque,

$$\mathbf{T} = \mathbf{r} \times \mathbf{F} \tag{12}$$

which yields, in differential form,

$$dT = B\,i\,r\,dr \tag{13}$$

that can be integrated across the radius r → 0, l to give the total torque.

Now in a Faraday generator, it is expected that this torque is also manifested in a direction opposite to that of rotation, analogous to the back emf experienced in a Faraday motor. It is well to note that this has historically been tested only with a two-piece Faraday generator since no one bas found a good reason to carry the magnets along with the rotating disk. In that case one finds an increased load on the drive motor and a substantial decrease in the output voltage of the generator.

To analyze the back torque or armature reaction, we can look at the angular momentum of a rotating body:

$$\mathbf{L} = \mathbf{I}\,\omega \tag{14}$$

Here, I is the "moment of inertia" which is defined uniquely for each object depending on its geometry and ω is the angular velocity. We can see in Figure 9 how I is defined for the type of magnets that were used in the generator. Now the torque can be defined as,

$$T = I\frac{d\omega}{dt} = \frac{dL}{dt} \tag{15}$$

and relating the power input to the torque applied, we may use the equation [69],

$$P = T\,\omega \tag{16}$$

which allows us to have the torque continuously applied even at constant angular velocity if the power is being dissipated in frictional forces and electrical generation. Thus, if a certain amount of power is measured for the drive motor of a bomopolar generator for a given ω, we can fmd the torque

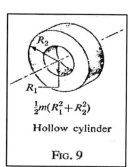

$\frac{1}{2}m(R_1^2 + R_2^2)$

Hollow cylinder

FIG. 9

being applied to overcome friction. If the output terminals are shorted, for example, to obtain maximum generation of current, one simply has to measure the new angular velocity and the new power input for the drive motor to find the increased torque. *Subtracting the two results, we have found the armature reaction the generator bas produced to counteract current output as Lenz's Law predicts.*

Measurement note: a cautionary statement is made here for those with only three-digit voltmeters. When two measurements are subtracted which may vary only by the last digit of a three-digit measurement, the error analysis doesn't allow one to claim more than ONE DIGIT ACCURACY in such measurements. (The formal treatment of error analysis is contained in the Appendix.) Any claim to more accuracy, without resorting to four-digit meters, is unscientific and amounts to committing falsehood.

As an interesting sideline, the torque, as seen from the above analysis, is related to the inertia of the object and the magnetic field it experiences. From Mach's Principle we obtain an explanation for the inertia of a body: its interaction with all of the extragalactic masses of the universe. From the previous general relativistic treatment, we find that the interaction of a rotating body with the rest of the universe is quite different than in the stationary case. The warping of space-time is different Therefore, the possibility exists that something as intrinsic as inertia may be affected by rotation. We are aware that the choice of rotation axis changes the moment of inertia. However, even the formula MR2 which is an integral part of all moments of inertia, has a nonlinear dependence on R which seems to indicate a sort of anisotropy. Furthermore, the concept of anisotropy of inertia is already a legitimate subject of inquiry [70][71]. In this same vein, it is worthwhile mentioning that there have been reports of changes in weight of rotating objects, specifically gyroscopes, that also may point to an avenue of investigation [72][73].

The measurement of back torque of a one-piece homopolar generator that, strictly speaking, has no stator is a mysterious undertaking. Jackson gives, in his textbook, the equation for the total torque on a current distribution [74] as (Gaussian units),

$$\mathbf{T} = \frac{1}{c} \int \mathbf{r} \times (\mathbf{J} \times \mathbf{B}) \, d^3 r$$

(17)

which compares to substituting Eq. (11) into (12). Though both are in MKS units, they really only differ from Eq. (17) by J which is *current density*. The magnetic field, as previously mentioned, is not apparently influenced by the rotation of the cylindrical magnet and provides the current with a basis for pushing against the "forward" rotation of the disk. To explain, when the magnets are stationary, scientists naturally assume that the current pushes against them or they assume the current uses them as a reference for producing torque. When the magnets rotate with the disk, however, that concept has to be modified as "the rug is pulled out from under one's feet" so to speak.

The experimental results that follow are not meant to be conclusive or even typical of what various designs of homopolar generators can do. The results are simply one person's investigation of a single design of an electrical generator that is unique in many ways.

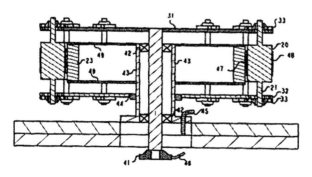

In 2004, a Searl -style orbiting homopolar machine was patented 6,822,361 by V. Roschin

EXPERIMENTAL RESULTS WITH DIFFERENT HOMOPOLAR GENERATORS

Speaker Magnet Generator

The first unipolar generator that I built, pictured in Fig. 10, used four speaker magnets, two on either side of a soft copper disk. The magnets were, on the average, three inches in diameter and magnetized axially. The output was in the range of a few millivolts when driven by an AC motor at about 2000 RPM. This model served to prove the "homopolar effect" which is hard to accept for anyone first faced with the phenomenon. The brushes used were 1/8" copper wire spring loaded to provide continuous contact. No power output measurements were made.

FIG. 10. Speaker Magnet Generator

One-Inch Diameter Generator

The second model that was built was a vertical shaft homopolar generator designed around two powerful, rare earth magnets rated at 8000 gauss. The inspiration for the design came from J.W. Then's article from the American Journal of Physics pictured in Fig. 11 [75]. As will be mentioned later, this design has a serious flaw in it, causing much lower voltage output than would be expected. However, Dr. Then from the University of Detroit, did not perform a voltage profile test along the length of the copper cup nor did he calculate the expected theoretical voltage.

Assuming that this was a viable

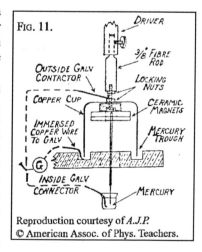

FIG. 11.

DRIVER

3/8" FIBRE ROD

OUTSIDE GALV CONTACTOR

LOCKING NUTS

COPPER CUP

CERAMIC MAGNETS

IMMERSED COPPER WIRE TO GALV

MERCURY TROUGH

INSIDE GALV CONNECTOR

MERCURY

Reproduction courtesy of *A.J.P.*
© American Assoc. of Phys. Teachers.

design, I built a similar model based on the copper cup idea. Using a one-inch I.D. copper pipe, I had it silver-soldered to a one-inch diameter copper disk. The magnets were then placed on either side of the disk, with the copper pipe going down into a liquid metal trough. Pictured in Fig. 12, one can see the upper and lower troughs which contained melted solder. The lower trough received the central shaft which became the opposite terminal of the generator. In the drawing of Fig. 13, one can see better how the pipe fit into the upper trough and the Weigand electric heaters (#PT-615) that were positioned below each trough. The AC electric current did not interfere with the output of the generator and was controlled by two separate VARIACs (variable AC voltage rheostat).

FIG.12.

The second generator served as a prototype of the full-scale model and demonstrated the regulated voltage output that is characteristic of this type of generator. Theoretically, the output voltage should have been about 13 millivolts, using the formula,

$$V = \frac{1}{2}\,\omega\,B\,(r_o^2 - r_i^2)$$

(18)

where ω is $2\pi(50\text{Hz})$ from 3000 RPM shaft, B is 0.8 Tesla, and r_o, r_i are the outer radius (1/16") and the inner radius (3/16") respectively, converted to meters.

Instead, the voltage output was about 0.15 millivolts; considerably lower than expected. I should have explored more fully the reason for such a major difference in voltage output. The cylinder, being six times longer than the thickness of the magnet, was producing a much lower voltage at the bottom, in the liquid metal trough, than at the top near the magnets. However, the design of the upper metal trough prohibited access to the rotating copper cylinder and I would not discover this phenomenon until a year later. I presumed instead that the solder was not conducting well.

The Unusual Phenomenon of Regulated Voltage

Using a digital voltmeter, the current

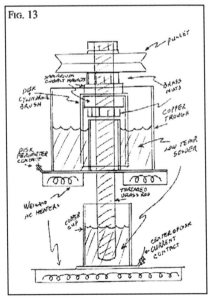

FIG. 13

output was monitored. It was found that the output current varied depending upon which scale was used, showing that the internal resistance of the meter was limiting the current output. The highest current output was measured on the 2 Ampere scale and registered 0.6 Amps output. This was the first demonstration of a variable output current that seeks to maintain the same generated voltage, under different resistive loads. This phenomenon is unique to the homopolar generator, seen only in electronic circuits, called a REGULATED VOLTAGE SOURCE!

The result of this effect is that maximum power can be delivered by designing the external circuit to be a low resistance load. The equations predicted this effect but it was a magical feeling to actually see it in action. My thesis adviser, Dr. Jonathan Reichert, witnessed this event in his lab at the University of Buffalo, but did not understand why the generator varied its current output until we talked about it. I suggested that it was behaving like a regulated voltage source and Dr. Reichert agreed. This discovery was impressive enough to physics professor Reichert to cause him to approve my Master's degree project, giving me the go-ahead for a full-size model.

With this small generator a GE current shunt #426, which monitors 75 Amps @50 mV, had an effective resistance of 666 microhms. It turned out that this was still too high to pull a measurable amount of current from the generator.

The back torque, calculated using $dT=Bir$ dr, came out to be 2.4 x 10^{-5} N-m, which was too small to have a noticeable effect even at 0.6A output.

In Fig. 14 we see a preliminary design that I came up with based on the cup or cylinder approach to current collection. Practical considerations forced some modifications to take place which will be discussed shortly. One can see from this design how Then's model influenced my generator approach.

Rotation of Magnetic Field Lines Tested

Before I describe the third generator, I would like to briefly talk about

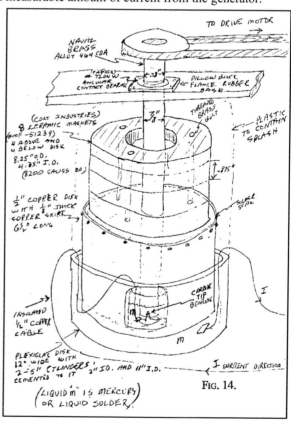

FIG. 14.

an experiment that shed some light on the nature of the magnetic field that powers the unipolar generator.

The first experiment, performed with the help of Dan Winter, from SS Electric in Buffalo, NY, assembled two rotating disks with magnets, in close proximity. (Fig. 15) We decided to test the idea that a Faraday generator might be influenced by a rotating magnet nearby. After Bruce DePalma had strongly emphasized that a "magnetic vortex" is created when a magnet spins, I was inclined to put the concept to a test, since this was the main esoteric reason why a one-piece Faraday generator differed in principle from a two-piece generator.

The test apparatus consisted of a copper disk, mounted horizontally, with an 8" magnet on it. One-half inch from this was another magnet, mounted on a wooden disk in a horizontal position as well. Both magnets were the Colt Industries, Crucible Division, Ferrimag 5 ceramic magnets with composition, $BaO \cdot Fe_2O_3$ that were later used in the third generator.

To set a baseline, the copper disk generator was run first without the other magnet assembly nearby, developing a 25 millivolt output. Then, the other magnet was put into place. It was found that the output of the generator increased about 10 millivolts (to 35 mV) when the magnetic fields were aligned and decreased about 10 millivolts (to 15 mV) when they opposed. The big question of whether or not the *rotation* of the nearby magnet would increase the generator output beyond 35 millivolts, was resolved very readily.

The rotation of the nearby magnet did not seem to affect "magnetic field lines" in the rotating homopolar generator. The output stayed at 35 millivolts without change, no matter which way the magnet was rotated. (Since the magnet and generator were separately belt-driven by electric motors, we can estimate the rotation speeds as exceeding 1000 RPM.) In the measurement of the output voltage, there was brush contact noise that caused some uncertainty in the measurement, so only two digits are reported. This experiment, as far as I can determine, has not been performed prior to my design of it. The results certainly diminish the role played by "field lines", which still appear today in engineering texts. This concept is only a human invention which does not correspond to a physical phenomenon, since the magnetic field is a homogeneous effect.

Fig. 15
An historic experiment testing the effect of a nearly stationary or rotating magnet of equal flux density on a homopolar generator disk ½" away from it. Note wooden disk holding magnet.

Actual Magnetic Field Profile

Another experiment of importance, showing the variations of the magnetic field as one traverses the radius of the magnet, was performed. Being influenced to use a shaft brush for one of the terminals by Tim Wilhelm of the Stelle Group in Illinois, who also was building a one-piece homopolar generator with liquid mercury brushes, I was aware that some of my voltage output would be counteracted by a reverse field going down the center of the stack of magnets.

Using one magnet as a representative sample, I used an A&I Industries Hall Effect Gaussmeter #100 to scan the magnetic flux density B, only 1/8" above the surface of the magnet. A ruler was placed on top of the magnet radially, so that the probe could be moved uniformly from the center to beyond the outer radius.

The results, shown in Graph #1, revealed that:

1. the magnetic field was not as strong as the saturated value of 3900 Gauss listed by the manufacturer (who suggest remagnetizing them after installation);
2. the peak of the field was not at the edge of the magnet as anticipated;
3. the reverse field in the center air space was about *half* of the strength of the magnetic field in the other direction.

The third result was of most concern for it would have to be taken into consideration in the theoretical calculation of the voltage output Also, it seems that only by virtue of the r^2 dependence of the output can the negative contribution of the central field be de-emphasized. In other words, the strength of the reverse field in the center doesn't matter as much as when such a reverse field appears at the outer edge because the generated voltage depends on the radius *squared*.

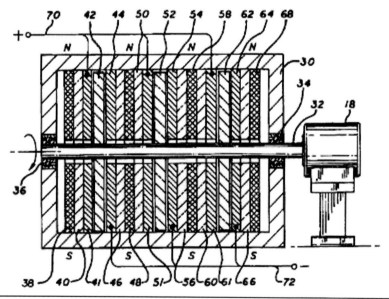

Richard Clark's patent 6,051,905 uses dielectric and conductor disks in a magnetic field

GRAPH #1.

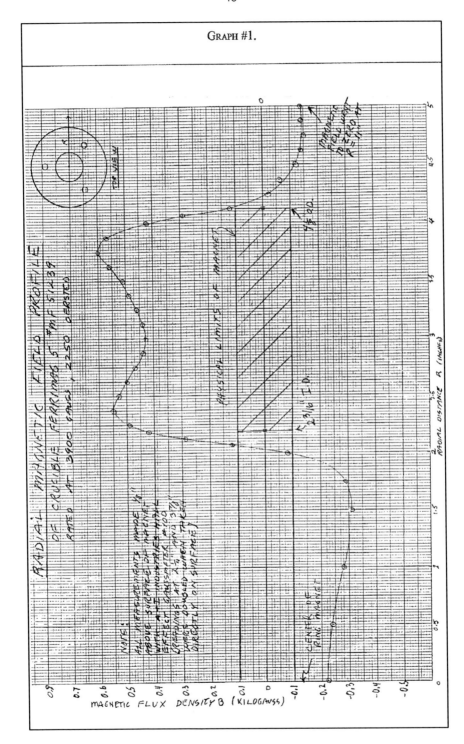

GRAPH #2.

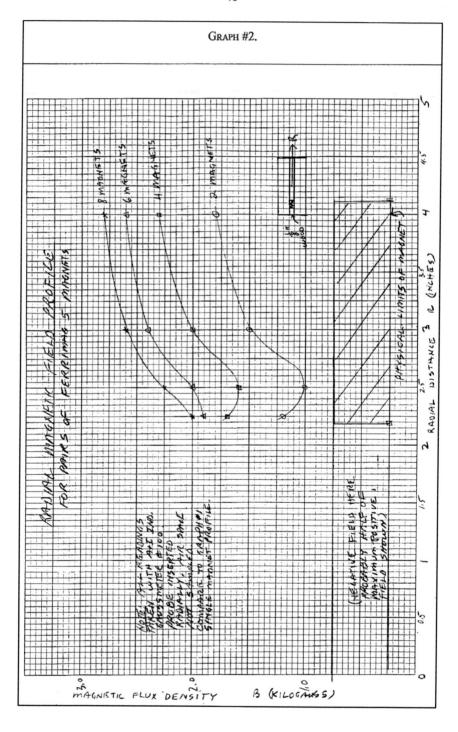

GRAPH #3.

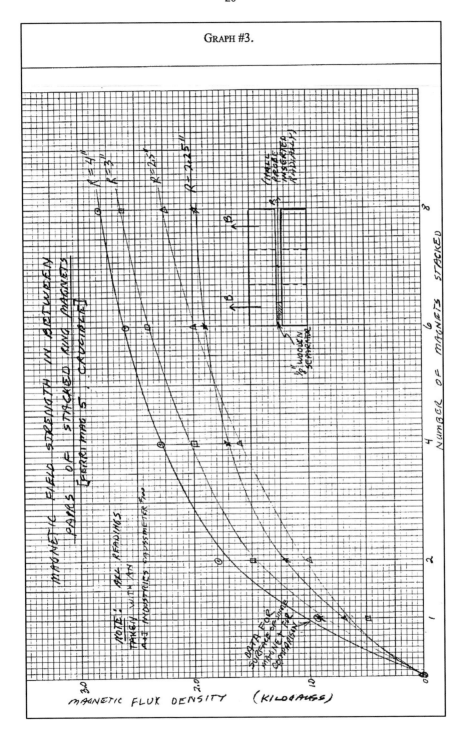

In Graph #2, a similar profile is made of the magnetic field B. This time, however, I looked at the area between the inner and the outer radius. First two magnets were placed, with opposite poles attracting, on top of each other. Only a 1/8" spacer separated the magnets. I probed the magnetic field radially, as before, at strategic distances and then added a magnet on top and bottom, for the next set of measurements. At the end, the field between the eight magnets was measured. With four on top and four on the bottom, it was similar to the situation that would be produced in the third generator.

The last experimental Graph (#3) simply restates the data contained in Graph #2 but dramatically demonstrates my reason for having four magnets on top of the copper disk and four on the bottom. One can see an almost linear increase in the magnetic flux density, at much of the radial distances, as each pair of magnets was added.

The Internal Resistance of the Homopolar Disk

Once the wooden frame of the generator was built the first test with a single magnet on either side was performed with a steel disk. Pictured in Fig. 16, the test also made use of two copper-impregnated carbon brushes that are usually better used at higher voltages, because of the contact resistance. Even substituting a copper disk, the one that would be used in all future tests, still revealed major contact resistance problems. After this test, I decided to proceed

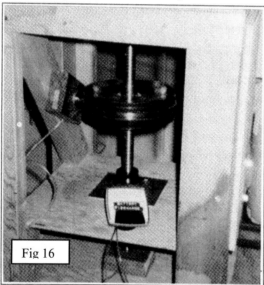

Fig 16

with the copper disk, based on the resistivity of copper which is about 1/10th of steel's resistivity. However, the relative permeability of steel is a thousand or more times that of air or copper, which should have dramatically increased the output voltage. I opted for a resistivity on the order of 1.7 microhm-cm instead of 18 microhm-cm or more which is characteristic of steel. Thinking that the high current in the medium necessitated low resistance, the choice probably increased the maximum

power transfer by an order of ten. Another way of stating this is that because of the low voltage output any resistive increase usually will significantly decrease the current output [76]. It would be interesting, however, to repeat some of the following experiments with a steel disk for comparison to resolve the question. As far as the final experiments are concerned, enough power was generated to measure armature reaction and completes the purpose of this project, using the copper disk.

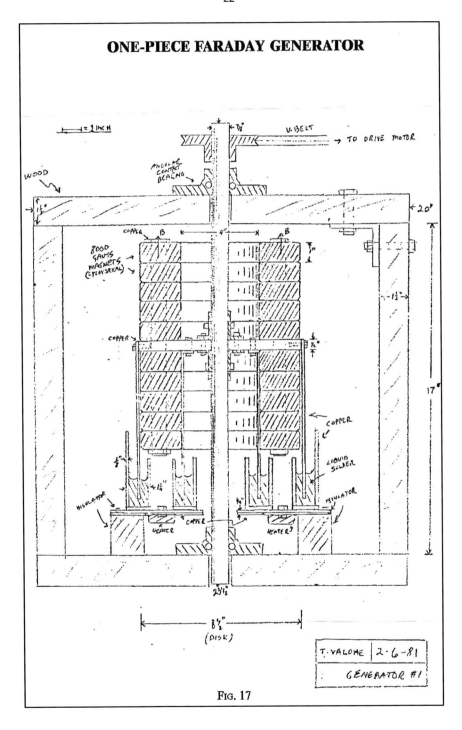

ONE-PIECE FARADAY GENERATOR

FIG. 17

The Internal Resistance of the Generator with Liquid Brushes

Shown in Fig. 17, the intended design for Generator #3 involved two troughs for liquid metal. One option which was decided upon included the removal of the inner solder trough seen in the diagram, replacing it with a small solder cup put directly under the Naval Brass shaft. This action tended to reduce the output since the reverse field would be creating a voltage in the opposite direction. However, due to the advice of Mr. Tim Wilhelm of the Stelle Group, Stelle, Illinois, I was convinced that the output voltage would not suffer very much.

As the machined parts from the Physics Machine Shop became available, I worked on designing a support for the solder trough and the external circuitry. Also, once assembled, I was interested in the internal resistance of the entire generator, with the liquid metal melted. Therefore, I put together a voltage-controlled current source (VCCS) ohmeter using a voltage regulator IC design that I had already published [77], and an op-amp VCCS. Adjusted for a constant current of 10.0 (to.01) milliamp output, the voltage across the object was directly proportional to the resistance of it. With this circuit, I was able to determine that the longest, direct resistance path through the generator, including the copper plates of the external circuit attached to the brushes, was below 10 milliohms.

Later, with Generator #4, which has a shortened cylinder brush, I was able to do an excellent resistance test, thanks to the Electronics Instruments Ltd. Milliohmeter (Model 47 A) borrowed from Mr. Tim Wilhelm. This instrument had a full scale reading of 1.2 milliohms, so it was well suited for the generator resistance test. With the liquid metal melted one hour before the test, I found a total resistance of the entire generator by disconnecting the current shunt on the front (see Fig. 18). Bolting the contacts of the milliohmeter to the upper and lower copper plates, I found the total resistance to actually be:

Fig. 18

$$R_i = 230 \pm 10 \text{ microhms} \qquad (19)$$

The contact resistance of the milliohmeter, measured by bolting the leads together, was found to be 30 ±10 microhms and included in the above measurement of Eq. 19. By comparison, the General Electric current shunt seen in Fig. 18, used for precisely measuring the current output, had 20.0 microhms of resistance. Producing 50.0 mV at 2500A, the 20.0 microhms was a necessary resistance and about the same as the contact resistance included in Eq. 19.

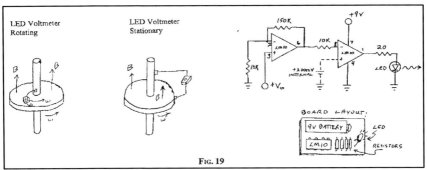

FIG. 19

(More Generator #4 Photos can be found on P. 91 and 92)

Test for Voltage Generation in the Rotating Reference Frame

This is a completely original experiment that I initiated to test for a measurable electromotive force (emf) or voltage in the rotating reference frame. For the first time a relativistic effect involving the Faraday generator has been detected in the laboratory. The Fig. 8 diagram explains that no voltage should be detectable on the rotating magnet, since thy electrostatic field completely compensates for the emf that is generated.

I built a LED voltmeter to test that theory. The circuit, about the size of the transistor battery that powered it, was designed to light the LED continuously until a voltage of more than 15 mV occurs at the terminal labeled "+Vin". In that case, the LED turns off until the voltage drops below 15 m V again. In that way, the LED will be visibly bright if the voltage on the rotating magnet does not exceed 15 millivolts (See Fig. 19).

Mounting the circuit securely on top of the generator magnets, the generator was started and brought up to speed. With no current output, the generator produced almost 100 m V, measured from the rest frame (laboratory reference frame), but still the LED circuit stayed lit I then tested the circuit in the rest frame to make sure it functioned with its solder soaked contacts. The LED turned off almost immediately as the generator was brought up to 1500 RPM.

The most dramatic part of this experiment was when r allowed the generator to produce a current output as well of more than 100 Amperes, while the LED circuit was mounted on it. Even though electrons were being moved through a potential difference, from the rotating frame, no voltage was detectable.

Since the LED circuit becomes part of the generator as it is rotating, it has been suggested that it does not function because it is a conductor itself. However, since the light stays lit, this demonstrates that the electrons of the LED circuit are not somehow overpowered by the effective electric field within the rotating reference frame.

I feel that this experiment has demonstrated the essential relativistic paradox of the homopolar generator.

The Shocking Truth About Generator #3

The first few tests that were performed in order to measure the back torque of the generator were characterized by a small percentage change between the situation with a load on the generator and that without a load. The results shown in this table are typical of generator #3.

7/26/82		Total Generated Voltage	Total Generated Current	DriveMotor Power Consumption	
Test	Speed				Comments
Open Cir.	1650 RPM	32.4 mVDC		530 Watts	no load
Closed Cir.	1650 RPM		125 A DC	533 Watts	4 Watts out

Notice that the output power is on the order of the wattage increase in the drive motor but very small in magnitude.

Another test done a few weeks later generated only 6 Watts at 2300 RPM. Using Eq. 3, the voltage output calculated taking the magnetic flux density to be 2800 Gauss or 0.28 Tesla from Graph #3. The inner radius of the magnets is 2.19" while the outer radius is 4.125". At 1650 RPM, the equation predicts a voltage output of **191 mV** not 32 mV!

Upon probing the generated voltage at points near the disk, at the top of the cylinder rotor, I found a voltage output of 500% more than what was generated at the bottom brush, or about 119 m V. Considering that the magnetic field is

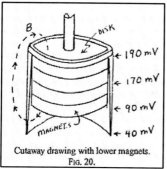

Cutaway drawing with lower magnets.
FIG. 20.

probably less than 0.28T, since the magnets are ½ " apart instead of 1/8 " as in Graph #3, the predicted voltage was not far off. In Fig. 20 is pictured a voltage profile done at about 2300 RPM with the brush trough removed.

The existence of such a voltage profile was a surprise to me as well as everyone else whom I spoke to. Professors were telling me that the cylinder, being symmetric with the magnets, should be able to conduct well and not be affected by the magnetic field.

However, the voltage profile revealed that even though the cylinder was a conductor, it was generating voltage differently along its length, depending on the relative density of the magnetic flux intersecting the cylinder!

This was very shocking since I had spent most of the summer in the physics lab of Erie Community College, where I was teaching during the regular school year, building and testing a very poor design for generating homopolar electrical power.

The Dramatic Redesign of the Cylindrical Conducting Brush

Based on the above voltage results, it was decided that I had to redesign the cylindrical conductor to obtain higher power output. To access the highest voltage possible, a very short brush system was deemed necessary. An actual size diagram is shown in Fig. 21 which illustrates how close the liquid metal could be to the copper disk. By the Fall, the new brush system (the 1.25" long cylinder in Fig. 21) was attached to the copper disk. Then, between semesters, tests were begun again. The results show the dramatic difference this redesign really made Generator #4, with the new brush, was ready by the Winter break.

The first tests were done at 1600 RPM producing 116 mV and 635 Amps for a total of 74 Watts of power out. Finally enough power was being drawn from the generator to look for a change in the motor input demand.

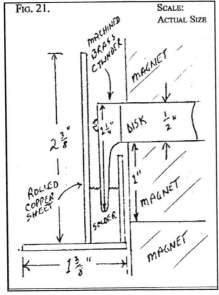

FIG. 21.

SCALE: ACTUAL SIZE

The Required Safety Calculations for Stress

Before any generator tests were performed, it should be mentioned that a stress calculation was performed, based on a failure mode suggested by Dr. Richard Dollinger, SUNYAB Electrical Engineering Department. Considering the tensile strength of the disk magnets, provided by the manufacturer, to be 4000 psi, the separation of two halves of the magnet was calculated while under the centrifugal force of rotation. The maximum RPM calculated was about 4300 RPM, shown in Fig. 22. Consequently, I set 3000 RPM as my reasonable limit. Also, to make the exposed upper magnets even more protected, I wrapped them with fiberglass twine and epoxy, with Dr. Dollinger's suggestion. It might be worth mentioning that the copper disk had a comparatively high tensile strength 0f 34,000 psi and was of no concern in the calculation of the maximum revolution speed.

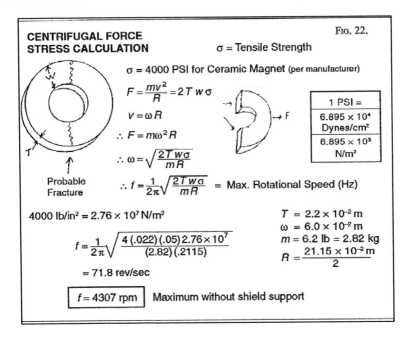

CENTRIFUGAL FORCE STRESS CALCULATION

FIG. 22.

σ = Tensile Strength

σ = 4000 PSI for Ceramic Magnet (per manufacturer)

$$F = \frac{mv^2}{R} = 2Tw\sigma$$

$$v = \omega R$$

$$\therefore F = m\omega^2 R$$

$$\therefore \omega = \sqrt{\frac{2Tw\sigma}{mR}}$$

$$\therefore f = \frac{1}{2\pi}\sqrt{\frac{2Tw\sigma}{mR}} = \text{Max. Rotational Speed (Hz)}$$

1 PSI =
6.895×10^4 Dynes/cm^2
6.895×10^3 N/m^2

Probable Fracture

4000 lb/in^2 = 2.76×10^7 N/m^2

$$f = \frac{1}{2\pi}\sqrt{\frac{4(.022)(.05)2.76\times10^7}{(2.82)(.2115)}}$$

= 71.8 rev/sec

f = 4307 rpm | Maximum without shield support

T = 2.2×10^{-2} m
ω = 6.0×10^{-2} m
m = 6.2 lb = 2.82 kg
$R = \dfrac{21.15 \times 10^{-2} \text{ m}}{2}$

Phototachometer for Rotation Speed Determination

In Fig. 18 (pg. 22) is a picture of the current shunt in use with attachment to the low resistance copper plates. The picture is actually of the Generator #4 which includes a foil splash barrier on the solder trough. Also seen is the foil covering on half of the circumference of the magnet on top used in the phototachometer circuit.

The phototachometer consisted of a Cadmium Sulfide (CdS) photocell mounted near the top of the rotating magnet along with a small light nearby. Half of the circumference was painted black and the other half had aluminum foil attached to it. The resistance of the CdS cell varied dramatically with each rotation, with a small battery attached to it, along with a fixed resistor. Using an oscilloscope to look at the voltage output of the CdS cell, a clean square wave was created on the screen. Thus, the period could easily be measured and the rotation speed calculated.

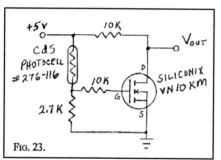

FIG. 23.

I also used a BK Precision Frequency Counter to count the square wave pulses for the sake of photographs and demonstrations, giving the revolutions per second directly in Hertz.

Fig. 23 shows the photocell circuit that was developed upon the suggestion of Bruce DePalma of Santa Barbara, CA during a phone conversation. Using a MOSFET improved the reliability of the circuit. The output, created when reflected light changed the resistance of the CdS photocell (Radio Shack 276-116), created a nice square wave on an oscilloscope once per revolution, since half of the circumference was covered with aluminum foil. Later on, an article was published in the American J. of Physics [78] that showed how to use the Commodore VIC-20 microcomputer as a pulse counter. The program given in the article worked very well and accurately substituted for a frequency counter, though my measurements were completed by then.

High Current Magnetohydrodynamics Causes Conduction Problem

At the high current levels that were now being produced, an unusual effect was created. Very often, when hundreds of Amperes were generated, the output became unsteady, conduction was intermittent, and the results were undependable. As can be seen with the strip chart recordings in Fig. 24, the effect was seen only with current generation. The test done 1/11/83 shows the current output at the bottom, in the range of 350 Amps, followed by a run (current shunt disconnected) measuring voltage only, in the range of 85 mV. At the top is the last run (current shunt connected) recording current in the range of 550 Amps but becoming even more intermittent.

This phenomenon is referred to in the literature by various terms. Dr. A.K. Das Gupta refers to it as the "electromagnetic pumping force due to the interaction of the brush current with the circumferential magnet fields" [79]. This magnetic field, in a circumferential direction, *is created by the radial current* just as the field around a straight wire carrying current, according to D.L. Lewis of the Central Research Laboratories [80]. This H_c is equal to $I/2\pi r$ and would be on the order of 100 A/m in my case. He mentions on p. 49 that turbulent flow can occur after the Reynolds number exceeds 2000. (The Reynolds number is a measure of turbulence in the mechanical engineering study of convection.) Eddy currents and magnetohydrodynamic losses then occur. According to Hong and Wilhelm, in the J. of Applied Physics, "Within the frame of linear magnetohydrodynamics, it is shown that the liquid-metal flow in the brush is always unstable if the brush transports current. In the absence of current flow (infinite load) the axial magnetic field stabilizes the liquid metal flow in the brush...." [81].

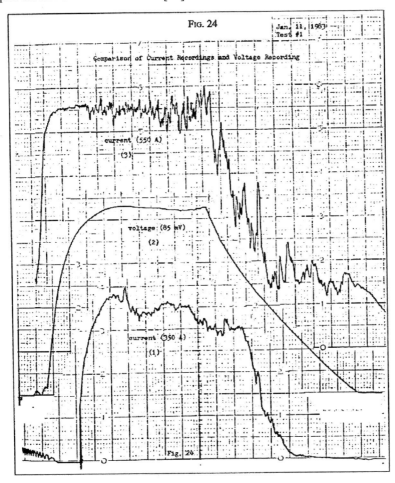

Qualitative Test for Back Torque

Taking all of the above details into account, I became aware that I could not hope to push the generator to the limits of my stress calculations. In February, I was fortunate to produce one test (Fig. 25) that succeeded, with a 380 Ampere output, in remaining stable. At first glance, a qualitative test can be made showing the presence of back torque by looking at the slow-down time for each case. Of course, the design of a one-piece Faraday disk generator was supposed to eliminate back torque or armature reaction according to Bruce DePalma, since the magnet rotates *with* the conducting disk. Surprisingly enough, when just voltage was produced (infinite load), it required 0.64 seconds to come to a

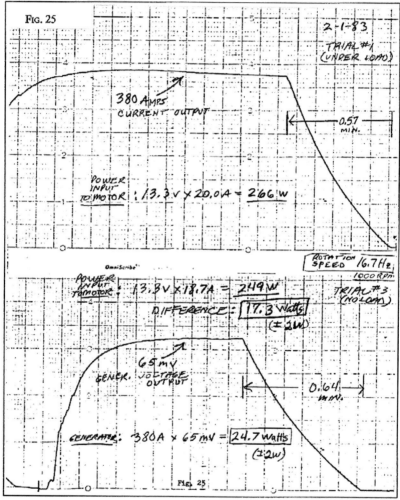

FIG. 25

2-1-83
TRIAL #1
(UNDER LOAD)

380 AMPS
CURRENT OUTPUT

0.57
MIN.

POWER
INPUT
TO MOTOR : 13.3 V × 20.0 A = 266 W

ROTATION
SPEED 16.7 Hz
1000 RPM

POWER
INPUT
TO MOTOR : 13.3 V × 18.7 A = 249 W

DIFFERENCE: 17.3 Watts
(± 2W)

TRIAL #3
(NO LOAD)

65 mV
GENER. VOLTAGE
OUTPUT

0.64
MIN.

GENERATOR: 380 A × 65 mV = 24.7 Watts
(± 2W)

Fig. 25

complete halt from 1000 RPM. However, when the above current was drawn from the generator, the time was shortened to 0.57 seconds, or about 89% of the above time. This demonstrates the existence of a force which is causing the generator some additional friction, drag, or back torque. From this qualitative test, it is hard to determine whether the turbulence of the liquid metal brush, discussed previously, is a significant contributor to this force. In this case, the conduction curve is remarkably uniform. One would tend to attribute most of the effect to the force of back torque (the interaction of the radial current and the magnetic field causing a motoring effect).

Quantitative Test for Back Torque

Looking at the power required by the motor before and after loading the generator, we can achieve a quantitative measure of the back torque created by the generator. We can also learn a few other facts about the generator as well. In the following chart, the increased load experienced by the motor with the generator ~ is compared to the open circuit generator load to find the back torque the generator has produced.

2/1/83 Test	Speed (RPM)	Total Generated Voltage	Total Generated Current	Drive Motor Power Consumption	Torque to Gener.
Open Cir.	1000	65 mVDC		249W	2.37 N-m
Closed Cir.	1000		380ADC	266W	2.54 N-m
Difference				17W	0.16 N-m

Using the formula $P = \omega T$ relating torque to applied power, the "Torque to Generator" column was calculated, in MKS units. Pushing against the magnetic field itself, the current in the generator has succeeded in producing a *back torque of 0.16 Newton-meters*. Using the above generated voltage, 65 mV, in the equation $V = \omega\phi/2$, where $\omega = 2$ ϕ and where $\omega = 2\phi$ and

$$\phi = \int_{r_1}^{r_2} \mathbf{B} \cdot \mathbf{da} = B\,(r_2{}^2 - r_1{}^2)$$

(20)

We can solve for the magnetic field needed to produce such a voltage. Calculating, we get $B = 0.157$ Tesla. Performing the same calculation for the 7/26/82 test, we find $B = 0.175$ Tesla with the average being 0.166 Tesla for B or about 1660 Gauss. This is the best measure of the mean effective magnetic flux density that the generator experiences. Notice that it is about half of the Graph #2 data measured with the four pair magnets 1/8" apart. It is good to mention the phenomenon associated with "armature reaction" actually displaces the field, causing a lower voltage output due to the interaction with the output current [82]. Furthermore, ceramic magnets do not have as much "coercive force" as neodymium or samarium cobalt magnets. Therefore, when stressed with the demagnetizing force of armature reaction, the magnets do not produce the same field as when unstressed.

Motor, Batteries, and Voltage/Current Measurements

For completeness, it should be mentioned that the lower RPM was achieved in this case by using three instead of five 6-volt marine batteries to run the GE motor. The DC motor used in all of these tests was a 24V, 20A, 3400 RPM, 1/2 Hp motor. Certain pulley ratios were used to change the RPM of the generator but also the number of batteries was adjusted to help in this case. Since the load on the motor changed less than 10% during the load/no load cycle, it was not expected that the motor's efficacy would vary significantly. Unfortunately, the manufacturer was not able to supply efficiency curves for this model when they were contacted.

The current to the motor was measured with TRW #4LPW-15 Watt, 0.01 ohm, 1% resistor by the voltage across it. Both current and voltage of the motor were monitored using three-and-one-half digit LCD voltmeters.

Error Analysis for Precision Limits

Noticing the discrepancy between the 25 Watts generated and the 17 Watts more demanded by the motor, it is useful to do an error analysis on the motor measurements. The Appendix contains an error analysis sheet used for teaching the method to Physics students at Erie Community College. This method is also used here. Accepting a ±1 digit error in the least significant digit of the measurements of voltage and current for the motor, the relative errors can be calculated. (One rationale for the error is that some fluctuations do occur when measurements are taken, so the least error will be one digit fluctuating, but it may be more.) Using the method outlined in the Appendix, the relative errors are calculated to be ±0.75% for voltage and ±0.5% for current. These seem like small errors but then we have to add them, since V and I were multiplied. In order to convert back to absolute error, we multiply by the value of the total power in Watts. The total absolute error is found for each multiplication to be ±3.3W and ±3.2W for each.

For the subtraction which was used to find the difference in the motor demand, most scientists forget the correct method used here. Subtraction loses most of the significant digits and therefore <u>loses</u> most of the accuracy. We have to admit a decline in the number of significant digits upon subtraction, or we are just fooling ourselves. The worst thing that seems to happen again and again in the "free energy" circles here is that the generator output looks like it is greater than 100% efficiency when we ignore error analysis. In this case, we have to <u>add</u> the absolute errors when doing a subtraction, to get ±6.5W. That is, the difference in the motor demand is uncertain by ±6.5 Watts. This answer actually takes account only of the meter error. Any human error would have to be added to the above calculation.

The conclusion from the above analysis is that in the 2/1/83 test, where the open circuit and closed circuit power consumptions were subtracted (266W-249W), we came up with only 17 Watts difference. However, this calculation has a ±6.5 Watt error!

Therefore, when we calculate the output of the generator with 65m V DC times 380A DC to get 24.7 Watts, the first correction we have to make is to limit the output power to 2 digits, since the voltage and current measurements are reported in two-digit accuracy, yielding 25 Watts. We cannot increase accuracy by multiplication! Secondly, the absolute errors for this calculation also need to be taken into account, adding upper and lower error limits to the 25 Watts. Then, if 6.5 Watts are added to 17 Watts, we get 24 Watts, which is the upper error limit for the motor demand calculation. This is almost equal to the 25 Watts that we calculated for the generator output.

Therefore, what initially looked like an energy excess coming from the "N-machine" homopolar generator is actually within the error limits of the motor demand. Under these circumstances, I cannot make claims for free energy as many other N-machine inventors have done. I can only hope that everyone becomes conscious of error analysis so more truthful science will result.

Equivalent Circuit of Generator for Maximum Power Calculation

Another interesting calculation that can be performed is pictured in Fig. 26. Using the known resistance of the GE current shunt, the voltage drop across it is found using the generator current output. The voltage drop across the brush is found using the voltage output minus the calculated internal resistance of the copper disk. The result shows the sizable voltage drop there which is, however, curiously smaller than the microhmeter measurement previously

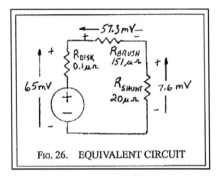

FIG. 26.   EQUIVALENT CIRCUIT

mentioned of 230 microhms. Without this voltage drop across the brush, one could follow Woodson and Melcher's method of calculating the maximum current and power that could be delivered by this generator [83]. The short circuit current I_{sc} would be equal to the open circuit voltage Voc divided by the internal resistance R_i. At 1000 RPM this equals 4.8 x 10^5A or about ½ megampere. The maximum power that could theoretically be achieved at this RPM is $V_{oc} \cdot I_{sc}$ or about 30 kW! Increasing the speed would linearly increase the power output as well. While being very impressive, it is idealistic and depends upon the low internal resistance. This calculation is useful in every case to determine the upper limit that any given homopolar generator can achieve.

Lower Speed Generator Back Torque Test Results

Choosing one other set of test results, we will now look at an experiment that replaced the 2.5" pulley with a 2" pulley on the motor. Since conduction problems were occurring from time to time resulting from overheating and oxidizing of the liquid solder, I thought that lower current production would cause less heating. Therefore, the next test results were conducted at 600 RPM. Fig. 27 shows the results that are summarized in the table:

7/18/83 Test	Speed (RPM)	Total Generated Voltage	Total Generated Current	Drive Motor Power Consumption	Torque to Generator
Open Cir.	600	43 mVDC	-	139W	2.39
Closed Cir.	600	-	240ADC	150W	2.21
Difference				11 W	0.18

Here the back torque is calculated to be **0.18 Newton-meters**, which is slightly larger than the 2/1/83 test. The effective magnetic field calculates to be 0.173 Tesla in this case. Since it is based on the recorded voltage and current produced by the generator, it is judged to be a fairly accurate measure of the magnetic field seen by the rotating disk. This would help explain an increased back torque to some extent. It should be mentioned that an average of effective magnetic fields <u>for six tests</u> came out to be 0.163 Tesla. This test may seem to be a little on the high side but the lower speed may explain the lower armature reaction and less demagnetization of the ceramic.

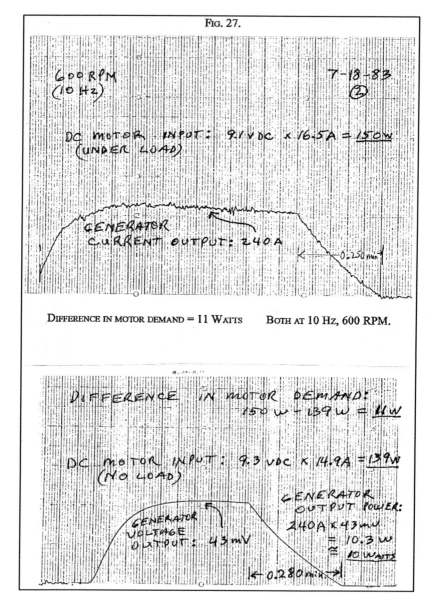

FIG. 27.

DIFFERENCE IN MOTOR DEMAND = 11 WATTS   BOTH AT 10 HZ, 600 RPM.

Approaching the calculation of back torque from another point of view, we can find the torque created by the passage of the generated current through the magnetic flux of the system. This equation,

$$T = \frac{\phi I}{2\pi}$$

(21)

yields **0.164 N-m** which is fairly close to the 0.18 N-m calculated from the motor's viewpoint. Of course, the correlation also shows in the comparison of the difference in power consumption of the motor (11 W) with the generated power (10W).

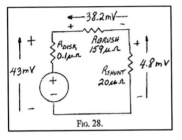

Fig. 28.

In Fig. 28 we see the equivalent circuit diagram for the 7/18/83 test. Interestingly, the comparison between this circuit and the 2/1/83 test shows only a 5% variation in the resistance of the liquid metal brush. This still is, however, the largest resistance in the system, which is the single most important limitation to the output power.

CONCLUSION

Recommendations for the Future

In conclusion, it should be mentioned that the test results shown in this report represent the "best" results that were obtained with the generator(s). Of course there were other test results which yielded irreconcilable power calculations, much of which were attributed to brush conduction loss or fluctuating meter readings. One example which is a bit different is the video tape that was made in September, 1983, by Dan Winter of the generator in action. It eliminated any chance of meter fluctuation error since I was able to use the "still action" control to copy down all of the readings at once. In that case, for some reason, the motor experienced two to four times the back torque that the generator was producing, based on the power measurements. I also tried, for the first time, the "closing the switch" method of holding the current shunt against the copper conductor to get voltage and then taking current output readings. Possibly this method introduced some loss due to poor conduction. However, cases like this one were difficult to account for.

For any future developments, I would be led toward a few variations such as disassembling the rotor and replacing the disk with the steel disk. Also, one of the directions that seemed important to Mr. Adam Trombly of the Acme Energy Research homopolar generator is to modify and attach an outside, steel cylinder to close the magnetic circuit. This would offer a path of low reluctance for over 90% of the magnetic circuit. Based on his verbal report of the results of his $250,000 project, this could offer an interesting improved generator, similar to the University of Texas, Center for Electromechanics, in Austin, Texas. The

Center conducted a study comparing various homopolar operating schemes and

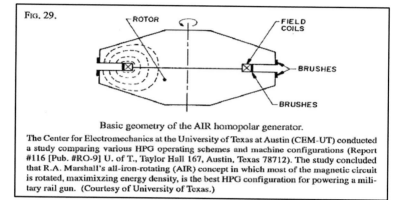

Basic geometry of the AIR homopolar generator.
The Center for Electromechanics at the University of Texas at Austin (CEM-UT) conducted a study comparing various HPG operating schemes and machine configurations (Report #116 [Pub. #RO-9] U. of T., Taylor Hall 167, Austin, Texas 78712). The study concluded that R.A. Marshall's all-iron-rotating (AIR) concept in which most of the magnetic circuit is rotated, maximixzing energy density, is the best HPG configuration for powering a military rail gun. (Courtesy of University of Texas.)

machine configurations [84]. The study concluded that R.A. Marshall's all-iron-rotating (AIR) concept seen in Fig. 29, in which most of the magnetic circuit is rotated, maximized energy density. Lastly, in the tradition of J.W. Then, who needed to publish a graph of galvanometer deflection vs. rev. /sec. to show that a one-piece homopolar generator would work as well as a two-piece, I have included my own graph of voltage vs. rev./sec. accumulated from a number of trials in Fig. 30. It demonstrates the linear dependence of *V on ω* .

As far as whether the one-piece homopolar generator can live up to the "N-machine" predictions of Bruce DePalma, Adam Trombly, and Paramabansa Tewari, I know that Dr. Marshall would have reported on anomalies years ago if the 90% closed magnetic circuit AIR generator had produced extra power output without corresponding power input.

Free energy from a rotating device will probably be found in the non-conducting disk design that Norman Paulsen first reported on in his book but was ignored by his Sunburst Community when Mr. Bruce DePalma came there in 1969. (See the reprint from Paulsen's book included, with permission, in the Appendix.)

Future Research Guide

In the last five years, research on homopolar or Faraday generators is not as easy to access through the literature searches because of the upsurge in magnetohydrodynamic (MHO) research. MHO uses ionized combustible gases in a magnetic field to generate electrical power. This may not be immediately apparent but suffice it to say that there are "Faraday-type" MHO generators as well. In fact, one of the articles in a recent search was entitled, "Distribution of Electric Fault Currents in MHO Faraday Generators".

Needless to say, Faraday-type MHO generators are not homopolar generators. Therefore, I have changed the name of the new edition of this book, though I wanted to give Michael Faraday credit for inventing a unique type of generator which still bears his name. In the earlier editions, I included an article about Faraday, from the N. Y. Times, which summarized the interesting flavor of excitement back in 1931 when his diary was first made public (100 years after

36

his generator experiments). It also mentions Faraday's theory of electricity and gravitation which wasn't confirmed until Einstein came on the scene. (My thanks to the N. Y. Times for allowing me to reproduce the article.)

Fig 30. Voltage Vs. Revolutions Per Second

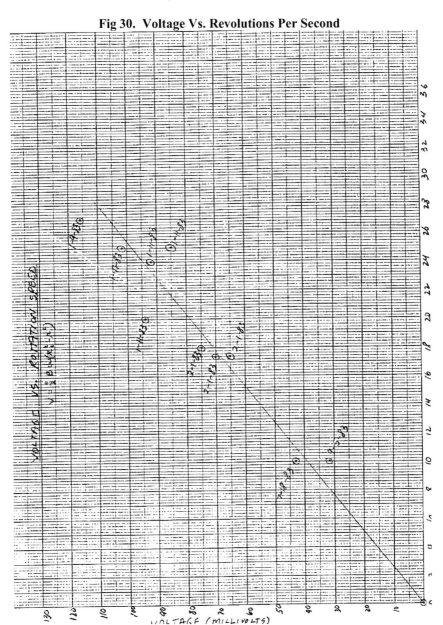

Other important people that have contributed to the science of homopolar generators (or "HPGs") include Einstein and Tesla. When Albert Einstein is mentioned, it is important to note that he also did some work theoretically predicting how a special type of homopolar generator would function. In the section of this book on the Field Rotation Paradox, we find a description of the Wilson experiment in which a dielectric is rotated in a magnetic field. At the beginning of the 20th century, scientists were concerned with any type of experiment that would have to take account of the motion of the elementary magnets composing a rotating magnet. As Tate points out [85], the hypothesis of "the stationary lines of induction" would have to be ruled out and so a non-conductor was necessary. Thus, the Einstein and Laub experiment with a non-conducting dielectric was perfect for fulfilling these conditions Tate outlined.

In the case of rotating a dielectric that was also magnetic, Einstein and Laub worked out a prediction of what the potential difference across it would be [86]. Today's ceramic magnets fall into this category though very few remember Einstein and Laub's equation. Five years later, Wilson and his son performed the experiment with steel balls imbedded in paraffin and confirmed Einstein's prediction [87]! (Also see Clark's magnetic dielectric patent on p. 17 of this book.) Tate believed, the abovementioned article, that the Einstein-Laub equation involved the "moving lines of induction theory" and required "that we take account of the translatory motion of the lines of induction attached to the individual elementary doublets." It is interesting to see the emphasis on imaginary lines of induction back in the early part of the 20th century though the description of them remains vague.

Last but not least, Nikola Tesla also contributed to the homopolar generator advancement with a few designs of his own. In an article entitled, "Notes on a Unipolar Dynamo", Tesla emphasizes the important effects of eddy currents generated by the rotation of the disk [88]. He believed they could be configured to strengthen the magnetic field. He even suggested that, once designed properly, the magnetic field could be gradually removed. "The current, once started, may then be sufficient to maintain itself and even increase in strength..." With an endorsement from Tesla for such free energy, this is actually the most viable method for increasing the efficiency of the N-Machine, using Optimum Spiral Current Path design.

In the Appendix, I have included reprints from a few conferences at which I presented the results of my HPG project, including the 1990 Tesla Symposium where I explored "The Homopolar Generator: Tesla's Contribution". The Intersociety Energy Conversion Engineering Conference (IECEC) paper summarizes my latest assessment of the work I performed on the homopolar generator.

Due to reader request, a step-by-step calculation of the voltage across a homopolar generator is included in the Appendix for those in need of help with the mathematics involved.

Naturally, the area of unipolar, homopolar, or Faraday generators will continue to grow as DC power comes back into use on a large scale. In the near future, superconductors will reach room-temperature and thereby make DC power much more efficient, safer, and less costly to transmit. Superconducting power transmission cables will be designed to carry large amounts of current without loss and the homopolar generator/motors will playa big role in power generation, utilization and possibly inverting for AC output. Possibly we will then see developments in the efficiency of these generators, beyond what is achieved even in the highly tuned research laboratories of today.

REFERENCES

[1]   *Technology Illustrated*, Sept. 83, p.64
[2]   *Cryogenics*, Sept.82, p.435
[3]   Zahn, M., *Electromagnetic Field Theory*, J.Wiley, NY   p.423
[4]   Ibid., p.425
[5]   Faraday, M., *Experimental Researches in Electricity*, QC 503 F21 1965, par. 217 (p.63)
[6]   Faraday, M., *Diary of Michael Faraday*, (pub. 100 years after his discovery of the Faraday generator)
[7]   Faraday, M., *Phil Trans. of Royal Acad.* 122, 183, 1832
[8]   Weber, W., *Pogg Annalen*, 1841 Bd. Iii, p.354
[9]   Preston, *Phil. Mag. S.*, 5, 19, 216, 1885
[10]   Plucker, *Pogg. Annalen*, 1852, p.357
[11]   Preston, *Phil. Mag.*, 33, 179, 1917
[12]   Poincare, H., *Ecl. Elect. xxiii*, 41, 1900
[13]   Kennard, *Phil. Mag.*, 33, 179, 1917
[14]   Barnett, *Phys. Rev.*, 2, 321, 1913
[15]   Valentiner, *Phys. Zeit.*, 6, 10, 1905
[16]   Hering, *Trans. AIEE*, 27, 1341, 1908
[17]   Pegram, *Phys. Rev.*, 10, 591, 1917
[18]   Djuric, J. *App. Phys.*, 9, 2623, 1976
[19]   Lowes, E, *J. Phys. D*: App. Phys. 11, 765, 1978
[20]   Sommerfeld, *Electrodynamics,* Academic Press, NY, 1955, V.III, p.285
[21]   Roentgen, *Ann. Physik*, 35, 264, 1888
[22]   Wilson, *Phil Trans.*, 204, 121, 1904
[23]   Djuric, J. *App. Phys.*, 46,687,1975
[24]   Pegram, p.252
[25]   Larmor, *Royal Soc. Trans.*, 1895A, p.727
[26]   Djuric, p.685
[27]   Then, J., *Am. J. Phys.* 30,414, 1962 [28] Then, J., p. 411
[29]   Crooks, et al., *Am. J. Phys.* 46, 729, 78
[30]   Lecher, E., *Ann. d. Phys.* 54, 276, 1895
[30]   Lecher, E., *Ann. D. Phys.* 54, 276, 1895
[31]   Hering, C., *Elec. World,* 51,559, 1908, Hering, C., *Trans. AIEE,* 42, 311,1923, and see ref. [16]
[32]   Blondel, A., *Electrician,* 75,344,1915
[33]   Cramp and Norgrove, *J. Inst. Elec. Eng.,* 78, 481, 1936
[34]   Cohn, G., *Elec. Eng.,* 68,441, 1949
[35]   Barnett, *Phys. Rev.,* 35, 323, 1912, Cullwich, *J. Inst. Elec. Eng.,* 85, 315, 1939
(36)   Moon and Spencer, *J. Frank. Inst.,* 260,214, 1955
[37]   Howe, *The Electrician,* Nov. 5, 1915, p.169

[38]   Zelany and Page, *Phys. Rev.*, 24, 544, 1924
[39]   Kimball, *Phys. Rev.*, 28, 1302, 1926
[40]   Cramp and Norgrove, *Proc. IEE* (London), 8, 487,1936
[41]   Das Gupta, *Am. J. Phys.*, 31,428, 1963
[42]   Feynmann, R., *FeynmannLectures on Physics*, Addison Wesley,Reading, MA, V.II, p.17-25,1964
[43]   Lombardi, *Am. J. Phys.*, 51,213, 1983
[44]   Landau and Lifshitz, *The Classical Theory of Fields*, 3rd ed., Pergammon, Oxford,1971, p.79
[45]   Lorrain and Corson, *Electromagnetic Fields and Waves*, W.H. Freeman & Co., San Francisco, 1970, p.226
[46]   Lewis, *J. Sci & Tech.*, 38,47,1971
[47]   Corson, *Am. J. Phys.*, 24, 127, 1956
[48]   Panofsky & Phillips, *Classical Electricity and Magnetism*, Addison Wesley, Reading, MA,p.l49
[49]   Cullwick, *Electromagnetism and Relativity*, J. Wiley & Sons, NY, 1962, p.143
[50]   Tate, *Bulletin Nat. Res. Council*, VA, Part 6,1922, p.79
[51]   Corson, p.129
[52]   Lorrain and Corson, p.663
[53]   Panofsky and Phillips, p.337
[54]   Becker, R., *Electromagnetic Fields and Interactions*, Blaisdell Pub., NY;p.378
[55]   Panofsky and Phillips, p.338
[56]   Trocheris, *Phil. Mag.*, ser.7, VAO,#310, p.ll50
[57]   Sagnac, *C.R.*, 157, 708, 1913
[58]   Schiff, Proc. *Nat. Acad. Sci.*, 25, 391, 1939
[59]   Marinov, S., *Found. of Physics*, V.8,n.1I2, p.137, 1978
[60]   Sommerfeld, v.m, p.363
[61]   Einstein, A., *The Meaning of Relativity*, Princeton Univ. Press, NY, 1950, p.61
[62]   Adler, Bazin, Schiffer, *Intro. to General Relativity*, McGraw Hill, 1957,0.257
[63]   Ise and Uretsky, *Am. J. Phys.*, 26,431, 1958
[64]   Webster, *Am. J. Phys.*, 31, 590, 1963
[65]   Webster, p.593
[66]   Trocheris, p.ll43
[67]   Cullwick, p.ll4
[68]   Adler, et al., p.258
[69]   Sears and Zemansky, *University Physics*, Addison Wesley, 1970 (All figures and equations in this section are from this textbook)
[70]   Drever, *Phil. Mag.*, "A Search for Anisotropy ofInertial Mass using a Free Precession Technique", 6, 683, 1961
[71]   Corconi & Salpeter, "A Search for Anisotropy of Inertia", Gravity Research Foundation, 58 Middle St., Gloucester, MA, 01930. (Winning essay on gravity for 1958)

[72]   Kozyrev, N., "Possibility of Experimental Study of the Properties of Time",
       NTIS, 5285 Pt. Royal Rd., Springfield, VA 22151, Report #JPRS-45238,
       5/2/68
[73]   Seiler, H., unpublished letter, 6/23/82, (Head Physician, Privatlinik, Bircher-
       Benner, Zurich, Switzerland)
[74]   Jackson, *Classical Electrodynamics,* J.Wiley & Sons, NY, 1975, p.173
[75]   Then, pAll
[76]   Lewis, pA8. lIt is found that for some operational requirements the use of
       copper may confer an advantage while for others, steel appears to offer a
       satisfactory design and is also cheaper."
[77]   Valone & Shih, *Electronics,* "Protected Regulator has Lowest Dropout
       Voltage", 4/ 24/80, p.130
[78]   Wunderlich and Shaw, *Am. J. Phys.,* 51, 797, 1983
[79]   Das Gupta, I.E. (I) *Journal E-L,* 50, 48, 1969
[80]   Lewis, pA8
[81]   Hong and Wilhelm, *J. App. Phys.,* 47,906, 76
[82]   Nasar, *Electromagnetic Energy Conversion Devices and Systems,* (TK
       2181, N37, 1970) p.127
[83]   Woodson and Melcher, *Electromechanical Dynamics,* J. Wiley & Sons, NY,
       p.288
[84]   Marshall, A.J., Report #116 Pub. #RO-9 from U of Texas, Taylor Hall 167,
       Austin, TX78712
[85]   Tate, p.93
[86]   Einstein and Laub, *Ann. d. Phys.,* 26, 532, 1908
[87]   Wilson, M. & H.A., *Proc. Royal Soc. London* A, 89,99,1913
[88]   Tesla, N., *The Elec. Eng.,* Sept. 2, 1891

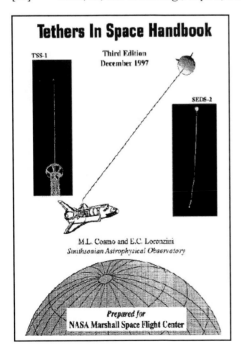

Tethers In Space Handbook

TSS-1

Third Edition
December 1997

SEDS-2

M.L. Cosmo and E.C. Lorenzini
Smithsonian Astrophysical Observatory

Prepared for
NASA Marshall Space Flight Center

In 1997, NASA started seriously experimenting with tethers in space. See "Failure Resistant Multiline Tether" patent 6,173,922 by Hoyt & Forward for example. "Electric current is then driven either towards bother ends of the tether or towards the supply on both sides. The schematic of current flow in the system is shown in FIG. 30. The action of these flowing currents across the geomagnetic field result in Lorentz forces on the tether. These forces result in a net torque on the tethered system. The physics of the rotational acceleration are equivalent to the physics of a homopolar generator." However, the scientists have consistently measured much less voltage and current than expected. The present book explains the action of an HPG trying to generate power in the rotating frame, which is like trying to measure voltage "on the disk" which will fail, as I have proven in the lab. The only contributing factor that tethers have going for them is really the electric gradient between high and low orbit plasma density. – T. Valone, 2012

APPENDIX

This revised Appendix has HPG formulas and patents, the Dr. Corson correspondence, an article from Dr. Inomata, Einstein's rotating dielectric articles, and a solution to the ball bearing motor. Developments that deserve mention are:

1. **Dr._Marc Millis** from NASA ("Challenge to Create the Space Drive", *J. of Prop. & Power*, V.13, No.5, 1997, p. 577) notes that Kennard [13] and Eagleton (p. 136 of this book) use the homopolar motor to illustrate a paradox of apparently imbalance magnetic reaction forces that may be a source for a new space drive.

2. **Heavy Electrons** in metals (Nature, V. 309, 21, 6/84) with a rare earth compounds (e.g. $CeAl_3$, UP t_3) have demonstrated an effective mass ($m*$) up to 200 times their true mass (m_e). Such metals are important for experiments such as the Searl disc and Hooper tube so the centrifugal force on the electron is utilized to enhance the HPG emf, designed so that the negative electrons are sent to the outer edge by both forces (see Hooper's # 3,656,013 patent, col.7, line 29)

3. **Armature reaction** has been claimed to be eliminated several tunes in the literature. Another techniques is to use a compensating shield such as seen in *Electromagnetic Energy Conversion Devices & Systems* by S. Nasar (Prentice-Hall, 1970, p.124-130) Designed for a drum HPG, it may be modified for a disk HPG.

4. **A cooling device** with a circulating inner liquid for outer liquid metal brushes is in the Ugrimoff patent of 1910 (#970,407) which has a centrifugal trough radial sliding contacts similar to the axial brushes on p.22 & 26 of this book.

5. **A homopolar transformer** has just been invented by Robert Smith in the U.S. Navy (# 5,821,659). It is reversible and has many taps for voltages.

6. **Patents** mentioned in this book can be obtained for $1.75 from patentee. com or $3.00 USPTO (www.uspto.gov) or www.google.com/patents

7. **Weber electrodynamics** (see page 3) is being revived with a recent test of the experiments of Muller (*Galilean Electrodynamics* May/June 1990, p. 92) and Kennard (p.3,4 of this book) by Wesley (*Found. of Physics Letters* V.3 No.5, 1990 p.471). Mencherini (Phys. Essays, V.6 no. 1, 1993, p.45) also defends Muller's HPG experiments and brings into question the Maxwell approach to unipolar induction.

8. **New liquid-gallium based alloy**, promises to be an environmentally safe replacement for mercury and 20 times more conductive. Developed by Professors James Rancourt and Larry Taylor of Virginia Polytechnic Institute and State University. The Virginia Center for Innovative Technology has licensed it to a company called NonMerc. It is recommended for homopolar generator liquid metal brushes.

9. **Geared Electromechanical Rotary Joint** developed by NASA, Goddard Spaceflight Center, Greenbelt MD (*NASA Tech Briefs*, 12/94) offers springy planetary gears that provide a low-noised electrical contact. The illustration shows a cross section of an inner gear with these small springy planetary gears between it and the outer ring gear. It is designed to overcome the disadvantages of sliding contact and rolling contact electrical contacts. They are made from beryllium copper which is a self-cleaning material. The average diameter is 6.35 mm with 13 teeth and designed to be slightly oversized.

APPENDIX I

HOMOPOLAR REFERENCE MATERIAL

Welding and Billet Heating With Homopolar Generators

By Jerel B. Walters and Ted A. Aanstoos

New processes for welding and billet heating based on the application of an old principle — the homopolar generator (HPG) — may soon be commercially available.

Research efforts over the past decade by the Center for Electromechanics, University of Texas at Austin (CEM-UT) have resulted in the development of a new design of the homopolar generator invented by Michael Faraday in 1831. By pulsing this high energy power source, CEM-UT has butt welded numerous materials and cross sections, including 6 in. (150 mm) in diameter API schedule 80 pipe and 90 lb/yd (45 kg/m) rail in less than 3 s. Small carbon steel and exotic alloy billets have also been heated from room temperature to forging temperature in less than 4 s.

CEM-UT performed its research with a 10 MJ HPG capable of making welds up to 10 in.^{2} (6450 mm^2) in area and heating steel billets weighing up to 10 lb (4.5 kg). To transfer the processes to industry, CEM-UT licensed its HPG technology to Parker Kinetic Designs Inc., Austin, Tex. Parker Kinetic Designs (formerly called OIME Research & Development) is currently producing a 6.7 MJ compact pulsed homopolar generator designed for use as a research power supply. Its prime application to date is as a power supply for electromagnetic launch research. A 15 MJ industrial homopolar generator is under development as a power supply for industrial applications, including welding and billet heating.

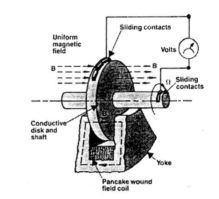

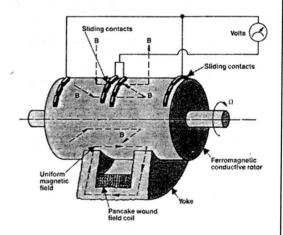

Fig. 1 — Schematics of disc and drum homopolar generators.

Operating Principles of The Homopolar Generator

The HPG is an electric machine which converts stored rotational kinetic energy into electric energy using the Faraday effect. It is a low voltage, high current device that is most advantageously operated in the pulsed mode, making it an excellent power supply for many applications that require short time, high power energy pulses. Pulsed mode operation of the HPG allows it to accept and store energy continuously from a low power source, and then deliver this energy to a load in the form of a controlled shape, high power pulse. The size of a pulsed mode homopolar generator is usually given in terms of its maximum amount of stored energy, which is typically expressed in megajoules (MJ).

The basic HPG consists of a cylindrical metal rotor spinning in a magnetic field. The rotor is supported at its ends by stub shafts mounted in low friction, high stiffness bearings. These bearings are in turn supported in bearing housings mounted in the machine's yoke. The yoke serves as both the generator's main structural component and, in most machines, as the return path for the applied magnetic field. This field is produced by one or more simple solenoids mounted inside the yoke.

Copper-graphite composite electrical brushes, and their associated bus bars and conductors, transfer current into or out of the rotor. The electrical portion of the HPG consists of a magnetic field coil powered by an auxiliary dc power source, and a generation circuit consisting of brushes, bus bars, and conductors.

There are two basic electrical configurations for rotational homopolar generators — disc and drum (see Fig. 1). Disc machines use an axial applied magnetic field in the rotor and a radial current flow to produce the stopping torque (Lorentz force) during the machine's

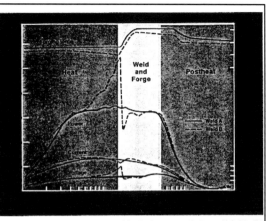

discharge. Drum machines use a radial magnetic field and axial current flow. Both types are usually powered by an external auxiliary prime mover such as a hydraulic motor.

Current Pulsing — The HPG's discharge circuit can be modeled as a high capacitance, low voltage capacitor. When the rotor is spinning at its maximum design speed, the machine is fully "charged." In this condition, with brushes lowered onto the rotor surface and field coil energized, the HPG will be producing its open circuit voltage at the output terminals. If this voltage is now switched across a load, a current will begin to flow out of the generator. Magnitude and shape of the current pulse will be determined by the discharge circuit's characteristic impedance.

The current interacts with the machine's magnetic field to rapidly decelerate the rotor, converting the stored rotational kinetic energy into electrical energy. As the rotor slows, the voltage it is producing decreases, which causes a drop in the magnitude of the discharge current. This process continues until the rotor comes to a full

stop and the terminal voltage and discharge current go to zero.

At this point, the HPG is ready to be disconnected from the load, have its brushes raised, and again motored to the desired discharge speed. Note that the HPG's rotor need not come to a full stop during a discharge. By killing the field coil excitation early in the discharge pulse, the brushes can be safely raised from the rotor in the no-current condition before it stops.

Thus, the rotor can be decelerated from full speed to some fraction of full speed, allowing a large machine to produce lower energy pulses.

Equations — Voltage output is determined by the equation, $V = \theta\omega/2\pi$, where $\theta = BA$ and $V =$ open circuit voltage, volts; $\theta =$ magnetic flux, webers; $\omega =$ angular velocity, rad/s; $B =$ magnetic flux density, tesla; and $A =$ area of swept magnetic field flux m^2.

Total energy available is a function of the rotational kinetic energy stored in the rotor, which is determined by the equation, $E = J\omega^2/2$, where $E =$ kinetic energy stored in the rotor, joules; $J =$ the rotor's polar mass moment of inertia, kg-m^2; and $\omega =$ rotor angular velocity, rad/s.

FARA-DRUM 10
Pulsed Power Supply

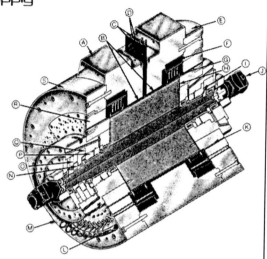

APPLICATIONS

There are numerous possible applications for the FARA-DRUM 10 pulsed power supply as a research tool in the scientific and military communities.

Coupled to a high energy density inductor and railgun this machine makes an ideal power supply for high velocity projectile research. It is also well suited for the production of pulsed high strength magnetic fields.

The FARA-DRUM 10 pulsed power supply can be used as a pulsed power source for high current switch testing or the generation of high energy electrical arcs. It is ideally suited for any laboratory application which requires high current pulses of electrical power.

A	Stator	K	Brush dust collection
B	Compensating conductor	L	Brush actuation manifold
C	Output terminal	M	Field coil terminal pin
D	Output terminal cooling tubes	N	Thrust rotor
E	Stator end cap (Non thrust end)	O	Outer thrust bearing
F	Field coil	P	Radial bearing (Thrust end)
G	Brush assembly	Q	Inner thrust bearing
H	Rotor shaft assembly	R	Brush access plug
I	Radial bearing (Non thrust end)	S	Stator end cap (Thrust end)
J	Hydraulic motor		

TECHNICAL SPECIFICATIONS

```
Maximum energy storage capacity ..................... 10 megajoules
Peak discharge current ........................... 1,500,000 amperes
Maximum open circuit voltage ........................... 100 volts
Maximum rotor speed .................................. 6,200 RPM
Magnetic flux density in air gaps ........................ 1.8 Tesla
Effective capacitance ................................. 2,000 farads
Impedance ..................... 7.1 microohms / 112 nanohenries
Maximum slip ring speed ...................... 186 m/s (610 ft/s)
Approximate dimensions ................. 1.2 m diameter X 1.8 m long
                                       (48 in diameter X 72 in long)
Approximate weight ........................... 10,000 kg (22,000 lb)
Motoring time to maximum rotor speed ..................... 2 minutes
Cycle rate ..................... Full energy discharge every 5 minutes
Discharge torque........................... 216,140 N-m (159,419 ft-lb)
```

Parker
Kinetic
Designs, Inc.

Post Office Box 26092 • Austin, Texas 78755 • Phone 512/834-0351

(See photo of the FARA-DRUM 10 on cover of this book)

FARA-LAB 60

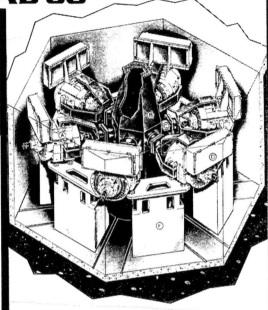

A   FARA-DRUM 10 pulsed power supply
B   Central hexagonal output bus
C   Coaxial bus configured for parallel circuit
D   Junction box
E   Output bus splitter
F   Generator pedestal

APPLICATIONS

New Modular Pulsed Power Supply For Research

The FARA-LAB 60 modular pulsed power supply has the highest current rating of any homopolar generator power supply in the world. It is comprised of six FARA-DRUM 10 pulsed power supplies, each of which can be connected to a common bus system. This provides the capability to interconnect the individual generators, forming various parallel and series circuit combinations. By so doing, the system can be configured to meet various load requirements, thus maximizing energy delivery efficiency.

All six of the FARA-DRUM 10 pulsed power supplies receive motoring power from a common 2,400 horsepower high pressure hydraulic system.

An automatic controller protects the modular power supply system from a wide range of accidents, including complete loss of site power. A low-impedance copper grounding mat protects personnel and equipment from system faults. Performance data from each generator is stored in computer memory during each discharge for rapid diagnostic capability.

The FARA-LAB 60 modular pulsed power supply is located in a sophisticated new pulsed power research facility at The University of Texas Balcones Research Center in Austin, Texas. It is owned and operated by The Center for Electromechanics, The University of Texas at Austin.

The system was designed by The Center for Electromechanics and is being manufactured and installed by Parker Kinetic Designs, Inc.

TECHNICAL SPECIFICATIONS

Maximum energy storage capacity . . . . 60 megajoules
Peak discharge current . . . . 9,000,000 amperes
  (Six machines in parallel circuit)
Maximum open circuit voltage . . . . 600 volts DC
  (Six machines in series circuit)
Maximum rotor speed . . . . 6,200 RPM
Magnetic flux density in air gaps . . . . 1.8 Tesla
Effective capacitance (per machine) . . . . 2,000 farads
Impedance (per machine) . . . . 7.1 microohms 112 nanohenries
Maximum slip ring speed . . . . 186 m/s (610 ft/s)
Approximate dimensions (per machine) . . . . 1.2 m diameter X 1.8 m long
  (48 in diameter X 72 in long)
Approximate weight (per machine) . . . . 10,000 kg (22,000 lb)
Motoring time to maximum rotor speed . . . . 2 minutes
Cycle rate . . . . Full energy discharge every 5 minutes
Discharge torque (per machine) . . . . 216,140 N-m (159,419 ft-lb)

Parker
Kinetic
Designs, Inc.

Post Office Box 26092 • Austin, Texas 78755 • Phone 512/834-0351

HOMOPOLAR FORMULAE

Voltage on the disk:
$$V_0 = \omega\phi/2\pi$$

where $\omega = 2\pi f$

f = frequency revolution per second

ϕ = magnetic flux in tesla-meter^2

V_0 = voltage in volts

Torque developed by current:
$$T = I\phi/2\pi$$

where I = current in amperes

T = torque in Newton meters

$$dT = B\,I\,r\,dr$$

opposes rotation of disk

$$T = BI \int r\,dr + \tfrac{1}{2} B\,\omega_m\,(r_1^2 - r_2^2)$$

$$T\,\omega_m = V_0\,I = \tfrac{1}{2} B\,\omega_m\,(r_1^2 - r_2^2)\,I$$

$$T = \tfrac{1}{2} BI\,(r_1^2 - r_2^2)$$

IR-drop developed by disk:
$$R = \int dr/2\pi\sigma tr = (\ln r_1 - \ln r_2)\,2\pi\sigma t$$

where σ is the conductivity of the disk in S/m

t is the thickness of the disk

r_2 is radius of shaft

r_1 is radius of the disk

R = resistance in ohms

Use $V = IR$ to find drop across disk & choose disk metal carefully

Terminal Voltage from disk: $V_t = V_0 - IR$

Power loss within the HPG: $W_L = I^2 R$ in watts

Output Power of the HPG: $W_0 = IV_t$ in watts

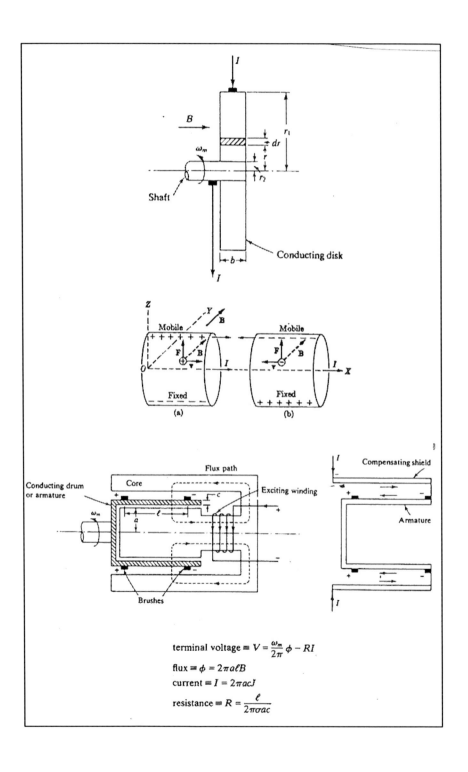

terminal voltage $\equiv V = \dfrac{\omega_m}{2\pi}\phi - RI$

flux $\equiv \phi = 2\pi a \ell B$

current $\equiv I = 2\pi ac J$

resistance $\equiv R = \dfrac{\ell}{2\pi\sigma ac}$

(**Note**: The following exchange of letters expands upon the theme introduced on pages 6-8 of this book where Dr. Corson and the book by Lorrain and Corson are mentioned. The emf on the disk from the rotating frame of reference is the theme of the discussion. The letters have been faithfully reproduced using OCR for reading clarity with signatures added.)

CORNELL UNIVERSITY
615 CLARK HALL
ITHACA, N.Y. 14853

June 26, 1984

Dr. Thomas Valone
Erie Community College
Main Street and Youngs Road
Buffalo, NY 14221

Dear Dr. Valone:

You have my permission to reprint anything you want from the American Journal of Physics 1956 article you refer to in your letter of June 18. I do not know whether the Journal requires permission to be granted before reprinting or not.

I wrote that paper, incidentally, as a result of the Moon paper in the Journal of the Franklin Institute--probably the 1955 paper you refer to in your list of references. Moon did not understand the concept of measuring things in two different coordinate systems moving relative to each other.

Sincerely yours,

Dale R. Corson

Dale R. Corson
President Emeritus

njh

8-16-84

Dr. Dale. R. Corson
Cornell University
615 Clark Hall
Ithaca, NY 14853

Dear Dr. Corson:

Thank you for your letter of June 26, granting me permission to reprint a diagram from your AJP article.

When you mentioned the Moon article and the concept of measurements in relative reference frames, it brought to mind the discovery that I have made in that regard. In the enclosed report on page 32 you will see a description of an experiment that I performed to test the existence of a measurable potential in the rotating frame of a one-piece homopolar generator. The voltmeter did not respond to the presence of over 100mV of emf throughout was simultaneously measurable in the rest frame.

This seems to be at odds with your prediction which I discuss on pages 10 through 12. Since this is a fundamental experiment which also has bearing on measuring a potential due to the- earth's rotation, etc., I would appreciate your comments on it before I send the manuscript to the publisher. Thank you.

Sincerely,

Thomas Valone

Thomas Valone Instructor Physics Unit
cc: Dr. Richard Dollinger,
SUNYAB EE Dept.,
Dr. Dennis Malone
SUNYAB EE Dept.

CORNELL UNIVERSITY
615 Clark Hall, Ithaca, NY 14853

September 17, 1984

Dr. Thomas Valone
Physics Unit
Erie Community College
Main Street and Youngs Road (Amherst)
Buffalo, NY 14221

Dear Dr. Valone:

I have returned to Ithaca for a few days and have your letter of August 16th. Unfortunately, I do not have the time to study your manuscript in detail so that I understand it fully.

In your statement on page 12 in which you refer to electrostatic fields I believe you misread my 1956 paper. There is a gradient of a scalar potential only if there is an accumulation of charge somewhere, and since in the discussion here, as long as there is a closed circuit, there is no accumulation of charge and therefore no electrostatic fields. The s statement t was there simply to point out that such fields are absent in the case discussed. I believe you will want to read my words carefully and correct what I believe is a mistake in your manuscript.

I have had no opportunity to study your experiment which you refer to in your letter and which you discuss on page 32 in your manuscript. You must be sure that your voltmeter is not changing the experiment. Is there a possibility that charges are accumulating somewhere in the measuring circuit so that electrostatic fields are being added to the ones you are seeking to measure?

Again, I do not have time to study your manuscript carefully enough, but are you distinguishing clearly between the concepts of potential which relates to the accumulation of charge and to electromotance having to do with the magnetic effects you are discussing?

I commend you for your experimental approach to the problem. You must be sure that you are measuring what you set out to measure, however, and not that plus artifacts introduced by the instrumentation.

Sincerely,

Dale R. Corson

ERIE COMMUNITY COLLEGE
Main Street and Youngs Road (Amherst) Buffalo, NY 14221

10-1-84

Dale R. Corson Ph. D.
Cornell University
615 Clark Hall
Ithaca, NY 14853

Dear Dr. Corson:

It was very nice meeting you in Rochester at the American Physical Society meeting. I must apologize for my over-eagerness in approaching you with my questions. I would much rather have had a few minutes with you just to hear your view of the hornopolar generator without pressuring you about my viewpoint. I thank you for your few comments that you gave me, including the suggestion that if the generator was an open-circuit then there would be an-electrostatic field present.

I did finally receive your letter when] returned and] see what you were trying to tell me at the conference.] seem to be attached to the classical interpretation given on page 7 of my thesis that since curl E = 0, the vector E is irrotational and therefore equal to the gradient of a scalar potential.

Whether or not there is an electrostatic field may be immaterial however. My real concern is the presence or absence of a measurable potential on the rotating disk, and whether it is electromotive or electrostatic.

Faraday believed that there was a potential within the rotating frame and set about to prove it by trying to measure the potential produced in rivers and streams by the earth's homopolar effect. There also have been a few articles recently, for and against this idea.

If there is a potential within the rotating frame, as your article proposes, two main problems seem to arise:
1) Attributing the case to the rotation of the external circuitry would be hard to imagine in the case of the earth
2) Residents on a magnetized, rotating space station would have an unlimited supply of electricity with no back torque (the two radial currents-generator and load- would create opposing torques).

I have enclosed a copy of the latest article on this subject (Lowes) in case you have time to look it over.

Lastly, instead of taking up your valuable time with this subject, would you be able to appoint or recommend a colleague or advanced graduate student to collaborate with on this important subject? I would like to resolve the many contradictions that exist in the literature concerning the homopolar generator and publish a review article in the American Journal of Physics.

Thank you very much Dr. Corson for your time and patience.

Sincerely

Thomas Valone

Thomas Valone
Instructor, Physics Unit

CORNELL UNIVERSITY
615 Clark Hall Ithaca NY 14853

January 4, 1985

Mr. Thomas Valone
Erie Community College
Main Street and Youngs Road (Amherst)
Buffalo, NY 14221

Dear Mr. Valone:

After I saw you in Rochester I was gone from Ithaca for an extended period and I received your October 1 letter only relatively recently. I believe your suggestion of finding someone to consult with you is a good one. I am not sure who such a person should be since I am not at all in close touch with physics activities at Cornell these days.

I have forwarded your letter to Professor Donald Holcomb, Chairman of the Department of Physics. Perhaps he will have someone to suggest or perhaps you could write to him directly seeking someone to talk with.

Best wishes.

Sincerely,

Dale R. Carson

Dale R. Carson

The Ball Bearing Motor Explained

The bearings in the ball bearing motor consist of precision-ground steel balls pressed tightly between inner and outer bearing races. The shaft is pressed into the inner bearing race. When the shaft, and inner race, turn, the balls roll without slipping. The balls rotate as shown, and also orbit around the inner race although at a slower rate than the rate of rotation of the inner race. Conversely, a torque which drives the balls to rotate will also drive the inner bearing race and the shaft to rotate.

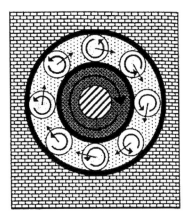

To understand how a torque is generated in the balls, it is easiest to imagine that we make the bearing races huge but the balls stay the same size. Then the races appear to be straight tracks, the bottom one stationary and the top rolling on top of the balls which are themselves rolling on the bottom track. Eliminating the curvature of the races makes the picture simpler but it is exactly equivalent.

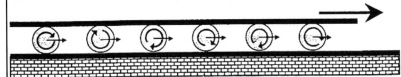

In the ball bearing motor, we have a large (~ 10 amp.) current passing between the outer and inner races through the balls. The current is always radial; this corresponds to a vertical current through the balls in our simplified picture. We only need to look at what happens with a single ball; the same process will be going on with all the balls and the torques generated will add. If 10 amps total are passing through each of 10 balls, the current of 1 amp through each ball is still a very substantial current. It is enough to magnetize the balls. This can be observed by placing the shaft of the motor in an arbitrary position and pulsing the current without starting the motor. The balls become magnetized in that position and the shaft will want to sit in that position.

(Reproduced with permission of Mark Gubrud)

Ampere's Law tells us that a vertical "North-South" current through a ball will produce a horizontal "East-West" magnetic field around the circumference of the ball, as shown. If the ball is made of a ferromagnetic material such as steel, it will become magnetized along the direction of the field. Note that this field wraps around the ball in a circle, it is not a polar field like the earth's magnetic field.

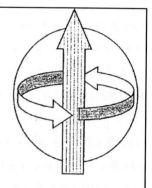

When the ball rotates, say to the right, the internal magnetization of the ball is dragged up toward a North-South orientation. Since the current is always vertical, the East-West magnetic field produced by the current forces the magnetization of the ball to change continuously back toward the East-West orientation. But this process lags due to the magnetic hysteresis of the steel. The net result is that the magnetization is partially dragged up toward the vertical, so there is now a component of the field which cuts across the current in one direction at the top of the ball and in the other direction at the bottom.

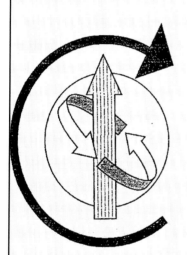

The Lorentz force law now tells us that the field cutting across the current one way at the top and the other way at the bottom produces forces which add up to a torque in the same sense as the sense of rotation. This explains why there is no torque when the motor is not turning, but once it gets a kick in either sense of rotation it develops torque in that sense.

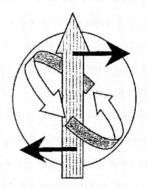

Note: The ball bearing motor consists of two ball bearings attached to an unmagnetized steel rod. or shaft. (Compare with the Kaplan patent of p. 168). When current is sent into one the rod starts rotating only if manually started. The circulating currents of the ball bearings and their resultant magnetic fields are similar to the armature reaction (current causing back torque) seen in the homopolar generator or conversely, the homopolar motor.

Science

Swoosh! It's a Railgun

A new electromagnetic launcher for earth and space

Ever since the city fathers of Florence ordered up brass cannon and iron balls in 1326 to defend themselves against the city of Lucca, in the first recorded use of explosive-powered metal artillery, gunsmiths have been trying to perfect their weapons. Guns have improved over the centuries—in range, accuracy and deadliness—but their firepower has always depended on the rapid expansion of exploding gases down a tube, which pushes the bullet forward. The maximum speed such gases—and thus the gun's projectile too

and abroad, the Vernean scheme shows promise of becoming a practical reality with far-reaching consequences: armor-piercing guns that can puncture the toughest steels, and perhaps a whole new era of space launchers.

The devices are called railguns, not because they sit atop railroad cars, like World War I artillery pieces, but because they consist of two parallel rails which act as both gunpowder and barrel. When the gun is fired, a powerful pulse of electricity goes down one rail. As the current

HOW THE DEVICE WORKS

1. When the railgun is fired, a powerful current goes from the capacitor bank into the two metal rails of a magnetic flux compression generator, creating a magnetic field.

2. A detonator ignites an explosive along one rail, pushing it against the other rail and driving the current from the flux compressor into the fuse behind the projectile.

3. The fuse vaporizes, creating a "plasma" (a gas that conducts electricity). The plasma current in the plasma interacts with the magnetic field produced by the current in the rails and provides the thrust to fire the projectile.

Source: Los Alamos Scientific and Lawrence Livermore Laboratories
TIME Diagram by Paul J. Pugliese

—can reach is severely constrained. None of the particles in the gases can travel faster than the speed of sound through the gas, at best about 10 km (6 miles) per sec.

Rockets, which are also driven by exploding chemicals, can exceed these sonic limits because the combustion takes place in the projectile itself. But rockets also operate under handicaps. So large are the fuel requirements for reaching orbital speed of 8 km (5 miles) per sec. that no one has yet been able to place a payload into orbit totaling more than 1% of the weight of the vehicle on the ground.

More than a century ago, visionaries like Jules Verne were suggesting a better way. A bullet-shaped vehicle, they claimed, could be propelled far faster by using powerful electromagnetic fields. Now, as a result of lab work in the U.S.

surges to the other rail, it vaporizes a metallic fuse in back of the bullet, creating a cloud of electrically charged particles, or plasma. Simultaneously, it generates a strong magnetic field between the rails, like those in an electric motor. The field exerts a force against the plasma, just as it would against a motor's rotor. But instead of spinning, the plasma moves forward, guided by the rails and pushing the projectile ahead of it. Not constrained by any sonic limitation, the plasma could, theoretically at least, approach the speed of light (300,000 km per sec.).

Revival of serious interest in railguns began a few years ago, when Physicist-Engineer Richard Marshall and his colleagues at the Australian National University in Canberra updated the old concept with some notable innovations,

including the plasma-creating fuse. They also increased the gun's muzzle velocity by resorting to an unusual power source: a huge homopolar electric generator which uses two rapidly spinning flywheels to build up and store electricity. In barely delivered as many as 500 megajoules of direct current—enough to light up a small city. Such a quick surge is essential for rapid buildup of the propelling magnetic field. Eventually, they were able to deliver the electromagnetic kick even quicker, and accelerated small plastic cubes at muzzle velocities of 6 km per second.

At the University of California's Los Alamos Scientific Laboratory and at the Lawrence Livermore Laboratory, scientists added another improvement: a magnetic flux compression generator, which increases the thrust of the magnetic field by squeezing it with a carefully directed explosive charge, a technology pioneered during nuclear weaponry research. When the gun is fired, the electric surge ignites the near end of an explosive strip placed just on the outside of the rails. As the detonation speeds forward, faster than the blink of an eye, it presses one rail against the other, confining the magnetic field between them in an ever smaller space and imparting still greater velocity to plasma and projectile. Teams led by Physicists Ronald Hawke and Max Fowler have fired half-inch projectiles down a railgun's square-bore barrel at an estimated 10 km per sec. They believe velocities of 150 km per sec. could be reached.

That will require much more research. One problem: single-shot railguns like the Los Alamos-Livermore machine must be painstakingly rebuilt after each firing. The projectiles also have an annoying habit of breaking apart when they leave the gun barrel. But the. remarkable possibilities—high-speed guns of almost every kind that can shoot through practically anything—ensure continued research, financed jointly by the Departments of Defense and Energy.

Unlike rockets, missiles launched by railguns would not leave fiery, polluting exhausts detectable by satellite. In a forthcoming issue, Physics Today reports that some scientists think that railguns, firing a stream of high-velocity particles at a target of deuterium and tritium, may offer the best way yet of achieving controlled fusion, a key energy hope for the future. Perhaps the most far-reaching application involves the space colonization ideas of Princeton Physicist Gerard O'Neill. He and some colleagues at M.I.T. are already building models of kindred electromagnetic launchers that they believe could be assembled on the moon and used to propel tons of lunar ores into space for construction of solar-powered space habitats. —By Frederic Golden. Reported by Melissa Ludtke Lincoln/New York

Reprinted with permission from Time, and Life, Inc.

Origin of the force on a current-carrying wire in a magnetic field

W. R. McKinnon, S. P. McAlister, and C. M. Hurd

National Research Council of Canada, Ottawa, Ontario, Canada K1A OR9

(Received 17 March 1980; accepted 23 July 1980)

What is the microscopic origin of the force $F = I.(i \times B)$ which acts on a wire of length $I.$ carrying a current i in a magnetic induction B? This deceptively simple question, which is at least 100 years old,[1] relates to a fundamental experiment in electromagnetism. Yet in the current literature[2] and in some basic textbooks[3] one still sees an explanation that is wrong, except for free electrons. Proper discussions of the problem are rare, and brief[4]; here we draw attention to the incorrect textbook arguments and provide a more detailed view of the origin of the force F than is generally available.

Let us refer to the arrangement of fields and current

493   Am. J. Phys. 49(5), May 1981   0002-9505/81/050493-02$00.50   © 1981 American Association of Physics Teachers   493

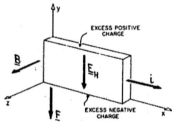

Fig. 1. This shows the arrangement of fields considered for an ideal conductor (Hall coefficient is negative) where in the steady state the electrons flow longitudinally along the negative x axis with a concentration gradient along the y direction.

the itinerant negative charges are piled up transversely, giving E_{II}, there is exposed positive charge on the fixed ions at the sample's other transverse extremity. The effect of F_{II} acting on this exposed charge is said to be the source of Ampère's force F. Thus the force on the itinerant electron system is in this view transmitted to the material of the conductor through the Hall field's effect on the stationary lattice of positive ions.

This argument gives the correct sign for F in the special case of a negative Hall coefficient (R) considered in Fig. 1, but it predicts incorrectly that the direction of F depends on the sign of R. To avoid this difficulty, one might argue that a positive R implies positive mobile charges (holes). The lattice must then have a net negative charge to preserve charge neutrality, and the direction of F is correctly predicted. However, experiments show[5,6] that the longitudinal current i comprises negatively charged particles whatever the sign of R. Furthermore, regardless of the sign of the charge carriers, the argument predicts incorrectly that there is no Ampèrian force when R is zero.[7]

The flaw in the above argument is the incomplete treatment of the electron-lattice interaction. For an electron with a velocity v, mass m, and charge $-e$, moving in a periodic potential, its k vector changes according to[8,9]

$$h\, dk/dt = -eE - e(v \times B). \tag{1}$$

In general, $h\, dk/dt \neq m\, dv/dt$, which implies[9] that the

shown in Fig. 1. Given that the induction B acts on the itinerant electron system in the conductor via the Lorentz force, the contentious point is how its influence is transferred to the material of the conductor to appear as Ampère's force F. The incorrect textbook argument involves the action of the transverse Hall field E_{II} on the lattice of positive ions. In an ideal conductor containing itinerant electrons with identical dynamical properties, E_{II} is established such that its effect in the steady state just balances the Lorentz force on each electron. The electrons thus move longitudinally under the influence of the primary electric field, but with a transverse concentration gradient. It is argued[2,3] that since

electron must feel an additional force F' caused by the positive ions. Thus

$$m\, dv/dt = -eE - e(v \times B) + F' = h\, dk/dt + F'. \tag{2}$$

F' is responsible for deviations from free electron behavior, such as a positive R, and vanishes for free electrons. F' will also be affected by deviations from perfect periodicity, which cause scattering of electrons, but here we need not enquire further about the nature of F'.

In the steady state in a fixed conductor the net transverse force on the n itinerant electrons must be zero. Thus

$$-neE_{II} - ne(v_d \times B) + F_t' = 0, \tag{3}$$

where F_t' is the net transverse component of F' and v_d is the drift velocity of the electrons. For a wire the latter is given by $v_d = L\, i/ne$. The transverse force (F_t) on the positive lattice comprises the force neE_{II} from the Hall field and the reaction force $-F_t'$. Thus

$$F_t = neE_H - F_t'$$
$$= -ne(v_d \times B) = L(i \times B), \tag{4}$$

with the second step following from (3). This is just the Ampèrian force F. Thus it is wrong to think in general that F is communicated to the lattice through E_{II} alone; both E_{II} and F' are involved, the latter being responsible for deviations from free electron behavior. The argument which neglects F' applies only to free electrons.

[1] E. H. Hall, Am. J. Math. 2, 287 (1879).

[2] A. Coombes, Am. J. Phys. 47, 915 (1979).

[3] See, for example, E. M. Purcell, *Electricity and Magnetism*, Berkley Physics Course, Vol. 2, (McGraw-Hill, New York, 1965), p. 219; or E. Della Torre and C. V. Longo, *The Electromagnetic Field* (Allyn and Bacon, Boston, 1969), p. 433.

[4] For example, W. E. Hazen and R. W. Pidd, *Physics* (Addison-Wesley, Reading, MA, 1965), p 378.

[5] G. G. Scott, Phys. Rev. 83, 656 (1961).

[6] S. Brown and S. J. Barnett, Phys. Rev. 81, 657 (1961).

[7] The Hall coefficient in several pure metals, including In, Al, Zn, and Cd, can be zero for suitable combinations of temperature and magnetic field strength.

[8] See, for example, J. M. Ziman, *Principles of the Theory of Solids*, 2nd ed. (Cambridge University, Cambridge, 1972), p. 171.

[9] A. B. Pippard, *The Dynamics of Conduction Electrons* (Blackie, London, 1965), p. 9.

THE ONE-PIECE FARADAY GENERATOR: RESEARCH RESULTS

Thomas Valone

Integrity Research Institute
1377 K Street NW, Suite 204
Washington, DC 20005

ABSTRACT

Faraday's disk experiments of 1831 have significance for a variety of reasons. From rail guns to Tokomaks to the origin of the earth's magnetic field, the Faraday generator has played a key role in present day science. Also called a homopolar, unipolar, or acyclic generator, it is the only one to produce electricity without commutation. Faraday's one-piece style of co-rotating the cylindrical magnet with the conducting disk is considered to be an unusual configuration and has eluded complete scientific explanation. To this day, prominent scientists can be found who believe it will not work since they operate with the flux line conceptualization. However, its importance is found in the connection to the earth's magnetic field, which evolves from a one-piece Faraday generator. A laboratory model is used to investigate the presence of back torque or armature reaction with the generation of electricity. For the first time, 1) the back torque of a one-piece homopolar generator has been measured, 2) the classification of the homopolar generator as a regulated voltage source has been experimentally determined, and 3) an effect, involving the lack of measurable voltage in the rotating frame, has been verified with a specially designed LED voltmeter. A back torque value of 0.17 N-m for a 25 Watt generator was obtained, in agreement with theory.

INTRODUCTION

The general homopolar generator (HPG) is one in which a disk or a drum is rotated *adjacent* to a magnet of the same size and shape. It has been suggested by DePalma that the one-piece Faraday generator (OPFG) may have the unusual possibility of the absence of back torque [1]. Subsequently, the author [2], Trombly [3], and Wil-

helm [4] began three independent experiments to replicate DePalma's results. Only one of us claim success in that endeavor, while Wilhelm and the author experienced back torque which compensated for the generated power in most cases. All three of the above scientists used liquid metal brushes in their experiments (Trombly-NaK; Wilhelm- Hg; Valone-low temperature solder) to reduce contact resistance. It is agreed that Trombly's sodium-potassium, having the viscosity of water, was superior to the other two. A major problem affecting all liquid metal brushes is the MHD instability caused by electrical conduction and motion in the presence of the magnetic field. None of us have calculated the measurable effect due to MHD that may have contributed to our results but they are expected to be negligible [5]. Referred to as an electromagnetic pumping force [6], the liquid metal becomes turbulent when the Reynolds number exceeds 2000. Eddy current and MHD losses then occur [7].

Eddy currents in the solid conducting disk are not a contributing factor to losses since there is no changing magnetic field. However, the motion of the conductor through the magnetic field, which remains stationary in space, whether or not the magnet rotates with the disk, creates the electromotive force (emf) measured from center to outer edge of the Faraday disk. A detailed discussion of the field rotation paradox may be found in my book, **The One-Piece Faraday Generator, Theory and Experiment** [2]. The simplest explanation for the operation of the HPG or the OPFG is the application of the Lorentz force on arbitrary radial segments as they pass through the magnetic field, thus explaining the force on the conduction layer electrons. Further molecular lattice effects of the motoring effect of back torque can be understood in terms of the Hall effect and the force on positive ions [10].

As the current is generated by the emf, a negative spiraling effect is seen as the disk rotation leads the radial current around the disk on its way across it. A further experiment is possible with a radially-segmented disk, to eliminate these eddy losses which tend to demagnetize the field. An alternative which Tesla proposed, is a *spirally-segmented disk*, which becomes a self-exciting Faraday generator (SEFG) [8], counter-ing demagnetizing effects. Tesla's suggestion eliminates the problem of the standard current flow creating a partial eddy current of its own. A wise note of Tesla's is to optimize the design of the spiral with the operating speed, thus prevent-ing any negative effect from excessive speed. In-tegrity Institute has plans to use computer model-ing for a spirally-segmented OPFG.

THE EARTH'S FARADAY DISK DYNAMO

Self-Sustaining Vs. Self-Exciting

One of the major reasons for interest in the OPFG is that the earth itself functions internally as a large OPFG. Moreover, the earth's OPFG is self-sustaining. "The crucial question is how the core liquid flows to act as a dynamo. Also a self-sustaining dynamo does not require a constant supply of magnetic field, it does require a con-stant supply of mechanical energy to keep the conducting material moving. In the case of the earth's core this means not only that the metallic fluid must flow in the right manner but also that some energy source must sustain the flow" [9]. Helical convection patterns called "rollers" created from conducting liquid metal are the best explanation of the mysterious secret of the earth's self-sustaining OPFG (SSOPFG).

In regards to the back torque of the earth's SSOPFG, Busse, Roberts, Lowes, and Wilkinson of the University of Newcastle upon Tyne are working on mechanical models of the earth's core to explain the changes in the fluid's speed and direction when the magnetic forces are large. A slightly different model that is being tested as well is the self-exciting OPFG (SEOPFG) which requires a spirally-segmented disk and/or exter-nal current-carrying coils as Tesla suggested. Since he noted that the armature current tends to demagnetize the field, in a normal solid disk con-figuration, Tesla felt that the subdivision of the disk would be an enhancement. In regards to these beneficial eddy currents, he writes, *"The current, once started, may then be sufficient to maintain itself and even increase in strength, and then we have the case of Sir William Thomson's 'current accumulator'"* [8].

A laboratory SEOPFG has been built by the Lowes and Wilkinson team [11]. Using metal rollers to simulate the earth's cylindrical eddy currents, the team found some interesting results after beginning with a few viscosity problems. "...a more efficient geometry was found, so effi-cient that the dynamo would self-excite in a com-pletely homogeneous state (i.e. with *no insula-tion*) at a much lower rotor speed than was believed possible" [12]. Upon achieving this breakthrough, their next goal is to look into the stability of the dynamo mechanism, hoping to ob-serve reversals of its magnetic field.

An illustration of a self-excited Faraday gener-ator (SEFG) is shown in Fig. 1, where the im-plication is that the model is a portion of the earth's SEOPFG [13]. The concept of the SEFG is used in some applications when an electromag-net is desired [14]. It is possible to use dual SEFGs, each exciting the other, by cross-connect-ing the windings. Furthermore, by creating two independent windings on each machine, with the fluxes adding on one and subtracting on the other, one can obtain two-phase alternating cur-rent [15].The AC power output of the dual SEFGs has self-limited oscillation of the mag-netic field polarities as well! Being a high cur-rent, low voltage device, the FG expands its range of applications with this AC improvement.

Through further study of the SEOPFG and the SSOPFG, we hope to strive toward Tesla's prediction of an energy accumulator or at least to approach the earth's amazing SSOPFG, (which is made entirely from molten metal). Whether the SEOPFG may become the free energy gener-ator of the future, solving home electrical power needs, as Trombly and DePalma believe, remains to be seen. (More information about free energy can be found in the other article by this author, "Non-Conventional Energy and Propulsion Methods" published concurrently in this IECEC **Proceedings**.)

One very pleasing discovery, that has not been found in the literature, was made with an early model of the OPFG. The OPFG, even the presence of a generated current, does not diminish or depress the emf, as normal voltage supplies and batteries do when loaded. The HPG and OPFG behave exactly as a *regulated voltage source* does. When tested at a fixed speed, the voltage remains the same no matter how much current is drawn from the generator [19].

Effects of the Earth's Faraday Generator

Historically, Faraday looked for the effects of the earth's OPFG, thinking that the electromotive forces (emfs) could be measured on the rotating disk. He tried to measure these emfs in rivers and streams [16]. Other scientists have committed a similar mistake, notably Corson [17], not knowing that such emfs are equally cancelled within the rotating frame by a self-created electrostatic field oppositely directed by the charge displacement [18]. Because **B** is not changing in time, curl **E** = 0. Therefore, the electric field that is created must be irrotational, i.e. electrostatic. (A lab test of the electrically neutral environment in the rotating frame is summarized in the Laboratory section.)

Though the emf of the earth's SSOPFG is not measureable on the surface of the rotating earth, some scientists believe the emf effect is most noticeable in the aurora borealis [20]. In fact a few have calculated the voltage that should be measurable from the pole to the equator in the magnetosphere [21]. Furthermore, some have even attributed the same HPG effects to the electromagnetic fields of stars [22].

RELATIVITY AND THE FARADAY DISK

Though space limitations prohibit a full theoretical analysis, most treatments of the HPG and the OPFG reviewed start with the Lorentz force to calculate the E field (E = v X B) and measurable voltage (emf). However, Becker notes in regards to the HPG, "we need the concept of the Lorentz force which is foreign to the Maxwell theory but is derivable by relativity theory" [23]. Then the nonvanishing divergence of the HPG effective electric field (E=Bwr, where w is the angular velocity) leads to a volume charge density for the generator, which correlates with the electrostatic field derived earlier. Library research revealed that special relativity can be used to describe the HPG and the OPFG, through use of the polarization/magnetization vectors of electromagnetism which are oppositely paired [24]. However, since the rotating disk is truly a non-inertial reference frame, general relativity must strictly be used [25]. Fortunately, since the curvature tensor vanishes, space is flat and the Lorentz metric is applicable, though various authors derive slightly different results using general relativity [26]. A table has been assembled to summarize the interesting relativistic facts that various authors have contributed to this subject (Fig. 2) [27].

LABORATORY RESULTS

A One-Piece Faraday Generator With Liquid Metal Brush

With three preliminary models, a fourth working prototype of the OPFG was fabricated using 8" ceramic magnets (four on each side of disk) and a 1/2" thick copper disk (Fig. 3). A General Electric current shunt (50 mV @ 2500 A) was used for accurate current measurement and a DC motor with 12 V battery power. Between Trombly, DePalma, Wilhelm and the author, however, this OPFG had the highest internal resistance, (which alone limits the theoretical maximum power output). Using an Electronics Limited Milliohmeter (Model 47A), it was measured at 230 microhms (+/- 10) with the current shunt disconnected. The GE current shunt contributed 20.0 microhms to the circuit while the contact resistance of the milliohmeter leads was about 30 microhms. Noting the contact resistance of copper brushes, the danger of mercury, and the wetting problem of mercury, it was decided to fabricate a circular trough with AC heaters for a low temperature solder (Wood's Metal) brush. Through one year of trial and error, it was discovered that the brush of an HPG has to be located as close to the disk as possible to obtain the maximum emf and current. Therefore, a special circular flange was designed (see Fig. 4) to pass through the circular trough filled with hot, melted solder.

Without the internal resistance of the liquid metal brush, the internal resistance of the copper disk and 1" brass shaft was measured to be about 0.1 microhm. Woodson and Melcher show that the maximum current can be calculated using the open circuit voltage, which yields about 500,000 Amps, at 1000 RPM. The maximum power that could therefore theoretically be delivered at that speed is about 30 kW [28]. While impressive, this shows the vital importance of a very low resistance brush system for high power output HPGs. For example, with the help of superconducting magnets, Northern Engineering Industries in England has designed an HPG capable of 1300 megawatts of continuous output [29].

Testing for Output and Back Torque

The 8" ring magnets used were the Ferrimag 5 #MF-51239 which have a 4" hole in the center, where the flux actually reverses. Though the center flux is of much lower intensity than the rest of the magnet area, the effect forced the the average magnetic flux density (B) to become a calculated quantity. Using the standard $V=wBR/2$, where R is the difference of the *squares* of the inner and outer radii, we solved for the average flux density experienced by the OPFG during open circuit emf production. For six trials, the average $B = 0.163$ Tesla.

With B determined, the torque delivered to the generator by the DC motor could be calculated for each trial, using $P=wT$. The GE motor was a 24 V, 20 A, 3400 RPM, 1/2 Hp motor. However, since the efficiency curve could not be obtained from the dealer nor from GE, we were forced to assume 100% efficiency for all power calculations. Since the load to the motor varied less than 10% between open and closed circuit generator operation, the efficiency variation was expected to be minimal, though the efficiency itself was most likely less than 100%. (See Error Discussion section for more information.)

In one sample trial, with stripchart results shown in Fig. 5, at 1000 RPM, the open circuit voltage was measured to be 65 mV (bottom graph) while the drive motor power consumption was 249 watts, which yielded a torque calculation of 2.37 N-m. At the same speed, the short circuit current was measured to be 380 Amps (top graph), with the drive motor power consumption going up to 266 watts, yielding a torque calculation of 2.54 N-m. Taking the difference of the two torques, *we find 0.16 N-m extra torque* was needed to drive the generator during power output. Therefore, this is an in-

direct measure of the back torque of the generator. A digital tachometer was used to verify the speed, which was maintained at 16.7 Hz (1000 RPM).

In spite of this back torque, and the accuracy of the voltage and current measurements, the drive motor power consumption increased by only 17 watts while the generated power was 24 watts, with an estimated error of +/- 2 watts. This anomalous power output, often referred to as "free energy" [30], cannot be explained readily. The clear current output line of this trial shows good continuous conduction without the turbulence that plagued many further tests as the solder overheated. However, after teaching physics for several years and emphasizing error calculations, it becomes apparent that the relative errors in the three place accuracy of the power calculation become a source of the problem when the *subtraction* is made to obtain the difference in the motor power demand. The relative error is calculated to be at best +/- 6 watts and at worst, +/- 12 watts. *Therefore, the 17 watts is really accurate to only one digit.*

A second sample trial is shown where conduction through the liquid metal was hampered slightly and turbulence is apparent in the current output graph. Here the generator was operated at 600 RPM, with 45 mV and 240 A produced. Drive motor power consumption was 139 W open circuit and 150 W closed circuit, yielding a difference of 11 W. Torque to the generator was 2.39 N-m open circuit and 2.21 N-m closed circuit, yielding 0.18 N-m difference which is again within 10% of the expected range, in spite of the relative error discussion above, *which applies to torque measurement/calculations as well.* In this case however, the power difference of 11 watts was almost exactly equal to the generated power of the OPFG. It may be possible that a loss was created in the erratic conduction through the brush, increasing the resistance of the brush and therefore, decreasing the current output. This would cause the generated power to drop as well. Fresh solder should probably be used for each trial since it oxidizes.

Comparing with the theoretical calculation of back torque (using $T = J \times B$) from the point of view of the torque generated from the passage of generated current through the magnetic flux of the system T=BRI/2 (with the same definition of R as above), yields 0.164 N-m which is in close agreement with the torque difference method above. This calculation shows that back torque is really the same as a homopolar motor (HPM) effect, analogous to the back emf in motors. Researchers therefore try to maximize HPG effect while minimizing the HPM effect. Utilizing a 1) closed path magnetic field, as Trombly and Kahn, 2) a low reluctance disk (iron or steel), and 3) a spirally-segmented disk will all contribute to changing the balance of the unaltered or "natural" HPG and OPFG.

Testing Rotating Frame Voltage

A test of the relativistic effect of a neutral electric environment in the rotating frame of the OPFG disk was performed, *even in the presence of generated current.* Using a modification of a previously designed voltage regulator which has an internal voltage reference [32], an LED voltmeter was placed on the rotating OPFG to look for the presence of any voltage surpassing an arbitrary 15 mV threshold. Tested in the laboratory rest frame, with the solder-soaked leads sliding on the shaft and periphery, the LED turned off almost immediately as the OPFG started turning, generating over 100 mV. Designing the LED voltmeter to *turn off* as it measured the voltage was of great value for the high speed rotor motion. Since the LED circuit becomes part of the generator as it is rotating, it has been suggested that it cannot function because it is a conductor itself. However, since the LED voltmeter is a 9 volt system, *and stays lit,* the electrons in the low voltage emf environment are not overpowered by the effective electric field within the rotating frame. The small circuit, about the size of the 9 volt battery that was used, is diagrammed in Fig. 6.

ERROR DISCUSSION

Besides the previously mentioned relative error discussion in third digit precision that shows up in subtraction of measured values, the perplexing counter argument to the anomalous Trial #1 centers on the DC motor's efficiency. If the efficiency is assumed to be about 90%, for ex-

ample, instead of 100%, then we have the interesting problem where the transfer function of the motor is a constant 0.9 multiplied by the torque or the battery power delivered. This means that the values recorded for the "torque to generator" would be 10% lower and the *difference,* being the back torque of interest, would be 10% less as well. This creates an even greater advantage to the free energy advocates, who would see the OPFG becoming over-unity in this example.

For future experiments, it is important to have efficiency curves for the motor in use and to measure to four-place accuracy wherever possible. The fascinating discoveries of the OPFG in the lab, the connection to the earth's own core activity, and the prediction by Nikola Tesla make the interest in the OPFG justifiably increase year after year.

REFERENCES

[1] Bruce DePalma, **DePalma Institute Report,** No. 1, 1978. (The DePalma Institute is located in Santa Barbara, CA)

[2] Thomas Valone, **The One-Piece Faraday Generator, Theory and Experiment,** pub. by Integrity Research Institute, 4th ed., 125 pgs. 1988. Also see "The One-Piece Homopolar Generator", **Proceedings of the First and Second International Symposium on Non-Conventional Energy Technology,** 1981, 1983. Cadake Industries Pub., Clayton, GA. Also see "The Homopolar Generator: Tesla's Contribution", **Proceedings of the International Tesla Society Conference,** 1986, Colorado Springs, CO. Preliminary lecture: The Symposium on Energy Technology, Hanover, W.Germany, 1980.

[3] Trombly and Kahn, International Patent #WO 82/02126 Adam Trombly has not published results of his experiments with the NaK OPFG, performed under the auspices of the Acme Research Corp., but presently can be contacted through the Earth First Foundation, Evergreen, CO.

[4] Timothy Wilhelm, **Stelle Letter,** Vol.15, No.9, 10/80.

[5] Hong and Wilhelm, **J. App. Phys.,** 47, 906, 76.

[6] A.K. Das Gupta, **I.E. (I) Journal E-L,** 50, 48, 69

[7] D.L. Lewis, **J. Sci. & Tech.**, 38, 47, 1971

[8] Nikola Tesla, "Notes on a Unipolar Dynamo", **Electrical Engineer**, Sept. 2, 1891, p.258.

[9] Carrigan & Gubbins, "The Source of the Earth's Magnetic Field", **Scientific American**, Feb., 1979, p. 118

[10] W.R. McKinnon, et al., "Origin of the Force on a Current-Carrying Wire in a Magnetic Field", **Amer. J. Phys.**, 49(5), May, 1981, p.493

[11] Hindmarsh,Lowes, Roberts, and Runcorn, **Magnetism and the Cosmos**, American Elsevier Pub. Co., 1965

[12] Hindmarsh, et al., p. 124.

[13] Carrigan and Gubbins, "The Source of the Earth's Magnetic Field", **Scientific American**, Feb., 1979, p.122

[14] Sears Patent #3,185,877.

[15] M. Zahn, **Electromagnetic Field Theory**, J. Wiley, NY, p. 423

[16] Michael Faraday, **Experimental Researches in Electricity**, reprinted 1965

[17] Lorrain and Corson, **Electromagnetic Fields and Waves**, W.H. Freeman & Co., San Francisco, 1970, p.226

[18] Panofsky and Phillips, **Classical Electricity and Magnetism**, Addison Wesley, Reading, MA, p.149 as well as Culwick, **Electromagnetism and Relativity**, J.Wiley & Sons, NY, 1962, p.143.

[19] Surprisingly, this was verified with only a 1" OPFG using Samarian-Cobalt magnets. As the resistive load varied, the emf did not change.

[20] Pogg, **Ann.**, 1852, p.357

[21] F.J Lowes, "The Earth as a Unipolar Generator", **J. Phys. D: App. Phys.**, Vol. 11, 1978, p.765

[22] Leverett Davis, Jr., "Stellar Electromagnetic Fields", **Physical Review**, Vol.22, No.7, Oct.1,1947,p.632. Also see: E.N. Parker, "Magnetic Fields in the Cosmos", **Scientific American**, Aug. 1983, p.44

[23] Richard Becker, **Electromagnetic Fields and Interactions**, Blaisdell Pub., NY, p.378

[24] Panofsky and Phillips, **Classical Electricity and Magnetism**, Addison Wesley, Reading, MA, p.338

[25] Adler, Bazin, Schiffer, **Introduction to General Relativity**, McGraw Hill, 1975, p.257

[26] Webster, "Schiff's Charges and Currents in Rotating Matter", **American Journal of Physics**, 31, 590, 1963 and also Ise and Uretsky, "Vacuum Electrodynamics on a Merry-Go-Round", **American Journal of Physics**, 26, 4341, 1958

[27] Sagnac, **Compt. Rend.** 157, 708, 1410 1913 and Schiff, **Proc. Nat. Acad. Sci.**, 25, 391, 1939.

[28] Woodson and Melcher, **Electromechanical Dynamics**, J. Wiley, NY, p.288

[29] **Cryogenics**, Sept. 1982, p.435

[30] Thomas Valone, "Non-Conventional Energy and Propulsion Methods", **Proceedings** IECEC, 1991

[31] Valone & Shih, "Protected Regulator Has Lowest Dropout Voltage", **Electronics**, April 24, 1980, p.130

LIST OF FIGURES

THE REAL STORY of the N-MACHINE

by: **Thomas Valone, M.A., P.E.**
Integrity Research Institute
1377 K Street NW, Suite 204
Washington, DC 20005
1-800-295-7674

Introduction

At long last, here is the whole story about the N-Machine and its inventor. It was *suppressed* by one "new energy" conference this year and may disturb the reader's equilibrium if read in its entirety.

Ever since 1831, when Michael Faraday invented the rotating magnet ("homopolar") generator which produces electricity without commutation, it has defied complete analysis because of its operation totally within a non-inertial reference frame. It is the basis for the earth's magnetic field, which is regarded as a "self-sustaining" homopolar generator (HG), since the field is maintained through the helical convection patterns of the molten iron core.[1] The simple HG's output voltage (Figure 1) is determined by the magnetic field (B), the radius *squared*, and the angular rotation speed.[2]

Nikola Tesla proposed that the homopolar generator could become self-excited with a spirally-segmented disk or with externally mounted coiled conductors.[3] Yet, to this day, his suggestion has not been exploited by scientists and experimenters interested in free energy.

Instead, the brother of horror filmmaker Brian DePalma decided that no improvement to Faraday's homopolar generator was needed to produce free energy. He extrapolated his kinetic energy anomalies from spinning ball bearings to spinning magnets in 1977. Bruce DePalma was fascinated by suspended gyroscopes. Calling Faraday's generator an "N-Machine," he also regarded it as a magnetized gyroscope. In his Simularity Institute Report #62 (7/16/79), he gives a one sentence summary of the new theory:

The absence of rotational drag when power is withdrawn from the machine validates the hypothesis of direct conversion of inertial

energy to electrical energy through separation of the energy aspects in a rotating disc which is magnetized to convert the inertial polarization into the positive and negative poles of electricity.

In a videotaped interview for the World Symposium on Humanity (4/12/79), as well as in Report #60, DePalma asserts,

If you put electricity into this N-Machine generator all you will get is a short circuit!! The N-Machine will not go around as a motor! ...Consequently, when you throw a load on the N-Machine you don't throw a load onto the engine or turbine which is turning it.... Now this is really important!

He had a novel concept about rotating the magnets with the disk of the HG:

Electrical loading of an N generator produces an internal torque between the conducting electrical disc and the attached ring magnets. However, since they are firmly cemented together this torque cannot escape from the machine and load the drive motor or engine (S.I. Report #60).

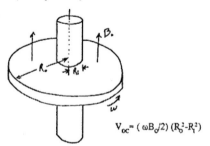

$$V_{oc} = (\omega B_o/2)(R_o^2 - R_i^2)$$

Figure 1. Calculation of Homopolar Generator Voltage:
This is a correction to the Vol. 5, Issue 4 <u>Extraordinary Science</u> (p. 25) equation of the homopolar generator.

Figure 2. Bruce DePalma, fascinated by suspended gyroscopes, developed a plethora of theories which led many to believe free energy was possible.

PHOTO CREDIT: Playgid July 1981

Apparently DePalma did not purchase a high DC current generator or a car battery to try the homopolar motor experiment, nor did he research the literature sufficiently:

* Prof. A.K. Das Gupta published a journal article revealing that the current in a homopolar motor's disk does not react against the magnet even if freely suspended;[4] therefore, disproving DePalma's "cemented magnet and disc" theory.

* Cramp and Norgrove rotated a disk below a cylindrical magnet, drew current from it and failed to find any slight movement of the suspended magnet with the help of a mirror and a beam of light.[5]

* Zelany and Page performed an experiment demonstrating that current into a radial arm firmly attached to a cylindrical magnet does cause the magnet to rotate;[6] disproving DePalma's "short circuit" theory.

Consequently, the one-piece homopolar motor will rotate when current is sent into it. Conversely, this also means that the one-piece homopolar generator naturally produces back torque (drag/"armature reaction") when current is drawn from it, because it also tries to act as a motor in the reverse direction.

After discovering these historical experiments, and circulating them, Tim Wilhelm, Adam Trombly and myself, each listened to DePalma's explanation about them. We were excited by the promise of free energy from the Germany conference on "Conversion of Gravity Field Energy" in 1980 and had already decided to build one of these one-piece Faraday generators, at considerable expense, in the early 1980s. Furthermore, we each hoped to be the first to measure an "over-unity" efficiency. In competition with each other, we were shocked to see the classically predictable "back torque" which slowed the N-Machine down when current was drawn from the generator. (Adam claims that his output exceeded his input but he accidentally destroyed his machine and never released his measurements.)

The N-Machine Story

In 1980, Norman Paulsen, another Santa Barbara resident, published *Sunburst, Return of the Ancients*, now in its 2nd edition, retitled as *Christ Consciousness*. This appeared to be an interesting autobiography with some unusual UFO stories associated with George Van Tassel. One such experience included a trip on a large saucer. Part of

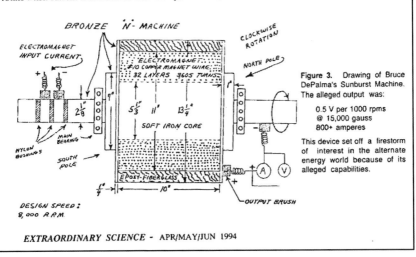

Figure 3. Drawing of Bruce DePalma's Sunburst Machine. The alleged output was:

0.5 V per 1000 rpms
@ 15,000 gauss
800+ amperes

This device set off a firestorm of interest in the alternate energy world because of its alleged capabilities.

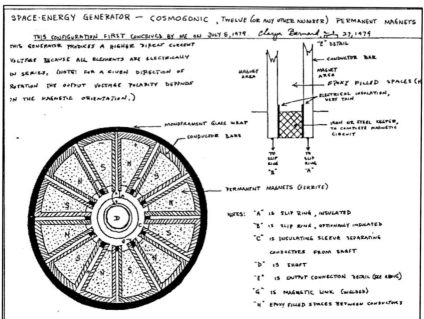

Figure 4. In this page from C. Bernard's lab notebook, Bernard expands on a twelve segmented version that he first conceptualized on July 8, 1979. The conductors were placed in series to increase the voltage.

the experience involved being shown the "engine room" and receiving a description of its operation. There were two disks rotating in opposite directions, either one of which provided electrical power for the ship.

Mr. Paulsen has since described these disks to me as *non-conducting disks* with magnets that had radial, instead of axial, magnetic orientation. (The homopolar generator has axial magnets because of the north/south direction of the magnetic field which is along the axis.) However, Mr. Paulsen did not override the Sunburst Community's interest in the DePalma generator, even though he recognized that it was substantially different than the one he experienced.

Seeing the Sunburst Machine

While visiting the Sunburst Community in 1980, I was privileged to see the $25,000 investment which they made in DePalma's 440-VAC powered N-Machine. As diagrammed in Figure 3, it has high resistance carbon brushes, along with an electromagnet design. They let me copy a couple of pages from the laboratory notebook of Charya

Bernard, who worked on several designs of magnetic disk configurations, before Bruce DePalma appeared (Figure 4). These designs try to reproduce what Norman saw on his trip but without the specifications that he mentioned to me. (Mr. Paulsen was not accommodating with the information because he was told at the time of his trip that the world was not ready for this new technology).

The story is that most of the designs that were built and tested did not work (note the circuitous conductor paths that are included in the drawing.) Unfortunately, Bernard died in 1979, so we didn't have a chance to converse on the subject. I am now continuing my research in the direction of electrostatic generators instead of unipolar or homopolar magnets.

Astronaut Ed Mitchell's Interest

After leaving California in 1980, I began corresponding with Bruce DePalma. He was helpful in describing in detail what had happened in all of his experiments and supplied any information requested. When I became involved in the project, Bruce was funded by the noted eye doctor Morgan Raiford and the Tanners, a Mormon family. After receiving material from Bruce, I informed Dr. George Ainsworth-Land, author of *Grow or Die*, about DePalma's ideas. The simplicity of the concept interested George and he began to research Faraday's writings to learn more.

George decided the generator was worth investigating and informed his friend, astronaut Edgar Mitchell, about Bruce DePalma. Mitchell was the sixth man to walk on the moon and was fairly influential in 1980, even before he founded the Noetics Institute. Together they flew to Santa Barbara to visit DePalma and evaluate his N-Machine's funding potential. Figure 5 shows a photo of the HG and motor combination which DePalma was working on at the time to attempt a self-running version. The homopolar motor has stationary magnets housed in the square wooden blocks on the right side of the central shaft.

The 1980 Gravity-Field Energy Conference

Dr. Hans Nieper describes the 1980 Gravity-Field Energy Conference in his book, *Revolution in Technology, Medicine, and Science*. DePalma sent me information regarding the conference since he was invited to speak there. He was advised not to attend because of the patent application that he was working on. Upon receiving this information, I felt my presence would be of benefit to gain information and by possibly giving a presentation in DePalma's place.

I had already decided to build a generator (as many scientists do when they learn of this strange method of generating electricity) to finish my Master's Degree in Physics. Arriving in Germany, I was equipped with my drawings and transparencies of my unique design for a one-piece HG. I met Adam Trombly who was building an expensive version of the one-piece HG with liquid sodium-potassium (NaK) brushes. Since Adam knew DePalma, we had a lot in common. He had several investors in his company called "Acme Energy Research" which had an operating budget of a few hundred thousand dollars. (Adam said that ACME was an acronym for *Acyclic Closed Magnetic Experiment*.)

Following the conference, I contacted Mr. Tim Wilhelm, whose organization, The Stelle Group, was also represented in Germany. Tim was working on a large one-piece homopolar generator, using mercury brushes, with the funding of the Stelle Group. He subsequently discovered a predicted amount of back torque and obtained no free energy output, which confirmed classical physics.

Dart Industries and DePalma

After the Mitchell/Ainsworth-Land journey to DePalma's garage, Justin Dart of Dart Industries was contacted for possible funding of an expanded project to prove the principle that the back torque, or drag of the generator when power is drawn from it, could be significantly lessened with the correct design (this is called the "N-effect" by DePalma).

Figure 5. The Hompolar Generator and motor combination which DePalma was working on during Edgar Mitchell's visit. DePalma was attempting to build a self-running version.

... Edgar Mitchell can be seen examining this version of the Homopolar Generator on P.73.

69

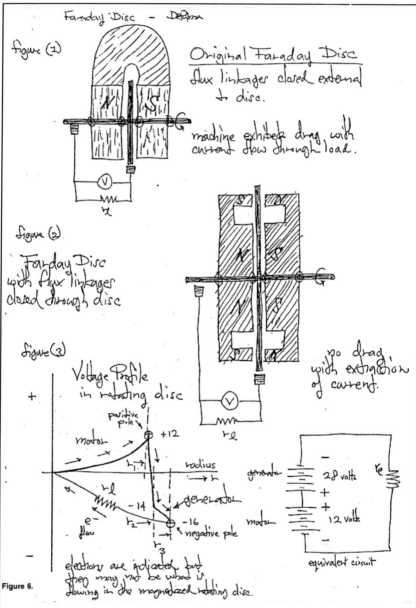

Figure 6.

From the Mitchell letter to Dart Industries dated 2/27/81, the project was thorough and steps for review and verification were built into the plan, with a proposed budget of $339,000.

Dr. D.C. White from MIT's Energy Lab was immediately called in to view DePalma's videotape of the Sunburst Machine, and to evaluate the validity of his claims. Dr. White states in his report (**Homopolar Handbook**, Appendix, 1994):

DePalma's problem stems from his very sloppy measurement of power into the drive motor. Careful instrumentation would show that the input drive power goes up when current is drawn from the homopolar machine.

You will recall that I noticed in his film that the ammeter in the drive motor circuit jumped (increased) when he drew power from the homopolar generator.

As a result of the Energy Lab consultation, two reactions occurred:

* Dr. D.C. White's report was like throwing water onto a fire, effectively casting doubts into the minds of everyone involved, except for DePalma;

* DePalma decided to sign a contract with Dr. Morgan Raiford instead of Mitchell and Ainsworth-Land.

Due to the unavailability of the Sunburst Machine and the poor quality of the video presentation, Dr. White's findings were not unexpected. However, it was still a letdown to learn of the withdrawal of the Mitchell/Ainsworth-Land/Dart team from the research.

Satellite News Coverage

To show how easily excitement can build in this uncharted area, *Satellite News*, a Phillips Publishing newsletter covering management, marketing and regulation of the satellite industry, decided to devote one page of their 2/15/81 issue to DePalma, Ainsworth-Land, and Trombly. With the title, *Researchers See Long-Life Satellite Power Systems in 19th Century Experiment*, we see quotes about "almost no drag" from DePalma, "50 kW of AC electrical power" from Trombly, and "pretty sure the Japanese already have something" from

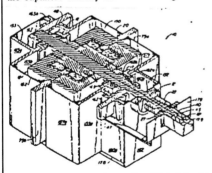

Figure 7. Adam Trombley's one-piece HG includes the concept of "completing the magnetic circuit" through an outer steel shell in his "closed-path" homopolar machine.

Ainsworth-Land. However, the end of the article was the clincher:

The power-in/power-out ratio for the Acme generator is not as high as the DePalma machine, but it still puts out about 3 to 4 times more electrical power than it takes to run the device. DePalma is building a bigger N-machine—a 250 kW version with a 2-ft diameter rotor.

DePalma Reverses His Theory

Adam Trombly's theory and design of the one-piece HG includes the concept of "completing the magnetic circuit" through an outer steel shell in his "closed-path" homopolar machine (International Patent #WO-82/02126). In 1983, this idea was also endorsed by DePalma (see Energy Unlimited, Summer 1984). However, the DePalma's Report #92 (2/2/84) entitled, "The Secret of the Faraday Disc," completely reversed his previous story, and surprisingly states,

On the practical side the operation of the machine is unaffected whether the magnets are rotated with disc or not...

In the same report, he goes on to say,

When the magnetic flux path is closed symmetrically through the disc instead of around the disc as in the early machines the drag associated with the flow of current disappears.

This new concept which actually decreases the voltage and decreases the power output, (as evident to those who have experienced this phenomena of reversed field through the disk). After losing over 80% of the theoretical voltage due to field reversal, I spent a whole summer redesigning my homopolar generator. Prior to this, DePalma sent me a letter (1/16/84) suggesting that I put iron slugs in the center of my ring magnets to enhance the field reversal through the center of the disk. This counter-productive suggestion was preceded by a 12/28/83 letter that DePalma would start attacking me if I didn't start mentioning him as the inventor of the N-Machine.

Marinov and Tewari Gain Attention

In 1984, Dr. Stefan Marinov, an Austrian physicist briefly promoted his "Perpetuum Mobile" which is an N-Machine motor-generator combination. (See *The Thorny Way of Truth,* Part II, Marinov, 1984.) Marinov claimed that when he attached the magnet to the disk, the braking effect disappeared.

Upon meeting Dr. Marinov in Switzerland, at the Swiss Association for Free Energy Conference in 1989, it appeared that he was an intelligent but eccentric physicist. This can be seen from his threat to "self-immolate" when he was unable to publish his N-machine nor his "coupled-shutters" article in a scientific journal *(Nature,* July, 1985, p.209). Assembling the work of other inventors, his books are mostly reprints and correspondence in contrast to his articles which are detailed. To the best of my knowledge, his experiments with the N-Machine were not published in article form.

With Trombly's consulting services, Paramahansa Tewari (a nuclear engineer from India) has designed several N-Machine motor/generator combinations with low contact resistance and a closed magnetic field path *(Magnets,* Aug 1986). Unfortunately, even his latest machine suffers from a large back torque, which brings into question his claim of free energy."

The Trombly-Kahn ACME Machine

Adam Trombly, a few years after the Raiford funding of De Palma 's project, described his fmal experiments to me with the Acme generator before the machine broke its axle sometime in 1982. The machine suffered what one scientist called "parasitic uniaxle breakdown." The iron core of the generator was powdered after this breakdown. How that could have happened is not well understood. An analysis showed a "flash process disaggregation along grain boundaries" which he feels any good metallurgist could correct by carefully regulating the amount of silicon iron.

Adam claims that the efficiency was close to 250 % when the device self-destructed, well below the rated level of output. Knowing how careful Adam had been in all of our conversations with calculations and instrumentation, I feel that he may have taken precise measurements. (Even power factor meters were used to determine the effective power output.) Whether or not the machine could actually power itself, which is what Adam bought a $10,000 DC to AC inventor for, is anyone's guess.

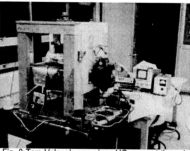

Fig. 8 Tom Valone's one-piece HG was put through a series of experiments to test for back torque.

Bruce DePalma's "Critique of the N-Machine Constructed by Trombly and Kahn" 10/15/85, is reprinted in *the Homopolar Handbook* Appendix, with permission of the DePalmar TIstitute. A complete copy of the Trombly patent is also included.

Adam's Acme generator has been kept from public scrutiny ever since it was built and even the lab notes and records have never been published (DePalma's report is the only written account of the TromblyKahn measurements). Ten years later, there is still a question about whether Trombly really built and tested an N-Machine. Trombly told me that his brush design was modified after the patent was issued for the U.S. patent application.

The U.S. Patent Office rejected the Acme Patent application the first time, on the grounds that the electrical generation method was impossible (homopolar generators usually have that effect on scientists). Adam quoted the Patent Office as saying, "No way will it work." Upon reapplying, the Patent Office rejected it a second time, claiming "prior art," even though the brush design was novel. (The electrical generation method has been public domain since the 1800s, therefore, the brush may have been the only patentable part of the machine.) Unfortunately, the Office of Naval Intelligence intervened shortly afterwards (since the U. S. military reviews all patent applications before the patent examiners have a look at them) and stamped Trombly's brush design "CLASSIFIED." He is now prohibited to talk about the NaK brush design without informing the Office of Naval Intelligence of the name of that person.

Adam believes that the project was a success. However, he doesn't think that all of the expensive design work the generator required was balanced by the reliability that he had hoped for. He thinks that there are other generators, such as the Gray Motor which offer high reliability along with over-unity performance.

My Homopolar Generator

During 1982 and 1983, my one-piece HG was put through a series of experiments to test for back torque. Using 8" disk magnets, there was sufficient voltage even at low rotation speeds to make accurate measurements. My unique contribution to the field was to use low temperature solder (Wood's Metal) for the brush design, cutting friction to a minimum.

The measurements of input power versus output power, which in most cases was below unity, the most direct experience of back torque was the deceleration time. When power was cut from the HG, it always decelerated at least 10% sooner with a closed circuit than with an open circuit. The record of experiments are detailed in the *Homopolar Handbook* along with photos and diagrams. My average measurement of the back torque was 0.17 N-m which was within classical limits.

Error Analysis
in N-Machine Measurements

As promised, the details of a simple error analysis will show how to avoid the trap of apparent over-unity efficiency when significant digits have not been accounted for. Assuming that voltage or current measurements are made to only 2 significant digits (SD's), the power calculations *must be* limited to 2 SD's to claim precision.

In my HG, one trial (2/1/83) resulted in 65mV generated voltage (open circuit) and a 380-Amp generated current, measured separately. This resulted in a calculated 25Watt output. However, the relative error sum (since there was a multiplication) is $10/380 + 1/65 = \pm 4\%$ or 8%. The

motor demand was 13.3V and 20.0 Amp open circuit and 13.3 V with 18.7 Amp closed circuit, yielding $\pm 1\%$ or 2% relative error.

Subtracting these power calculations of 266 Watts and 249 Watts, we get 17 Watts of motor power difference, which appears to be less than the generated power and maybe something to get excited about. However, there is a 1% error built into both power measurements, yielding about 3 Watts doubled (since there is a subtraction, errors are added), or ± 6 Watts of error in the motor power measurements.

This means that the 17 Watts must have an error range (error bars) of 23 Watts maximum and 11 Watts minimum. Now the 25 Watts of generator output has a 4% measurement error (1 Watt), which brings the error range up to 26 Watts and down to 24 Watts.

Calculating the over-unity efficiency here involves $25/17$ or 150% which seems exciting until we consider adding the relative errors (for multiplication or division relative errors are added). 1/25 is a 4% error but 6/17 is a 35% error.

The sum yields the final relative error in the efficiency calculation ($\pm 40\%$) which is just about the extra amount over unity!

Therefore, it is not prudent to assert that free energy was there or over-unity efficiency was measured. Note that the 35% error in the 17 Watt value arose from two bigger numbers being subtracted. Whenever subtraction takes place, significant digits are lost since we maintain the same precision but the difference is a small number.

Hopefully, this example will help other researchers with their work in this field.

Conclusion

With Tesla's suggested modifications to the HG, it may turn out to be what he called, a *current accumulator*. Tesla realized that one has to use the output current path to an advantage, counteracting the natural motoring effect. Even in its classical two-piece form, it has been commercially designed to be over 90% efficient. Perhaps with a truly novel approach, the HG can exceed 100% efficiency. In any case, we need to keep in mind a few guidelines:

* A demonstration of drag-free generation of current should be a prerequisite to any claims for over-unity power output in a homopolar generator.

* It is advantageous to use P=IV for power measurement, taking V from the open-circuit voltage and I from a commercially available current shunt in the microhm range. The HG maintains the same output V whether under load or not making this method superior to squaring the current times the resistance (as Tewari likes to do).

* A DC drive motor should be used, powered by batteries, instead of an AC motor which introduces power factor errors.

* It helps to remove the current symmetrically from the current-collecting brush system to optimize any drag-reduction designs. A sheet of copper soldered to the stationary brush is suggested.

Lastly, it is worth mentioning some of the heavy weights in the homopolar area for those wishing to do further research.

The Center for Electromagnetics at the University of Texas at Austin[9] is a good resource since they have been constructing one-piece HG's since 1980 for fusion and rail-gun experiments. Their Compact HG (pub. #PR-8) has a 90% closed magnetic path and a one-piece design which has challenged the Trombly claim to free energy since 1980. 10 kW HG machines from as early as 1958 are described in the literature.[10] Westinghouse has been a leader in homopolar design with 3000 horsepower machines using NaK brushes.[11] The first practical superconducting homopolar motor was developed at the International Research and Development Co. Ltd. in Britain with a 3250 HP rating and tested at the Fawley power station for driving a cooling water pump.[12] It has a unique slotted disk design (radial slots) for water-cooling and radial current enhancement along with a series/parallel arrangement of the armature segments.

The first few years of the 1980's were very exciting to me. As our collective knowledge continues to grow, stretching the boundaries of science and awareness, the future has to improve._TV

References

1 Carrigan & Gubbins, "The Source of the Earth's Magnetic Field", Scientific American, Feb., 1979, p.118 (see also: T. Valone, "The One-Piece Faraday Generator: Research Results", Proceedings of the Intersociety Energy Conversion Engineering Conference, 1991.)

2 Thomas Valone. "The Homopolar Generator: Tesla's Contribution", Proceedings of the 1986 International Tesla Society Symposium, p.6-32

3 Ibid., p.6-38

4 A.K. Das Gupta, "Unipolar Machines. Association of the Magnetic Field with the Field-Producing Magnet", American Journal of Physics, V.31, p.428, 1963)

5 Cramp and Norgrove, "Some Investigations on the Axial Spin of a Magnet and on the Laws of Electromagnetic Induction", Proc. IEE (London), Vol. 8, p.487, 1936

6 Zelaney and Page, "Torque on a Cylindrical Magnet Through Which a Current is Passing", Physical Review Vol. 24, p. 544, 1924

7 Thomas Valone, The Homopolar Handbook: A Definitive Guide to Faraday Disk and N-Machine Technologies, 1992, Integrity Research Institute, 1377 K Street NW, Suite 204, Washington, DC 20005, $20 postpaid.

8 My analysis of Tewari's 1993 paper to the IANS Conference is available for free upon request.

9 Center for Electromagnetics, U. of Texas at Austin, Taylor Hall 167, Austin, TX 78712.

10 D.A. Watt, "The Development and Operation of a 10 kW Homopolar Generator with Mercury Brushes", IEE (London), June, 1958, p. 233

11 Witkowski, Arcella, Keeton, "Vital Support Systems for Liquid Metal Collector Homopolar Machines", IEEE Trans. on Power App. and Sys., Vol. PAS-95, No.4, 1976, p.1493

12 Appleton, "Advances in Homopolar Machine Design", Electrical Review, 4/4/69, p.488

Astronaut Edgar Mitchell examining Bruce DePalma's N-Machine. See his proposal to Dart Industries on P. 149

Figure 9.

EXPLOITATION OF GRAVITY FIELD ENERGY

HANNOVER 1980

by Thomas F. Valone

558 Breckènridge St., Buffalo, NY 14222

Bruce DePalma, inventor of the N Generator, has asked me to describe my experiences at the Germany Symposium of Gravitational Field Energy (Nov. 27, 1980) for this magazine. I will try to be candid about what probably was the most progressive conference ever held concerning energy technology.

THE SPEAKERS

My first encounter, the day before, involved the amiable coordinator, Dr. Hans Nieper, and the group of speakers. Dr. Nieper, it turns out, is a cancer doctor who is famous for his successful Lactrile treatments.[1] The group of speakers were Dr. Nieper, Rudolf Zinsser, Dr. Shinichi Seike, Richard Kinnegar, Joachim Kirchhoff, Adam Trombly, along with the entrepreneur, Dr. John Raiford, and myself.

As I was introduced to Dr. Seike, in the lobby of the Hannover Intercontenental Hotel, I found myself grasping his business card instead of his hand. Dr. Seike is a bit eccentric but he is a good physicist as I found out in the next few days.

He spoke to me about the gravitational effects of Nuclear Electronic Resonance which no one in this country has explored. Usually we physicists look at NMR (Nuclear Magnetic Resonance) only, when the nucleus is explored.

RUDOLPH ZINSSER

At dinner, Adam Trombly and I were interrupted by Dr. Nieper re-introducing Rudolph Zinsser as the foremost German expert on gravitation. Then the friendly, white-haired Zinsser began to describe his 10 years of research to us as I reached for my tape recorder. There was an excitement in the air as Adam and I struggled to comprehend Mr. Zinsser's patented pulse generator (US #4,085,384) causing an unprecedented 3 to 5 hour force from a brief "activation" of only 90 seconds. We were shown a 6-inch plexiglass cylinder with two aluminum plates inside submerged in a water dielectric. He described the small activator in front of us energizing an object suspended in a vacuum.

Dr. Zinsser showed us graphs recording the angle of deflection of the object which was labeled in terms of force. A maximum of 8 dynes manifested within ¼ hour of activation, slowly dropping to zero about 5 hours later. He said everything could be scaled upwards without difficulty. In comparing the impulse delivered to power input, he said it was at least

10,000 times the ratio obtained from chemical rockets (based on Dr. Peschka's analysis).[2] I am really glad I met Rudolph Zinsser who certainly destroyed my conventional notions of force and energy.[3]

That night I briefly shook hands with John Searl in the restaurant when he arrived. However I learned the next day that he was sent back to England by Dr. Nieper to maintain "a certain credibility level". It seems that Mr. Searl had no demonstration model (which no one else had!) and no concise speech prepared. John Searl is known for his various, high voltage, anti-gravity saucers he has built over the years.[4]

NIEPER N-MACHINE

The conference began the next day with Dr. Nieper giving a long slide presentation on his shielding theory of gravity. About 300 people were there from as far away as New Zealand for this event. He showed a few slides of the N-machine he had built based on photos sent by Bruce DePalma. (Unfortunately, Bruce was advised not to go since he had no patent application filed.) Because of brush friction, the motor-generator combination was not self-sustaining.

KIRCHHOFF TALK

Next came Mr. Kirchhoff, a diplomat from E. Germany, speaking on the *Collision which is Programmed by Inertia of Natural Science vs. Crisis of Lack of Energy*. A slide of Dr. Peshka's article about Mr. Zinsser's work was included.

ZINSSER LECTURE

The third speaker was Rudolph Zinsser. The talks so far had been given in German with Dr. Nieper translating sporadically but this time Mr. Zinsser did both. **He explained his kinetobaric effect by the "chaos" that's created in the center of mass by the trigger energy. He repeated the description of random (about 1 mm) oscillations that continue for years afterwards—a side effect he says he has now eliminated.**

DR. SEIKE'S PRESENTATION

Dr. Seike was next with many slides, most of which were from his book, *The Principles of Ultra Relativity*[5]. He started with a description of the Mobius strip and resultant "double solenoid". He proceeded into the **three phase oscillator which increases frequency in about 3 days.** Seike included the theory of his harnessing tachyon or "imaginary mass current" for his devices. Next he showed the oscillator from P. 291 of his book and emphasized the barium titanate used. (It was also 3 phase.) The energy density of the G-field was noted as he presented the possibility of a "G Power Generator". This turned out to be an electrical generator (P. 265) which increases from 2 to 40 volts in three months absorbing "g-energy".

STONE MELTED

The last amazing topic mentioned was Dr. Seike's circuit for melting a stone (P. 251). Even though there is a 400V, 300ma source added, the slide of the melted stone was very impressive (P. 273). As was right when he mentioned that this is not possible with a comparable welder's gun. At first I thought the power source invalidated his claim.

He also mentioned that the stone will totally disappear if the "flare" is sustained. **Apparently the circuit generates a visible tachyon-electron arc, usually only possible with voltages 10 to 100 times higher.**

Dr. Seike noted that g-power comes from a negative energy state and uses p-type semiconductor material. He promises to talk about imaginary acceleration by tachyon propulsion at the next meeting!

STELLE & TROMBLY N-MACHINES

Mr. Kinnegar from Dallas was next, talking about the Stelle group's N-machine, which also was a Faraday motor and generator combination. He had many detailed slides. They also had brush friction problems and plan to use mercury next.

Adam Trombly, director of Acme Energy

Research in San Rafael, talked about his "state of the art" NaK liquid brush N-machine which should be completed soon. His design eliminates that major obstacle of brush friction which has plagued other models.

VALONE PRESENTATION

Then I talked briefly about Bruce DePalma's Sunburst generator, the highest power (8kW) N-generator yet built. I had a few transparencies, including one of the Santa Barbara *News-Press* (3-30-80) article of Bruce with his picture. I felt that at least they could see what he lookedd like since he was mentioned so much! I also outlined my M.A. project which involves testing the back torque of an N-generator.

BORGE FROKJAER-JENSON

Lastly, the mysterious Borge Frokjaer-Jenson spoke a few words.[6] He said that he was associated with groups in Denmark and Sweden and had tested the DePalma machine. They have also discovered a transformer that puts out three times the input power (e.g., 3 watts for 1 watt). When I met him personally, he would not volunteer any more information. I have since wondered whether it is related to the Alexander patent (#3,913,004) that has the same claim!

THE DAY AFTER

That was the major part of the conference. The next day Dr. Nieper met with the speakers and some other invited people in hopes of coming to some international agreement about energy inventors and their support. The date for the American conference was set. The night after the conference, all of the speakers were received at Dr. and Mrs. Nieper's house for a cordial get-together.

It was exciting meeting poorly funded experimenters from European countries as well as successful inventors looking for more ideas at the conference. By the way, the overwhelming and beautiful book, *UFO...Contact From the Pleiades*[7], talks about tachyon propulsion for the Pleiades crafts and describes effects similar to Searl's saucers.

Germany is a friendly place and has high quality in most of their products. On the way to the airport coming home, I met a taxi driver who had been a POW in World War II and was sent to Texas for a year. In the airport I saw Dr. Seike again and he asked me if I knew anything about UFOs. He admitted receiving help from his UFO contacts. It's about time we received some help, isn't it?

PROCEEDINGS & NEXT CONFERENCE

George Hatthaway, a consultant in Ontario may be the organizer of the next conference. He has just compiled the text of the conference for distribution[8]. Also, the Mittelstands-Institut in Hannóver should have the proceedings available presently.[9] Thank goodness for Dr. Hans Nieper.

REFERENCES

1) *Let's Live*, June 1980, P. 144.
2) *Raumfahrt Forshung*, W. Peshka, Feb. 1974. (translated by Don Reed)
3) Rudolph Zinsser, Junkerrech 34/ Weierbach, D-6580 Idar-Oberstein, W. Germany (send at least $5 when requesting information)
4) John Searl, 17 Stephen's Close, Mortimer, Reading, Berkshire, RG7-3TX England (same for Mr. Searl)
5) Dr. Seike's book (fifth edition) is available for $40 plus a few dollars for shipping from his G research Lab, 2-1, Ohmiyachoh 1, Uwajima City, Ehime (798), Japan.
6) Borge Frokjaer-Jenson, Prins Valkemars Vej 34, DK-2820, Gentofte, Denmark.
7) This Cadillac of UFO books finally substantiates a 5 year, 150 visit, UFO experience in Switzerland and is available for $24.95 plus $3 shipping from Genesis III Publications, P.O. Box 32067, Phoenix, AZ 85064, You will be overwhelmed too.
8) George Hatthaway, Hatthaway Consulting Services, 85 Alcorn Ave., Toronto, Ontario M4V-1E5, Canada.
9) Mittelstand-Institut, Augustinerweg 20, 3000 Hannover 21, W. Germany.   ###

The Homopolar Generator:
Tesla's Contribution

Thomas Valone, M.A., P.E.
Integrity Electronics & Research
558 Breckenridge Street
Buffalo, NY 14222

Abstract

With the continued interest in Faraday or homopolar generators, it is good to review Tesla's experiments in this field. Tesla proposed several methods for increasing the output of the generator, including the "current accumulator." In this paper, the range of homopolar generators Tesla experimented, the Forbes Unipolar generator and my work on the one-piece homopolar generator will be discussed. We will look at why Tesla believed that he could build a self-sustaining dynamo.

Introduction

This paper will center on a very simple but very intriguing device that is a model of the planet earth (see Figure 1). It's the unipolar, acyclic, or homopolar generator which is also referred to as a "Faraday disk dynamo" after Michael Faraday who discovered it in 1831. (Hence, the title of my book, The One-Piece Faraday Generator, available through High Energy Enterprises, PO Box 5636, Security, CO 80911.) Note the self-sustaining nature of the earth model that's presented in the following Scientific American article. (For your convenience, the article, "Modeling Magnetism: The earth as a dynamo," by S. Weisburd is reprinted in full.) [Science News, V.128, p.220, 1985] They are describing an unusual mechanism of the earth which pumps current in a spiral manner strengthening the magnetic field, as described by Tesla in the following pages. (This could have great significance for a new, liquid metal Homopolar Generator if someone wants to try a novel approach. The article says, "F.H. Busse proved that by virtue of the dynamo action of the fluid motions, the magnetic field could increase substantially from a small initial value"-p.124). It appears to be a "free energy" device, with no dissipative effects, but the theory, as well as my experiment, has shown that a one-piece homopolar generator should exhibit back torque. Therefore the earth should be slowing down quite noticeably. However, it's not appreciably slowing, so there must be a method nature uses to avoid the back torque.

Modeling Magnetism: The earth as a dynamo

In 1600 William Gilbert, the physician of Queen Elizabeth I published a treatise on magnetism called *De Magnete*, in which he dispelled the notion that lodestones are attracted to heavenly bodies. Instead, he concluded from an experiment with a spherical lodestone that the earth itself is a giant magnet.

Centuries passed before scientists developed any reasonable ideas as to what causes this geomagnetism. The main, dipolar part of the earth's field clearly resembles that produced by a bar magnet. But it has become apparent that the field could not arise from permanently magnetized minerals in the earth. Most of the earth is too hot for such materials to retain their magnetism for long, and in order to create all of the changes observed in the magnetic field, solid magnets would have to scurry around within the earth--an impossible feat that would result in massive upheavals of the planet. Moreover, earthquake data indicate that the outer region of the core is a fluid.

Scientists believe this outer core is a rotating liquid made principally of molten iron and nickel, which conduct electricity. This view of the core has led to the only surviving idea out of many theories (including the notion, once considered and then dropped by Albert Einstein and others, that magnetism is an inherent property of all rotating masses).

Forty years ago Walter M. Elsasser at the University of California at San Diego and Edward C. Bullard of the University of Cambridge in England developed the "self-exciting dynamo" model for the core. The illustration below ... [Figure 1] ... shows a simple example of a dynamo invented by the 19th century British scientist Michael Faraday. When the metal disk spins in the initial presence of a magnetic field, currents are generated in the disk. In a self-exciting dynamo, these currents are fed into a solenoid, or coil, which creates a magnetic field of its own.

If the spinning fluids of the earth's outer core act like the disk in the dynamo, the earth could similarly produce a large magnetic field, provided there was a small magnetic field around at the beginning. (The small field that pervades the galaxy would be a good candidate, according to some scientists.) Another provision would be that the core fluids keep moving, and the unanswered question here is what energy source is responsible for doing just that.

Of course, the actual core movements must be considerably different from and much more complex than a spinning disk. So the present focus of research is to devise complicated flow patterns consistent with the magnetic field's behavior--its reversals, secular variations and now possibly the jerk.

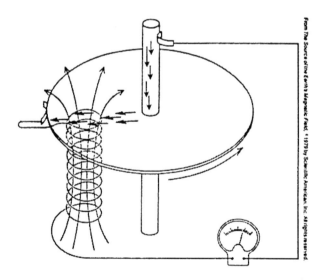

Figure 1. In this self-sustaining Faraday disk dynamo, an electric current (small arrows) in the copper disk reinforces the magnetic field of the coil (from "The Source of the Earth's Magnetic Field" by Scientific American, 1979).

Another interesting aspect of the earth as a unipolar generator (the title of another journal article) is the electromotive voltage that is produced in the rotating armature. Faraday thought it would be measurable in the rotating reference frame. He looked for a voltage in rivers and streams. My experiments with a small LED voltmeter, described in my book, show that no voltage is measurable in the rotating environment. The reason is that (see Figure 2) there is an equal and opposite electrostatic field created when a charge displacement is induced by the Lorentz force. This essentially maintains a neutral environment on the disk, even during sizable current flow, that will act as a voltage regulator. I could measure a voltage across the rotating disk in the stationary lab frame but my LED voltmeter could not measure even a millivolt when one hundred times that was present in the lab frame. In other words, we can't draw power from the earth's homopolar generator while rotating with it.

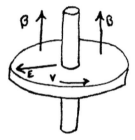

Effective Electric Field set up by $E = V \times B$

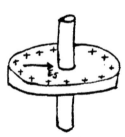

Results in a charge displacement that causes an external electrostatic field in opposite direction. (E_s)

Figure 2. Charges displace until equilibrium is established. Fields cancel within a disk. This explains why a constant voltage will be maintained across the disk even during high current output.

To calculate the voltage generated with an homopolar generator (Figure 3), we find that the equation depends upon the magnetic flux density, rotational speed, and the radius of the disk squared. The internal resistance is the only thing that limits the power output of the device. It is important to note also, before going on with the aspects that relate to Tesla's article, that all of the recent experiments that have reported anomalous effects have all been done with the one-piece Faraday generator, the one with the magnet rotating with the disk. (Dr. Stephan Marinov, on p. A-73 of my book, has a couple of published articles to this effect. Also, Dr. P. Tewari just published "Generation of Electrical Power from Absolute Vacuum by High Speed Rotation of Conducting Magnetic Cylinder" in Magnets, August 1986, p. 16, based upon his experiments, not to mention Trombly and DePalma.) We notice that the one-piece is closer the a model of the earth as well.

Calculation of the HOMOPOLAR GENERATOR Voltage

As seen in Electromechanical Devices by Woodson and Melcher, p.287 & 289, we use,

$$V_{oc} = \frac{\omega B_o}{2} (R_o^2 - R_i^2) \tag{1}$$

where V_{oc} is the open circuit voltage, R_o is the outer radius of the disk, R_i is the inner radius, and ω is the angular frequency (or the frequency of rotation in Hertz multiplied by 2π).

Now if we have a disk generator with the following characteristics:

$R_i = 1cm = 0.01$ m
$R_o = 10$ cm = 0.1 m
$\omega = 3820$ rpm = 400 rad/sec
$B_o = 10,000$ gauss = 1 Tesla = 1 Wb/m²

then we can calculate the open circuit voltage. It should come out to be:

$V_{oc} = 2.0$ volts

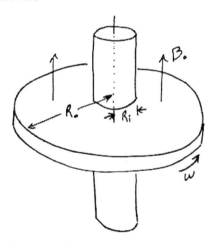

Figure 3. Calculation of the homopolar generator voltage.

Back to Nikola Tesla's article, we see that he performed a few experiments with models of the device and published the results and theory in an article entitled, "Notes on a Unipolar Dynamo" (Electrical Engineer, Sept. 2, 1891, p.258).

(Nikola Tesla's article is reprinted in its entirety on P. 171 of this book.)

The general design, shown in Figure 4, is discussed in the first portions of Tesla's article, (also reprinted in Inventions, Researches and Writings of Nikola Tesla, by Thomas C. Martin). "... such a machine (the homopolar generator) differs from ordinary dynamos in that there is no reaction between armature and field." It is a key sentence which Tesla qualifies by limiting the circumstance to magnets that are weakly energized.

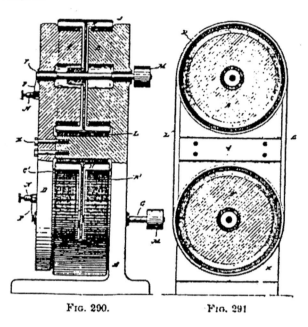

FIG. 290.   FIG. 291

Figure 4. Tesla's Design: Coupling two homopolar generators together for higher output and better brush conductivity.

In my experimentation with strong (almost 1 Tesla field strength) ceramic magnets mounted on a copper disk, I was able to measure the reaction between the disk (armature) and field which is technically labelled "back torque" (the force which slows down the spinning disk when current is drawn from it). We can ask, "How does the one-piece homopolar generator experience back torque when there is no stator, only a rotor?" The best explanation that I could come up with when I measured it is the following: The electrons in the armature (disk) current push against the magnetic field, not the magnet, causing the reaction force. By the way, it's just the radial component of the current that contributes to the back torque, according to the traditional methods for applying the torque equation.

Tesla, however describes it as a reaction between the magnetic field set up by the armature current and the electromagnet's coil current. This is probably equivalent to the equation of torque (T) being equal to the current density crossed with the magnetic flux density (JxB). He also notes another aspect of the generator that is a key to reducing back torque, the symmetry of the external circuit:

... Considered as a dynamo machine, the disc is an equally interesting object of study. In addition to its peculiarity of giving currents of one direction without the employment of commutating devices, such a machine differs from ordinary dynamos in that there is no reaction between armature and field. The armature current tends to set up a magnetization at right angles to that of the field current, but since the current is taken off uniformly from all points of the periphery, and since, to be exact, the external circuit may also be arranged perfectly symmetrical to the field magnet, no reaction can occur. This, however, is true only as long as the magnets are weakly energized, for when the magnets are more or less saturated, both magnetizations at right angles seemingly interfere with each other.

For the above reason alone it would appear that the output of such a machine should, for the same weight, be much greater than that of any other machine in which the armature current tends to demagnetize the field. The extraordinary output of the Forbes unipolar dynamo and the experience of the writer confirm this view ...

Symmetrical External Circuit

We note that Tesla refers to the "external circuit" which is made to be "perfectly symmetrical" to reduce the reaction to zero. This was a popular notion, which still may have profound significance. Adam Trombly, the builder of the most successful "over-unity" homopolar generator in recent history, also emphasized to me the symmetry of the external circuit in his design in order to reduce back torque). It is believed, according to the theory noted by G.W. Howe in The Electrician, (Nov. 5, 1915, p.169), and others, that the torque or "reaction" in a unipolar generator, that tends to slow down or retard its motion (and thus keep its efficiency less than 100%) is due to the interaction between the magnetic flux and the current-carrying conductors in the external circuit. Our present theory only looks at the armature current and the magnetic field but this aspect of the force may be the neglected part. The next section refers to the eddy currents that are set up in the disk with external symmetry. They tend to magnetize the field, which is a beneficial effect. A disk without external symmetry pulling current off from one spot (like my generator, to a great extent) will tend not to contribute to reinforcing the field.

It's interesting to note that Howe also published an article 37 years later entitled "A Novel Form of D.C. Motor" (Wireless Engineer, Nov. 1952, p.285) in which a spiral path homopolar generator is described. It was subsequently built by Ku and Kamal a short time later (see J. Franklin Inst., v.258, 1954, p.7) and tested.

Tesla also notes in the next paragraph that in all other motors and generators "the armature current tends to demagnetize the field" which may be greatly reduced in his design of a unique Faraday generator.

Beneficial Eddy Currents

The next illustration (Figure 5) of a unipolar dynamo with relatively small magnets demonstrates a principle that Tesla wishes to exploit. He points out that path "n" will tend to predominate because the current will choose the path "which offers the least opposition." He believes that the currents in such a generator tend to reinforce the magnetic field and may even "continue to flow" when the field magnet is turned off (assuming electromagnets).

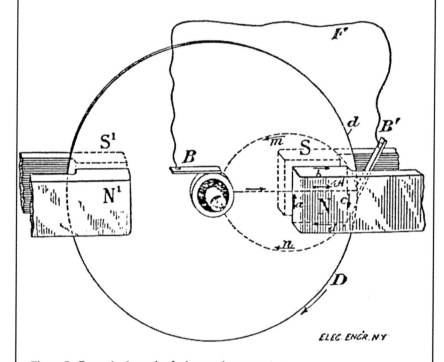

Figure 5. General schematic of a homopolar generator.

... In consequence of this there will be a constant tendency to reduce the current flow in the path A B' m B, while on the other hand no such opposition will exist in path A B' n B, and the effect of the latter branch or path will be more or less preponderating over that of the former. The joint effect of both the assumed branch currents might be represented by that of one single current of the same direction as that energizing the field. In other words, the eddy currents circulating in the disc will energize the field magnet. This is a result quite contrary to what we might be led to suppose at first, for we would naturally expect that the resulting effect of the armature currents would be such as to oppose the field current, as generally occurs when a primary and secondary conductor are placed in inductive relations to each other. But it must be remembered that this results from the peculiar disposition in this case, namely, two paths being afforded to the current, and the latter selecting that path which offers the least opposition to its flow. From this we see that the eddy currents flowing in the disc partly energize the field, and for this reason when the field current is interrupted the currents in the disc will continue to flow , and the field magnet will lose its strength with comparative slowness and may even retain a certain strength as long as the rotation of the disc is continued ...

... If the latter [disc] were rotated as before in the direction of the arrow D, the field would be dragged in the same direction with a torque, which, up to a certain point, would go on increasing with the speed of rotation, then fall off, and, passing through zero, finally become negative; that is, the field would begin to rotate in opposite direction to the disc. In experiments with alternate current motors in which the field was shifted by currents of differing phase, this interesting result was observed. For very low speeds of rotation of the field the motor would show a torque of 900 lbs. or more, measured on a pulley 12 inches in diameter. When the speed of rotation of the poles was increased, the torque would diminish, would finally go down to zero, become negative, and then the armature would begin to rotate in opposite direction to the field.

Tesla notes further on that this effect depends upon the "resistance, speed of rotation, and the geometrical dimensions of the resulting eddy currents." He then suggests that "at a certain speed there would be a maximum energizing effect," presenting the intriguing notion that the field is being dragged in the same direction as the rotation of the disk until a maximum is reached where the field would tend to reverse as the rotation speed is increased. He is proposing here that there is a phase relationship between the field concentric to a conducting disk, as illustrated by a split phase AC motor analogy. We will see shortly an illustration with solid and dotted spiral lines on a disk which demonstrates Tesla's "phase" relationship. Depending upon the direction of the spiraling eddy currents, clockwise (path "n") or counter-clockwise (path "m"), the magnetic field will tend to be in the same direction as the external magnetic field or opposing it. Thus it is reasonable to assume that as the disk increases speed, the current may start out spiraling, say, in a clockwise manner reinforcing the external field, and then reverse to a counterclockwise spiral as the speed increases. A good computer simulation of the variables involved would reveal this relationship and may suggest, as Tesla does, an optimum speed of operation for self-generation.

Another article that reinforces Tesla's ideas is "A Laboratory Self-Exciting Dynamo" by Lowes and Wilkinson, reprinted in Magnetism and the Cosmos, in 1965, by NATO Advanced Study Institute on Planetary and Stellar Magnetism in the Departments of Physics and Mathematics at the University of Newcastle upon Tyne. On page 124, they mention that "a more efficient geometry was found, so efficient that the dynamo would self-excite in a completely homogeneous state (i.e. with no insulation) at a much lower rotor speed than was believed possible." Their design is based upon conducting spheres or cylinders rotating like eddy currents in a conducting medium (also see page 126 of Sci. Amer., "The Source of the Earth's Magnetic Field," 1979).

My Experiment With Field Rotation

I'd like to mention that I have tried the experiment of rotating an 8" disk magnet on a non-conductive (wood) disk within one centimeter of a copper disk (and vice versa), along with the help of Dan Winter in Buffalo, NY (see Figure 6). We were unable to find an effect of rotating a symmetric magnetic field on the output voltage though we didn't look at the output current which is what Dr. Tesla is referring to.

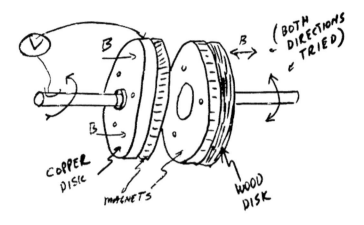

Figure 6. Dragged rotating field experiment.

Here, it is important to also note experiments (described in my book) by Cramp and Norgrove (1936) and Das Gupta (1963) which have failed to find any torques on a non-conductive magnet adjacent to a conductive disk carrying current. In fact, several scientists have proposed, as Mr. Klicker mentioned at the Tesla 1986 Conference, that no experiment can resolve whether the magnetic field is rotating if it is symmetric. However, this may not have a bearing on the phenomena that Tesla is talking about concerning the "dragging" of the field, since he concentrates on the spiraling currents.

Removing The External Magnetic Field

The next part of Dr. Tesla's article proposes that in a solid disk, as described above, we may be able to find that the field magnet may be removed while the generator disk is kept rotating. Tesla suggests that, due to favorable eddy currents, the entire generator may continue to function and even increase in output when the speed is increased, forming a fascinating "current accumulator."

> To return to the principal subject; assume the conditions to be such that the eddy currents generated by the rotation of the disc strengthen the field, and suppose the latter gradually removed while the disc is kept rotating at an increased rate. The current, once started, may then be sufficient to maintain itself and even increase in strength, and then we have the case of Sir William Thomson's "current accumulator." But from the above considerations it would seem that for the success of the experiment the employment of a disc *not subdivided* would be essential, for if there should be a radial subdivision, the eddy currents could not form and the self-exciting action would cease. If such a radially subdivided disc were used it would be necessary to connect the spokes by a conducting rim or in any proper manner so as to form a symmetrical system of closed circuits ...

In the next illustration (Figure 7), we see a suggestion for giving the disk an additional push from the generated currents by leading them through conductors that pass into coils. Here, the coils then encounter a reverse polarity magnetic field which tends to give the coils a small amount of push. This effect may not work at all but tends to lead the reader into thinking about curving the generated currents to an advantage.

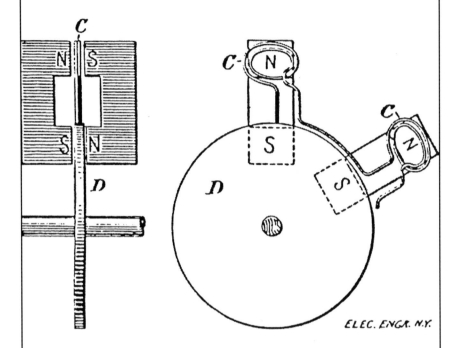

ELEC. ENGR. N.Y.

Figure 7. Possible enhancement to give discs an additional "push."

Sub-Dividing The Disk

The suggestion of sub-dividing the disk is now discussed, in order to "do away with the field coils" entirely! As illustrated in Figure 8, sub-dividing the disk spirally (actually cutting the disk in radial directions that spiral outward) tends to create a self-generated magnetic field.

... But a unipolar dynamo or motor, such as shown in Fig 292, may be excited in an efficient manner by simply properly subdividing the disc or cylinder in which the currents are set up, and it is practicable to do away with the field coils which are usually employed. Such a plan is illustrated in Fig. 295. The disc or cylinder D is supposed to be arranged to rotate between the two poles N and S of a magnet, which completely cover it on both sides, the contours of the disc and poles being represented by the circles d and d' respectively, the upper pole being omitted for the sake of clearness. The cores of the magnet are supposed to be hollow, the shaft C of the disc passing through them If the unmarked pole be below, and the disc be rotated screw fashion, the current will be, as before, from the centre to the periphery and may be taken off by suitable sliding contacts, B B', on the shaft and periphery respectively. In this arrangement the current flowing through the disc and external circuit will have no appreciable effect on the field magnet.

But let us now suppose the disc to be subdivided spirally, as indicated by the full or dotted lines, Fig. 295. [Fig 8; ed. note] The difference of potential between a point on the shaft and a point on the periphery will remain unchanged, in sign as well as in amount ...

We note here that in AC induction motors, eddy currents have to be controlled by laminating the core to obtain a reasonable efficiency, which demonstrates the same principle. As the illustration shows, the dotted path of radial current generation is the preferred path of current that suffers the standard "back torque" and goes in the opposite direction to the rotation of the disk in a usually successful attempt to slow it sown. (My generator slowed down from back torque rather well, to my disappointment.) However, if the disk is subdivided in the solid line manner, the current generated will now enhance the magnetic field (since rotating currents generate magnetic fields).

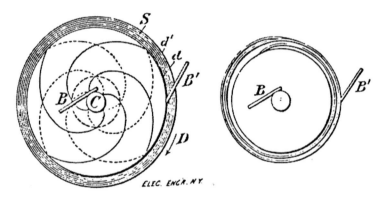

Figure 8. Spiral Disc Detailed.

At this point I would like to propose that the etched disk for sale by Borderland Research Foundation, in the pattern of a golden mean spiral, may be an interesting unipolar generator for the Tesla experiment proposed.

Of course, as Figure 8 shows, we may use an external spiral or coil encircling the disk to obtain a similar effect. Note the similarity between this drawing and the first one (from <u>Scientific American</u>) which is a model for the earth's core.

Forbes Dynamo

The Forbes dynamo is now discussed, from Figure 4, which seems to be simply a very efficient homopolar generator modified with two disks for higher voltage. For that example, Tesla proposes using the external coil but also a conductive belt, in what turns out to be a very innovative idea for increasing conductivity and decreasing resistance of the dynamo. The current is thus extracted only from the shafts of both generators.

... Instead of subdividing the disc or cylinder spirally, as indicated in Fig. 295, it is more convenient to interpose one or more turns between the disc and the contact ring on the periphery, as illustrated in Fig. 296. [Fig 8; ed. note]

A Forbes dynamo may, for instance, be excited in such a manner. In the experience of the writer it has been found that instead of taking the current from two such discs by sliding contacts, as usual, a flexible conducting belt may be employed to advantage. The discs are in such case provided with large flanges, affording a very great contact surface. The belt should be made to bear on the flanges with spring pressure to take up the expansion. Several machines with belt contact were constructed by the writer two years ago, and worked satisfactorily; but for want of time the work in that direction has been temporarily suspended. A number of features pointed out above have also been used by the writer in connection with some types of alternating current motors.

Noting that his work on these generators has been suspended in the recent past, Tesla abruptly ends a most entertaining article unequalled in all of the homopolar literature. [Note: More information on Forbes and his dynamo can be found in Robert Belfield's article, Jour. IEEE, Sept. 1976, p.344.]

RELATIVITY COMPARISONS	
Rectilinear Motion	**Circular Motion**
- No voltage developed when bar and meter move together	- Voltage not developed when disk and meter move together, but electric field is generated
- No difference between motion of observer and charge: $M_i = V \times P_i$	- Difference between rotating charged sphere or rotating observer (Schiff, 1939) B Field vs. no field - Ring currents developed causing magnetic field for sphere rotation
- No absolute motion detectable	- Absolute Rotation measured (wrt inertial frame) Sagnac, Marinov; see Marinov, Foundations of Physics Vol. 8, 1978 p.137
- Special Relativity applies	- Special relativity doesn't apply
- No volume charge by special relativity transformation laws	- Volume charge: $E = V \times B$ $D = \varepsilon_o E$ $\rho = \nabla \cdot D$ $\rho = -2\varepsilon_o \omega B$
- No forces for uniform, constant velocity	- Centrifugal and coriolis forces generated

Relative Motion

In order to help some researchers distinguish between what they believe is true for the linear motion and what really happens on a rotating disk, I have included a couple of charts, not published previously. In Figure 9, we see the left hand column contains some major aspects of rectilinear motion taken from a classical physics text. On the right is my rotational analog to each of the same experiments, i.e., rotate the magnet (+) but not the meter (-) nor the disk(-), etc. Notice that the results are the same whether we rotate the magnet or not (to the best of our knowledge).

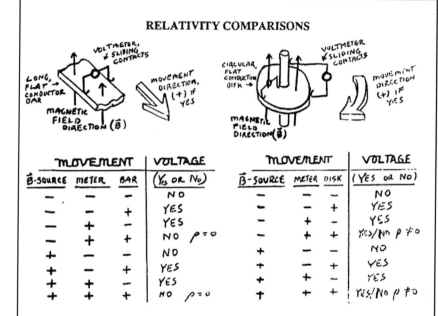

Figure 9. Comparison between linear and rotational motion.

The only debatable part comes when we rotate the meter and the disk with or without the magnet rotating. Here if we ask about an "emf" or electromotive force, we know that here is one present (yes), or if we ask if there is a nonuniform charge density, we answer yes, but if we ask about "voltage", the reaction of a meter, in the rotating frame, we have to answer no. (I placed a small, specially designed voltmeter on the disc to test this unusual effect.)

The Relativity Comparison Table is a comparison between linear and circular motion in a more theoretical fashion. Notice the many differences present for any rotating object.

My $1000 Homopolar Generator

When I came back from California in 1980, after a trip exploring the $25,000 generator that Bruce DePalma had built at the Sunburst Community (now called The Builders), I was determined to build one myself. This evolved into a Master's Degree project for the Physics Department at Buffalo's State University. Thanks to Erie Community College, I was able to test it at the school, in one of the labs.

In Figure 10, we see the results of a typical run. At the top, the trial was performed with the circuit closed, generating about 380 Amps and the DC motor demanding 266 Watts. Note the slowdown time here was about 0.57 minutes. Next, at the bottom, we see the test run with the circuit open, generating just voltage. Here the motor demand lessened to 249 Watts. Note the slowdown time is now longer (0.64 minutes) showing less "resistance" with the lack of back torque. The last verification of this analysis is the comparison of generated power (about 25 Watts) and the difference in the motor demand (about 17 Watts in this case). They are about the same.

(See P. 29 for strip chart recording)

Figure 10. Current run charts for the $1000 generator.

In Figure 11, we see the results of another trial. Here the generated power and the difference in the motor demand was even closer -- less than 1 Watt between them. Quantitatively and qualitatively we see evidence for the existence of back torque in a one-piece Faraday generator. The output of the generator tended to be compensated by the increase in the motor demand for power from the batteries.

(See P. 33 for strip chart recording)

Figure 11. Additional run charts.

We know that a decrease in resistance of the system, from 1 milliohm down to about 1 microhm (recommended by Adam Trombly) would improve the performance. Also some of the design ideas of Tesla's would also contribute to a more self-sustaining generator.

The last few figures show various pictures of my generator. They are the best photos of my large generator with 8" ceramic magnets. For more information, including a complete copy of the Trombly-Kahn patent application, I would recommend my book, The One-Piece Faraday Generator.

Fig. 12. Homopolar generator – rotating.
Square wave on Oscilloscope is the photocell circuit output.
Background: Digital frequency Counter, oscilloscope, power supply.
Foreground: DC motor, 2 Variacs for Heaters, 3 Digital Voltmeters.

Figure 13. Homopolar generator – rotor removed. Note 8" ceramic magnets with non-magnetic brass bolts.

Fig. 14. Homopolar generator with strip chart recorder shown on left.

Fig 15. top view of liquid metal (low temp solder) trough.
Thrust bearing is seen in center. Bottom right is photocell.
Aluminum foil covers heater coil surrounding brush (trough).

This paper published in the Proceedings of the International symposium on New Energy, April 16-18, 1993, Denver, CO

ARMATURE REACTION IN THE HOMOPOLAR GENERATOR
by
Thomas F. Valone, M.A., P.E.*

Abstract
    The investigation into the one-piece homopolar, unipolar or Faraday generator as a new energy source must involve a treatment of the armature reaction or back torque. Appearing as an increased load on the drive motor when power is drawn from the homopolar generator, it tends to counter the output of the homopolar generator. Based upon the interaction of the electron and the atomic lattice of the conducting disk, the armature reaction creates a physically spiraling effect on the generated current as it moves in a magnetic field. This intrinsic mechanism of radial current draw has a rich history which is highlighted in this paper. Methods for ameliorating its effect are included. Much of the material for this paper is taken from the book, The Homopolar Handbook: A Definitive Guide to Faraday Disk and N-Machine Technologies by Thomas Valone.

Introduction
    Popular in "free energy" circles is the N-Machine designed by Bruce DePalma (1979), shown in Figure 1. It proposes to use a homopolar motor to drive a homopolar generator, which supplies the electrical power to turn the motor. The only difference between the two is that the magnets are mounted on the disk for the generator making it a one-piece, co-rotating device, while the motor has stationary magnets. We can treat the torque produced by the current traversing the motor disk as an armature reaction for investigative purposes, which normally will have a back emf (glectromotive ~orce) counteracting its input. However, the armature reaction of the one-piece homopolar generator was explained away by DePalma and those after him in the free energy (new energy) arena. "Electrical loading of an N generator produces an internal torque between the conducting electrical disc and the attached ring magnets. However, since they are firmly cemented together this torque cannot escape from the machine and load the drive motor or engine" (DePalma, 1979, page 3).

---

* Consulting Engineer, Integrity Institute, Washington, DC

94

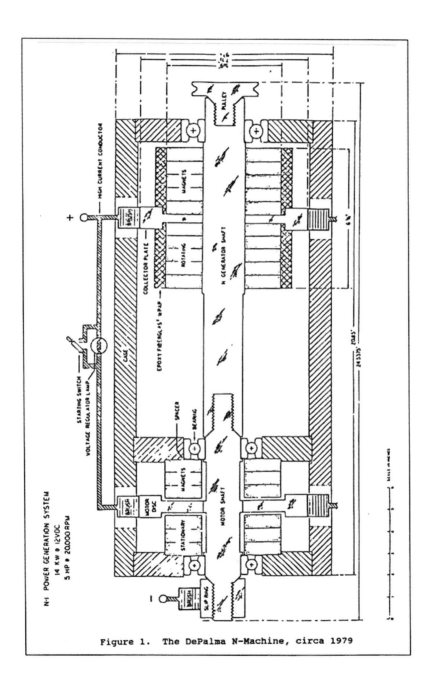

Figure 1.   The DePalma N-Machine, circa 1979

His recreation of Michael Faraday's original experiment (1832, page 12S) has a 150-year history which fills the scientific literature. Most of the controversy centers around the question of the rotation of the field with the magnet and there are easily one hundred journal articles (83 references are cited in my book) to wade through. Unless the simple problem entitled back torque, "rotational drag" or armature reaction is addressed by free energy enthusiasts, the scientific community will continue to ignore claims of "over-unity" efficiency as it has for the past decade.

Origin of the Force

Back torque is developed in any homopolar generator when current is drawn from it. The electrons are being pushed from their radial path by the magnetic field and interacting with the atomic lattice to produce a reaction force or torque. The macroscopic physics involves the Lorentz force with $F=qv \times B$ or Ampere's force with $F=L(i \times B)$. However, the microscopic origin of the force is pointed out by McKinnon et al., (1981, page 493). This force is actually due to a transverse Hall field and the excess positive ion concentration of the lattice. They emphasize that both contribute to the net force but in some metals (Al, Zn, and Cd) the Hall coefficient can be zero or the opposite sign with suitable combinations of temperature and magnetic field strength.

History of the Torque Controversy

Only in the 20th century does there appear to be published articles dealing specifically with the torque developed in a homopolar motor and the relationship between the current into it and the magnetic field. (A "conducting magnet" mentioned in older articles is identical to a one piece homopolar machine, where the magnet and disk are attached together, which is the basis of the N-machine.)

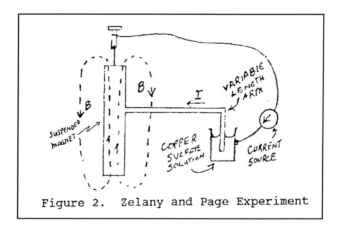

Figure 2. Zelany and Page Experiment

In 1915, Prof. G.W.O. Howe writes, "A very interesting and at first sight very puzzling problem is the nature of the mechanical reaction which must oppose the driving torque when current is taken from the rotating disc" (Howe, 1915, page 169). He concludes that the torque is due to a reaction between the flux of the magnet and the circuit external to the disk.

In 1924, Zelany and Page (1924, page 544) made a test of the torque on a homopolar motor. They attached "the external circuit" to the magnet by means of a radial arm, as I have drawn in Figure 2. The radial arm was exposed to the returning magnetic field of the magnet and therefore caused a torque in the opposite direction to that within the magnet. Thus probing the extent of the magnetic field, it wasn't until the radial arm reached thirty times the radius of the magnet that the resultant torque went to zero. (For 8" ceramic ring magnets, this distance is much less as shown in Figure 3.)* This showed that it is possible for the external circuit to experience a torque due to the current passing through it. However, this does not prove that the torque within the magnet is related to the torque on an external circuit.

This experiment was also repeated by A.L. Kimball who considered the flux of a magnet to be fixed to the magnet. He concluded that the torque was the result of the "reaction between the external flux of the magnet and the fixed external circuit which is not carried by the magnet" (Kimball, 1926, page 1302). This is similar to G.W.O. Howe (1915, page 169), who asserted the same conclusion a decade earlier, though his article was not cited.

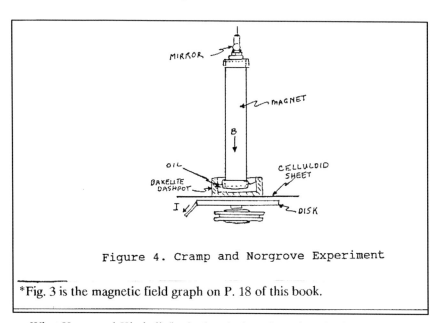

Figure 4. Cramp and Norgrove Experiment

*Fig. 3 is the magnetic field graph on P. 18 of this book.

What Howe and Kimball (both electrical engineers) and others have sought to explain is the mystery of the torque being created within the conducting magnet without an apparent equal and opposite reaction which would conserve angular momentum. In 1936, Cramp and Norgrove performed an experiment illustrated in Figure 4. They rotated a disk below a cylindrical magnet, drew current from it, and calculated its back torque. "Assuming the electromagnetic torque to react upon the magnet" (Cramp and Norgrove, 1936, page 487) they looked for any slight movement of the suspended magnet with the help of a mirror mounted on the top of it and a beam of light. No movement of the magnet was detected at any speed of the disk.

A similar experiment was performed by A.K. Das Gupta (1963, page 428) when he mounted a disk and magnet freely and then passed current into the disk. with the idea that the adjacent magnet might react to the torque developed in the disk, he looked for, but could not detect, any movement of the magnet. In this case a disk magnet was used which had more surface area exposed to the 50 amp current in the disk.

When the above two experiments were brought to DePalma's attention in the early 1980's, he changed his explanation of the "N effect". Echoing Adam Trombly's work (Trombly and Kahn, 1982) with a $290,000 one-piece homopolar generator, he writes, "When the magnetic flux path is closed symmetrically through the disc instead of around the disc as in the early machines the drag associated with the flow of current disappears" (DePalma, 1984, page 4). Today, this design method of Trombly's still remains an intriguing compensation technique to reduce armature reaction.

Angular Momentum in a Conducting Disk

Though Howe, Kimball, and even Das Gupta demonstrate that the external circuit can react to the presence of the magnetic field, it still does not resolve the angular momentum question that becomes apparent when one studies the lack of its conservation in the above experiments.

Richard Feynman, a Nobel Prize winner, also proposed a similar paradox in his Lectures (Feynman, 1964, page 17). In his example, charged metallic spheres mounted on a plastic disk cause it to rotate when a coaxial electromagnet on the disk suddenly interrupts its current and thus, its magnetic field. Its resolution, as well as the resolution of the torque controversy, was made clear in an article by G. Lombardi, (1983, page 213) as well as in a textbook by Landau and Lifshitz (1971, page 79).

Lombardi points out that static electromagnetic fields have angular momentum and that this must be considered when computing the total conserved quantity. The angular momentum depends upon the three-dimensional integral of $r\times(E\times B)$ in the above-mentioned textbook.

Thus, with the electromagnetic field carrying the conservation of angular momentum for torque produced in a conducting disk, this opens a theoretical approach path for new energy physicists seeking over-unity.

Measurement of Back Torque

In the classical treatment of the torque on a Faraday disk motor, we may take the equation for the Ampere force on a current loop in a magnetic field, $F=Li\times B$, where i is the current vector, L the radial distance, and B the magnetic flux density. This equation is then substituted into the definition for torque, $T=r\times F$, which yields, in differential form, dT=Bir dr, which can then be integrated across the radius to give the total torque.

In a Faraday or homopolar generator, it is expected that this torque is also manifested in a direction opposite to that of rotation, analogous to the back emf experienced in the homopolar motor. To analyze the back torque, we can look at the angular momentum of a rotating body, L=Iw. Here, I is the "moment of inertia" which is defined uniquely for each object depending on its geometry and w is the angular velocity. For a ring magnet, I is defined as m/2 times the sum of the squares of the radii, where m is the mass of the magnet. The torque can then be defined as T=I(dw/dt) which is the same as T=(dL/dt).

However, the direct measurement of this quantity is difficult unless a prony brake is employed. Therefore, relating the power input to the torque applied, we may use the standard equation, P=Tw, which allows us to have the torque continuously applied even at constant angular velocity if the power is being dissipated in frictional forces and electrical generation. Thus if a certain amount of power is measured for the drive motor of a homopolar generator, for a given w, we can find the torque being applied to overcome friction. Then, if the output terminals are shorted, for example, to obtain maximum generation of current, one simply has to measure the new angular velocity and the new power input for the drive motor to find the increased torque, subtracting the two results, we have found the back torque the generator has produced to counteract current output as Lenz's Law predicts.

Inertia and Mach's Principle

The torque, as seen from the above analysis, is related to the inertia of the object and the magnetic field it experiences. From Mach's Principle, we obtain an explanation for the inertia of a body: its interaction with all of the extragalactic masses of the universe. From a general relativity treatment (Valone, 1983, page 14) we find that the interaction of a rotating body with the rest of the universe is quite different than in the stationary case. Therefore, the possibility exists that something as intrinsic as inertia may be affected by rotation.

We are aware that the choice of rotation axis changes the moment of inertia. However, even the formula MRR, which is an integral part of all moments of inertia, has a nonlinear dependence on R which seems to indicate a sort of anisotropy. Furthermore, the concept of anisotropy of inertia is already a legitimate subject of inquiry in physics with the work of Corconi and Salpeter (1958) as well as Drever (1961, page 683).

Conclusion

As engineers and physicists with graduate degrees are eventually attracted to the new energy and free energy technologies, the one-piece homopolar generator looms as a simple yet mysterious rotating machine. The only generator which can produce DC electricity without commutation still has not been fully utilized. Yet the effect of torque being created when current is passed through the disk is so fundamental that if closing the magnetic field path through the disk does not diminish the current flow significantly, the Trombly idea can be tested with a closed-path homopolar motor. If the motor does not move when current is sent into the disk, then back torque has been licked once and for all.

Though the Trombly/DePalma method for cancelling or diminishing its effect has been proposed, Nikola Tesla's idea of spirally-segrnenting the disk directly addresses the phenomena of armature reaction (Valone, 1986, 1988). The optimal Spiral Homopolar Generator Project is now underway with a team from Alaska and my design assistance.

References

Corconi and Salpeter (1958). "A Search for Anisotropy Inertia" , Gravity Research Foundation, of Gloucester, MA, winning essay on gravity for 1958.

Das Gupta, A.K. (1963). "Association of the Magnetic Field with the Field-Producing Magnet", American Journal of Physics, page 428.

DePalma, Bruce (1979). The N-1 Power Generation System Diagram was obtained from Joe Beldon of the Sunburst Community when I visited them in 1979 to investigate the generator they had paid DePalma to build.

DePalma, Bruce (1979). "Extraction of Electrical Energy Directly from Space: The 'N' Machine", Simularity Institute Report #60, March 9.

DePalma, Bruce (1984). "The Secret of the Faraday Disc", DePalma Institute, Report #92, February 2.

Drever (1961). "A Search for Anisotropy of Inertial Mass Using a Free Precession Technique", Philosophical Magazine, Vol. 6, page 683.

Faraday, Michael (1832). "Experimental Researches in Electricity", Philosophical Transactions of the Royal Society Vol. 122, page 125.

Feynman, Richard (1964). Lectures on Physics, Addison Wesley, Reading, MA, Vol. II, page 17.

Howe, G.W.O. (1915). "Some Problems of Electromagnetic Induction", The Electrician, Nov. 5, page 169.

Kimball (1926). Physical Review, Vol. 28, page 1302.

Landau and Lifshitz (1971). The Classical Theory of Fields, 3rd ed., Pergammon Oxford, page 79.

Lombardi (1983). American Journal of Physics, Vol. 51, page 213.

McKinnon, McAlister, and Hurd (1981). "Origin of the Force in a Current-Carrying Wire in a Magnetic Field", American Journal of Physics, Vol. 49(5), page 493.

Trombly and Kahn (1982). "Closed Path Homopolar Machine", International PCT, World Intellectual Property Organization, International Publication Number WO 82/02126, International Application Number PCT/US81/01588

Valone, Thomas (1983). The One-Piece Faradav Generator: Theory and Experiment, Master's Thesis SUNY at Buffalo, Physics Department (subsequently incorporated into the book: The Homopolar Handbook: -A Definitive Guide to Faraday Disk and N-Machine Technologies, Integrity Institute, Washington, DC.)

Valone, Thomas (1986). "The One-Piece Faraday Generator, Tesla's Contribution", Proceedings of the International Tesla symposium, International Tesla Society, Colorado Springs, CO.

Valone, Thomas (1988). "The One-Piece Faraday Generator, Tesla's contribution", Third International Symposium on Non-Conventional Energy Technology, Planetary Association for Clean Energy, Ottawa, Ontario.

Zelany and Page (1924). Physical Review, Vol. 24, page 544.

APPENDIX III

Wilhelm Report:
The Stelle Homopolar Machine
(built to DePalma's specifications)

The Stelle Group

STELLE, ILLINOIS 60919   815-949-1111

investigations of the n-effect, one-piece homopolar dynamos, and miscellaneous field effects

-july 10, 1981 status report

contents

- PHASE I AND PHASE II REPORTS
- PROJECT HISTORY/PHASE I
- PROJECT CORRESPONDENCE/PHASE I
- "N" TECHNICAL PAPER
- PROJECT HISTORY/PHASE II
- CALCULATIONS/PHASE II
- TELEPHONE LOG/PHASE II
- PROJECT CORRESPONDENCE/PHASE II
- LAB NOTES/PHASE II
- RESEARCHED BIBLIOGRAPHY

COPY

BY:

Timothy J. Wilhelm   7/10/81

TIMOTHY J. WILHELM

7/23/81

Tom,
Good Luck! I'm eager to
hear about your results.
                    Tim

Stelle Letter

OCTOBER 1980 • Volume 15, No. 9

Stelle's Experimental Energy Converter Presented In West Germany

Physicist Tim Wilhelm, director of Stelle's Office of Technology, tests the output of the tachyon energy converter he built.

"Testing Bruce De Palma's N-Machine"

A priority task to be completed in accomplishing one
of The Stelle Group's major goals involves putting into
practical use a device that operates on the basic premise
alluded to in this paragraph:

"...gravity and magnetism, which are different manifesta-
tions of the same force, are inherent in the axial spin
of particles. One day men will derive more power for
motors directly from this source than they shall ever
achieve from fuels, electricity, or nuclear disintegra-
tion."

To date, our approach to dealing with this task has been
solely the searching out and investigation of presently
existing devices that would meet our needs with little or
no development work required. Also to date, amongst the
many inventions we have investigated, nothing viable or
sound has been found. All of them have been either fraudu-
lent or just plain impractical and unsound. Through my
experience in these dealings, it has become quite apparent that what is needed is: A sound footing in proven
basic scientific "knowledge," a "theory" (much more complete than what is contained in The Ultimate Frontier)
that can be submitted to testing from which new scientific knowledge can be gleaned, and a great deal of
logical thought and persistent effort to transform newly
gained knowledge into a working device which will meet our
needs.

This present investigation ("Testing Bruce De Palma's
N-Machine") takes a major step out of the context of
our previous searchings and into the preferred strategy
I have described above.

I recently met with Mr. DePalma at which time he shared
with me his background, his theories, and the current
level of detail that he has developed on his N-Machine
concept. His theory and current state of development are
seen in the attached article, "Rotation of a Magnetized
Gyroscope". In summary, DePalma's claim is that he has
discovered that a magnetized gyroscope will generate a
D.C. electrical potential, in homopolar fashion, between
the periphery and the center of the rotating magnetized
mass. Further he claims that when current is drawn from
this "generator" it does not experience an opposition
torque anywhere nearly equal to the electrical power
consumed. In other words, he states, Lenz's law does
not apply. At first glance one can see that this is an
odd electical generator in that it has only a rotor, no
stator. Having no stator, what then is there for a back-
torque to torque against? Maybe nothing, maybe something.

My purpose in this investigation into the operation of
DePalma's N-Machine is to empirically validate the claim
that this device exhibits no back torque (per Lenz's Law)
when current is drawn from it through an external electrical load. A small experiment by Jeff Campau seemed to
indicate that, when current is imposed on a one-piece
homopolar machine from an external power source, the
resultant motor effect is not strong enough to cause
rotation, even at fairly high currents. His observations
may lend some credence to the claim that the device is
not subject to Lenz's law, but further experimentation is
needed to make absolute substantiation.

If indeed a device can be built which generates electrical
power while experiencing no back-torque under load, a
machine would then be feasible which could drive itself,
with power to spare. Aside from meeting a primary need
in the fulfillment of our purpose, the impact of such a
device upon current economics, politics, and the social
order in Stelle could be quite major.

t: The finished apparatus used in this investigation is
seen in the enclosed 35 mm slides. Slide No. 1 shows a
good full view of the test device, not including the
cable and shunt used to short-circuit this small generator
during testing. The disk-armature used is a six-inch
diameter steel disk and the shaft is a nonmagnetic alloy
of unknown composition. Current pick-up was made with
large carbon brushes as seen in slide No. 6. Brush
holders for both the disk brushes and shaft brushes are
aluminum and are seen in slides No. 3, 4, 5, 6, 7, and 8.
The field magnets are epoxied together and to the disk
with a ¼" thick steel plate epoxied at both ends of the
rotor assembly for providing a drillable surface needed
to dynamically balance the machine. The magnets themselves are a ceramic grade 5 composition and, as seen in
slides #15, 16, and 17, do not have a very high tensile
strength.

Drawings illustrating the details of each basic component
of the test apparatus are also enclosed.

For testing the apparatus, the following test equipment
was used:

Output Voltage - Simpson 0-1.5V DC Voltmeter

Output Current - Simpson 50 mV meter with an Empro
50 amp x 50 mV shunt

Circuit Resistance - E.T.L. Model 47A milliohmmeter

Results and Conclusions -

Our completed generator yielded the following:

$\omega \cong$ 6900 RPM

B (estimated) $\cong$ 15,000 Gauss

E (measured) $\cong$ .23 Volts

I (measured) $\cong$ 4 Amps

$R_{int.}$ (measured) $\cong$ .05 Ω

$R_{ext.}$ (estimated) $\cong$ .005 Ω

Observations -

Voltage was a bit lower than expected, probably due to inaccurate estimate of flux density in the magnetic circuit. Current was also lower than expected due to the internal resistance being higher than expected. High resistance was due to the use of a bare steel generating disk. The disk surface proved not only too hard for proper interface with the brushes, but also quickly built up an oxide layer that added further resistance at the brush-to-disk contact point. To help correct the problem, a thin layer of copper plating was applied to the disk's peripheral surface. This one modification lowered the internal resistance from .35 Ω to .05 Ω. However, .005 Ω would be more in the desired range.

Unfortunately, our testing of the generator is incomplete due to the machine being damaged beyond usefulness before tests for "back-torque under load" could be made. Centrifugal force caused one of the magnets to break loose (at 6900 RPM) thus destroying the balanced rotor assembly. For further models, it is concluded that a fiber wrap or metal sleeve around the magnets will be an absolute must.

Although we were not able to get as far as desired in our testing, we have spoken with other persons working on this concept and all "feel good" about its viability:

Jeff Campau (Electronic Engineer) - tested a very small model for motor effect and could not get it to spin under its own force when current was pumped in, and yet it generated current (per all equations) when rotated axially.

Adam Trombly (M.S., Physics and Astronomy) - Mr. Trombly has every faith in the "N" concept and is presently doing material stress calculations for a future test model.

The Sunburst Community (who had directly worked with Bruce DePalma) - reports that they have successfully tested a bench model; no back-torque and more power out than in.

I recommend that we pursue building a second test model, coupled to a homopolar motor as the drive source. We should view our first model as an exercise in new concept acclimation, and make appropriate design

107

changes in the second model that will overcome the problems inherent
in the first. The second model should be sized and fabricated for
self-sustained operation, similar in design to DePalma's "N-1 power
system". A design and budget will be forthcoming on this recommended
next step.

Respectfully submitted,

Timothy J. Wilhelm, 9/12/80

Timothy J. Wilhelm

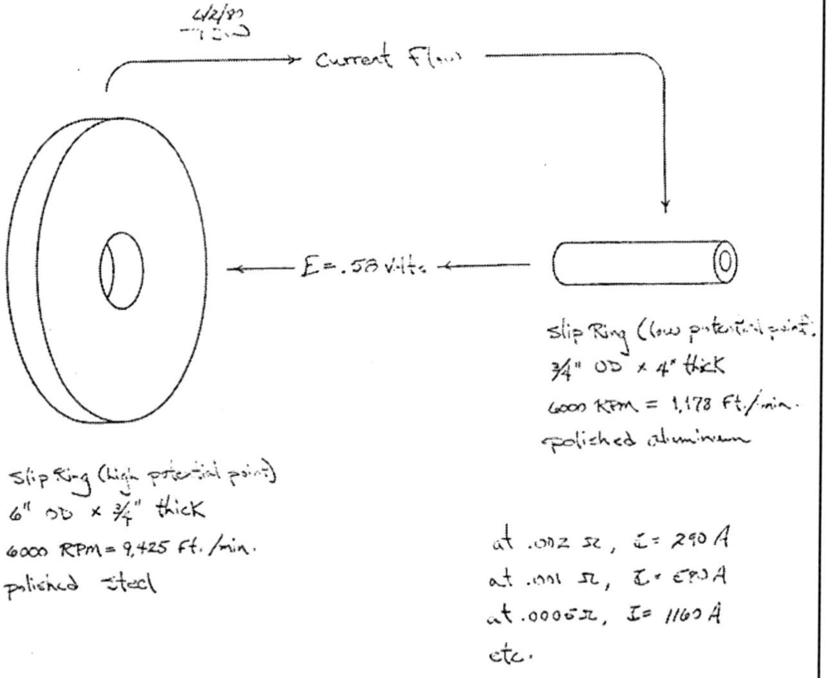

PROJECT EXPENSE SUMMARY

Trip to meet with DePalma	$ 449.55
Model #1 Hardware	130.00
Dynamic Balancing	92.00
Mis. Expenses (gasoline, travel, etc.)	75.58
Meters	118.72
Total project expenses	$ 865.85

PROJECT 043.2/PHASE 2

Testing a One-Piece Homopolar Generator for Back Torque
when Submitted to Electrical Loading.

   As has been stated before, one of The Stelle Group's
major/priority objectives is to discover, develop, invent,
or procure a means for extracting useful work and motive
power from the abundance of field forces that permeate the
universe. Our previous work "Testing Bruce DePalma's
N Machine", was a recent effort in that direction.
Although, as previously described, we were not able to
perform all the tests necessary to prove or disprove the
validity of the N-effect, we did learn several things of
which we were not previously aware:

1. That it truly is possible to generate an EMF with a
    one-piece electrical generator (only a rotor; no stator)
    per the mathematical relationships used in conventional
    homopolar machines.

2. That this so called "N-machine" initially appeared to
    exhibit practically no motor effect relative to its
    generative output, and if this could be proved to be
    true, it would indicate a lack of back-torque as well.

Further, we came to the understanding that the so-called
"N-machine" is, in actuality, a basic, one-piece homopolar
generator. This type of device has been known of (albeit
by few people) since the late 1800's. Thus, the machine
itself cannot be considered an invention of Bruce DePalma.
However, the modern recognition of the so-called "N-effect"
(a lack of back-torque in a one-piece, homopolar generator
when electrically loaded), if indeed it proves to be valid,
seems at this point anyway to be to Mr. DePalma's credit;
it would be a newly-discovered principle of nature.

Given the primacy of our goal and the lack of conclusive
data from our initial tests, we pursued obtaining feedback
from others doing work similar to ours. Library research
on general homopolar technology was initiated at this time,
as well.

We discovered that work done by others in the past (Faraday,
Howe, Then, Das Gupta, et.al.) indicated that the one-
piece homopolar generator is indeed a unique and seemingly
paradoxical machine in the conventional context of electrical engineering. Further, we learned that very few people,
even among electrical engineers familiar with homopolar
technology, knew much of anything about the one-piece
generator. On April 14, 1981, I had a telephone conversation with a Mr. H. O. Stevens, a research engineer with
the U.S. Dept. of Navy at the David W. Taylor Naval Ship

Research and Development Center. His area of specialty
was liquid metal brushes in homopolar machines. Not only
did Mr. Stevens think that some of the results of Das
Gupta's tests were impossible (that the field magnets of
a homopolar motor do not experience any reaction torque
when an imposed current causes the disk to spin), but he
had never before even heard of any such thing as a one-
piece homopolar generator, let alone believe that it would
work. But obviously it does work, as we have proven.

Besides the theories and reported test results from Bruce
DePalma, we also obtained feedback from two other physicists
doing very similar work: Mr. Tom Valone, from New York
State, doing a special investigation of the one-piece
machine and its back torque characteristics as part of his
work on a M.S. degree in Physics, and Mr. Adam Trombly,
a California physicist who reportedly has recently obtained
$100,000 to build a state-of-the-art one-piece homopolar
dynamo for analyzing the back-torque phenomenon. Both of
these gentlemen are confident that there is validity to
the supposition that the one-piece homopolar exhibits
less than the normally expected back-torque. Our purpose
in pursuing this project is to prove this supposition
ourselves, conclusively, one way or the other. And further,
to glean as many insights into the nature of fields and
their related forces as we are able to obtain from this work.

The final setup used in our phase 2 experiment is
seen in the enclosed 35mm slides, numbers 21 through 36.
Slide No. 24 shows the actual generator. Slide No. 25
shows the 5 H.P., 3∅, 480V AC drive motor and clutch used
to spin the generator. Slide #29 shows the large knife
switch used to short circuit the generator, and the 3,000
amp/50 mv shunt used in the external circuit to take current
readings. The heavy copper bar in the external circuit
connects the brush on the disk periphery, through the switch,
to a mercury pot that contacts the generator shaft on the
underside of the frame.

Also enclosed herein is a set of the construction drawings
for the phase 2 machine which shows the originally-intended
configuration of a one-piece and two-piece homopolar
composite machine. Although these drawings do not show the
"as-built" configuration, they do illustrate the details of
most of the components used. A complete schematic of our
as-built/final setup is shown in Fig. "A".

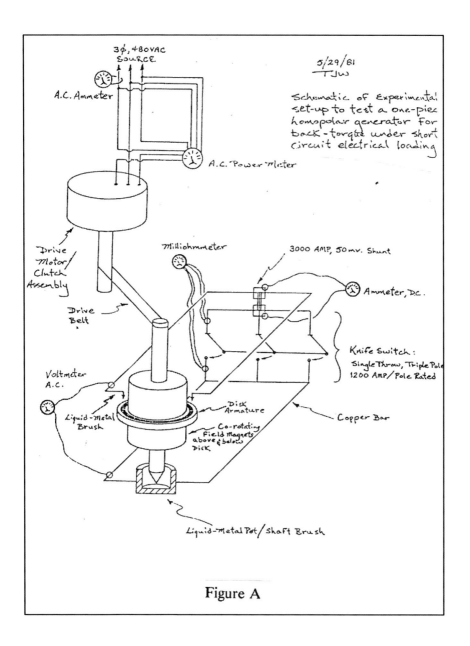

Figure A

111

Test equipment used is as follows:

For measuring Generator Voltage	Simpson 0-1.5V D.C. Voltmeter
For measuring Total Circuit Current Generated	Simpson 50mv meter with an Enpro 3000 amp x 50 mv shunt
For measuring Circuit Resistance	E.T.L. Model 47A milliohmeter
For measuring Drive Motor Current Draw	Amprobe model RS-3 clamp-on AC ammeter.
For measuring Drive Motor Voltage	Sencore Model FE27 Field Effect Multimeter
For measuring Drive Motor Power Consumption	General Electric model AB40, 0-6000 watt, 3∅, 480V AC Power Meter

1) Check apparatus for proper setup.

2) Check static resistance of circuit to insure good connections and thus high current.

3) Disengage clutch.

4) Start drive motor.

5) Engage clutch and take generator up to full speed.

6) Measure and note the following:

   angular velocity, generated voltage, current draw through any one leg of drive motor input, drive motor power consumption.

7) Close knife switch.

8) Measure and note the following:

   angular velocity, generated voltage, current draw through any one leg of drive motor input, drive motor power consumption.

9) Repeat steps 6, 7, and 8.

10) Calculate what the conventionally-expected back-torque in the generator (and the subsequent increased power consumption in the drive) motor should be after closing knife switch.

Qualitative Test For Back-Torque Under Load

Test Date - 5/6/81
        TJW

Static Resistance - Total closed-circuit resistance= .864mΩ

Dynamic Test -

Switch Position	w	Total Generated Voltage	Total Circuit Current	Observations and Assumptions
open circuit	4700 RPM	0.4 Volts	---	--
closed circuit	4700 RPM	(0.1 Volts across switch)	ammeter needle pegged at 3000 amps & as generator heated up current dropped & settled at 2400 amps	No apparent visible or audible strain on drive motor. Drive motor current increased by approximately ½ ampere.

Run-Down Test - Run generator up to 4700 RPM with switch open, turn off drive motor and time how long it takes to run down to dead still. Then run generator with switch closed, turn off drive motor and time how long it takes to run down to dead still.

	Run-down with Switch Open	Run-down with Switch Closed
Trial #1	1 min., 5 sec.	48 sec.
Trial #2	1 min., 15 sec.	55 sec.
Trial #3	1 min., 20 sec.	1 min., 5 sec.

Quantitative Test For Back-Torque Under Load

Test Date - 5/13/81
        TJW

Static Resistance - Total closed circuit resistance = 1.07 mΩ (increase in static resistance probably due to oxidation in mercury brush)

Dynamic Test -

Switch Position	w	Total Generated Voltage	Total Circuit Current	Drive Motor Power Consumption	Observations and Assumptions
open circuit	4725 RPM	0.4 Volts	--	1850 watts	--
closed circuit	4725 RPM	(0.1 Volts across switch)	1200 amps continuous	2400 watts	Δ power of drive = 550 watts

Calculated Δ Power of Drive Motor -

Conventional Back-Torque T should have been = $\dfrac{\emptyset \ I}{2 \ \pi}$

$\therefore \ T = \dfrac{\emptyset \ I}{2 \ \pi} = \dfrac{(3.2 \times 10^6) \ (120)}{2 \ \pi} = .6 \times 10^3$ dyne.cm = 849.672 oz.in

Δ Power required to maintain 4725 RPM = $\dfrac{wT}{6.3 \times 10^6}$ (in H.P.)

$\therefore \ \Delta P = \dfrac{wT}{6.3 \times 10^6} = \dfrac{(4725) \ (849.672)}{(6.3 \times 10^6)} = .637254$ H.P.=475.2 watts

475.2 watts $\div$ 85% efficiency = 559.06 watts

Also- .4 volts x 1200 amps $\div$ 85% efficiency = 564.71 watts

n

ns: It is seen in the results of our "Quantitative Test
For Back-Torque Under Load", that our one-piece homopolar
generator definitely appeared to exhibit the conventionally
expected back-torque when submitted to electrical loading.
But it should be noted that the reason for this outcome
might be other than the clasically assumed and accepted
Lenz's Law. Soliciting feedback on our results lead to
the proposal that other possible reasons for the results
we obtained may be related to either M.H.D. frictional
losses in the liquid-metal brushes, or some quality of
permanent magnets that would yield different results than if
electromagnetic field magnets were used, or some other
reason not yet obvious. However, our calculated M.H.D.
losses in the mercury brush is less than eight watts.
Also, our library research thus far indicates that there
are no observable differences in the action of electromagnets, compared to permanent magnets, in their conventional
application as field magnets in homopolar generators (one
exception being a December 17, 1980 report published by
Bruce DePalma titled, Performance of the "Sunburst" N
Machine). Therefore, at this point in time, my best conclusion regarding our test results is this:

That a one-piece homopolar generator, of the type and
configuation illustrated in this report, does exhibit
back-torque when electrically loaded, per Lenz's Law,
and thus cannot be considered as a viable device for
tapping free energy from space and converting it to a
useful form.

However, I still feel that it is essential to maintain an
open mind to the possibility of circumventing Lenz's Law.
As already stated, there may be an as-yet-unobserved cause

for our test results that may be easily avoided, thus
yielding different results. Or perhaps, changing the
configuration of our external circuit may lead to a
lessening of back-torque. In any case, the pursuit must
continue.

During the construction of our test device, we experienced
difficulty in getting the rotor properly dynamically
balanced. In dealing with this situation, we learned
the importance of including deflection and resonance calculations as part of the shaft design process, and the need
for prestressing the shaft material prior to machining.
These considerations should be given high priority in any
future work with rotary machinery.

Concurrent with the physics research performed in this
project, some legal research was performed as well. It
was learned from Mr. Donald W. Banner, former U.S. Commis-
sioner of Patents and Trademarks, and presently a professor
at John Marshall Law School in Chicago, that all U.S.
patent applications are reviewed by a security team repre-
senting the U.S. Dept. of Defense during the first six
months subsequent to their submission to the U.S. Patent
Office. Reflecting on this information may be useful in
the future when making administrative/directional decisions.

In conclusion, I would like to note that new information
gained during the progress of this project has lead to
several new and potentially valid assumptions concerning
the nature of and relationships between electricity, magnetism, and gravity. Experiments are now being designed and
a paper is now being written in preparation for a third
phase of this project. I trust it will take us another
step closer to our goal.

Timothy J. Wilhelm
6/10/81

115

6/8/81
TJW

MHD LOSSES IN MERCURY BRUSH DUE TO EDDYS CAUSED BY ELECTRIC CURRENT :

$$\text{MHD Power Loss} = \mu K \frac{V^2}{2} \coth \frac{Kt}{2} \text{ per unit area}$$

where, $K^2 = B^2/\mu\rho$

μ = viscosity of Liquid Metal in $N \cdot s/m^2$
ρ = resistivity of Liquid Metal in Ω/m
B = Flux density in wb/m^2
t = radial depth of Liquid Metal in m
V = velocity of moving wall in m/sec

For our application, using Hg :

μ of Hg = 1.55×10^{-3} $N \cdot s/m^2$

ρ of Hg = 9.84×10^{-3} Ω/m

$B = .45$ Wb./m^2

$t = 6.35 \times 10^{-3}$ meters

$V = 71.8$ m/sec

$K = \sqrt{B^2/\mu\rho} = 115.23$

$$\frac{\text{MHD Power Loss}}{m^2} =$$

$$\left(\frac{1.55 \times 10^{-3} N \cdot s}{m^2}\right)(115.23)\left(\frac{71.8 \times 71.8}{2}\right) \coth\left[\frac{(115.23)(6.35 \times 10^{-3})}{2}\right] =$$

$$(460.38)\left(\coth 3.66 \times 10^{-1}\right) =$$

$$(460.38)(2.85) = 1.3 \times 10^3 \text{ watts}/m^2$$

Surface area of stationary wall = 6.1×10^{-3} m^2

$\therefore$ Total MHD power loss = $\dfrac{1.3 \times 10^3 \text{ watts}}{m^2} \times \dfrac{6.1 \times 10^{-3} m^2}{1}$

$$= 7.93 \text{ watts}$$

Page 1 of 2

Equations Pertaining to Disk-Type Homopolar
Machines
3/16/81
TJW

Generator Effect - (Generated EMF/volts)

$$\varepsilon = \frac{B \omega r^2}{2 \times 10^8}$$

B - gauss

ω - rev./sec.

r - radius, cm.

10^8 abvolts (cgs) = 1 volt

Motor Effect - (Output Torque/dyne·cm)

$$T = \frac{\phi I}{2\pi}$$

ϕ - maxwells =
$\quad$ B (gauss) × Area (cm^2)

I - abamperes =
$\quad$ amperes × 10^{-1}

- (Output Power/Horse Power)

$$H.P. = \frac{2\pi \omega T}{(12)(16)(33,003)}$$

ω - radians per minute

T - oz·in

12 - in/ft

16 - oz/lb.

33,003 - Ft·lb/HP·min

- (Back EMF Due to Rotation/volts)

$$\varepsilon_b = \frac{\omega \phi}{2\pi \times 10^8}$$

ω - rev./sec

ϕ - Maxwells =
$\quad$ B (gauss) × Area (cm^2)

10^8 abvolts (cgs) = 1 volt

$$\frac{\omega \phi}{2\pi \times 10^8} \times \left(\frac{B \times \pi r^2}{\phi}\right) = \frac{B \omega r^2}{2 \times 10^8}$$

Page 2 of 2

3/16/81

—TJW

-(Impressed Current/amperes)

$$I = \frac{\left(E - \frac{\omega\phi}{2\pi \times 10^8}\right)}{R}$$

E- impressed EMF (volts)

$\frac{\omega\phi}{2\pi \times 10^8}$ — back EMF (volts)

R- total circuit resistance (ohms)

Mechanical force & stress —

- (Force Due to Rotation /lbs.)

$$T = \frac{4\pi^2\omega^2 \rho h r^3}{3g}$$

ω - rev./sec.

ρ - material density (lbs./Ft.^{3})

h - thickness of Disk (Ft.)

r - radius of Disk (Ft.)

g - acceleration due to gravity = 32 ft./sec.^{2}

- (Tensile Stress/psi)

$$S_t = T/A$$

T- Tensile force due to rotation (lbs.)

A - Radial cross sectional area of Disk (in^2)

118

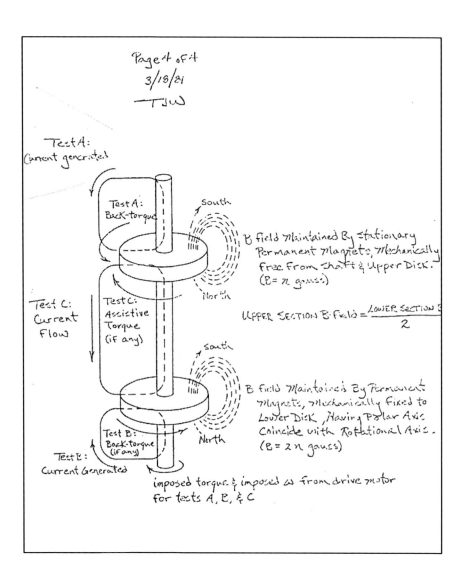

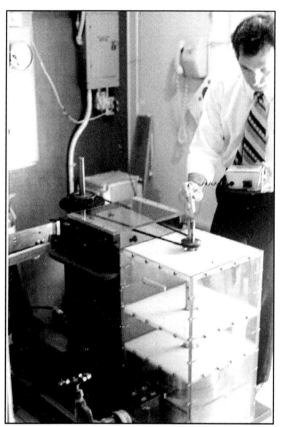

Photos of the Stelle one-Piece Homopolar Generator with Mercury Brushes

To the left:
T. Wilhelm is testing the rotation speed with a tachometer.

Below:
Photo of the complete Stelle Machine, encased in airtight plastic to protect from mercury vapor. Note the large copper bus bar for the output current.

RESEARCHED BIBLIOGRAPHY:

1) Zelany & Page, *Physical Review*, Volume 24, pg.544, 1924
2) Kimball, *Physical Review*, Volume 28, pg. 1302, Dec., 1926
3) Williams, *Michael Faraday*, pages 202-205.
4) Crooks, Litvin & Matthews, *American Journal of Physics*, Vol. 46, pg. 729, 1978
5) Das Gupta, *American Journal of Physics*, Volume 31, pg. 428, 1963
6) Valone, Thomas, private paper, "*A Test for the Back Torque of a One-Piece Faraday Generator*", 1981.
7) Tesla, *The Electrical Engineer*, September 2, 1891
8) Noeggerath, *A.I.E.E. Transactions*, June 28, 1912
9) Lamme, *A.I.E.E. Transactions*, June 28, 1912
10) Boning, *Wireless Engineer*, Volume 29, No. 350, pg. 285, Nov. 1952
11) Ku & Kamal, *Journal of the Franklin Institute*, July, 1954, pg. 7
12) Weldon, et.al., *Transactions of Int. Conference on Energy Storage, Compression, & Switching*; Torino, Italy; Nov. 5-7, 1974
13) Weldon, et. al., University of Texas, *CEM Publication No. PN-43*
14) Weldon, et.al., *Welding Journal*, May, 1979
15) Weldon, et.al., University of Texas, *CEM Publication No. PN-51*
16) Gully, University of Texas, *CEM Publication No. PN-65*
17) Thomsen, *Science News*, Volume 119, pg. 218
18) Watt, *Journal, Institution of Electrical Engineers*, pg. 233, June, 1958
19) Das Gupta, *AIEE Transactions*, Pt. III, Volume 80, pg. 567, Oct. 1961.
20) Das Gupta, *AIEE Transactions*, October 1962, pg. 399
21) Klaudy, chapter from unknown resource book titled, "*The Graz Homopolar Machine*"
22) Strough & Shrader, *The Review of Scientific Instruments*, Volume 22, No. 8, August, 1951
23) Lewis, *Journal of Science & Technology*, Vol. 38, No. 2, pg. 46, 1971
24) Hong & Wilhelm, *Journal of Applied Physics*, Vol. 47, No. 3, pg. 906, 1976
25) Johnson, Hummert & Keeton, *IEEE Transactions*, Vol. PAS-95, No. 4, pg. 1234, July/August, 1976
26) Witkowski, et.al., *IEEE Transactions*, Vol. PAS-95, No. 4, Pg. 1493 July/August, 1976
27) Carrigan & Gubbins, *Scientific American*, Feb. 1979, Pg. 118
28) Book titled, *Atoms, Stars & Nebulae*, pg. 86, Author unknown.
29) Woodson & Melcher, *Electromechanical Dynamics*, Pgs. 283-329 John Wyley & Son, 1968
30) Bureau of Navy Personnel, *Basic Electricity*, pages 353, 373, & 374, Dover No. 0-486-20973-3
31) Feynman, *Lecture Series on Physics*, Vol. II, sections 17-2, 17-3,& 17-4·
32) Webster, *American Journal of Physics*, Vol. 31, Pg. 590, 1963
33) McKinnan, et.al., *American Journal of Physics*, Vol. 49, Pg. 493, 1981
34) Martin, *Physical Basis for Electrical Engineering*, pgs. 37-60, Prentice Hall, 1957
35) Winch, *Electricity and Magnetism*, pgs. 377-379, Prentice Hall 1963
36) Then, *American Journal of Physics*, Volume 28, No.6, pg. 557, 1960
37) Then, *American Journal of Physics*, Volume· 30, pg. 411, 1962

ON THE ELECTROMAGNETIC BASIC EQUATIONS FOR MOVING BODIES

by A. Einstein and J. Laub
Annalen der Physik V. 26, 1908, p. 533
(translated from the German by Integrity Research Institute)

In a recently published treatise, Mr. Minkowski* explained the basic equations for the electromagnetic processes in moving bodies. In view of the fact that this work, in relation to mathematics, makes great demands on the reader, we do not think it unnecessary to differentiate, in an elementary way, the important equations in this paper, which, by the way, essentially agree with Minkowski's paper.

1. Derivation of the Basic Equations for Moving Bodies

The adopted way is the following: We introduce two systems of coordinates K and K' which are both acceleration-free, but moving in relation to one another. If there is matter in the space that is at rest in relation to K', then the laws of electrodynamics of bodies at rest, which are presented by the Maxwell-Hertz equations, are valid with regard to K'. If we transform these equations to the system K, we will obtain immediately the electrodynamic equations of moving bodies for the case in which the velocity of matter is constant, spacially and temporally. These obtained equations are also valid, apparently at least at the first approach, when the velocity distribution of matter is arbitary. This assumption is justified in part also by the fact that the result obtained this way is rigorously valid in the case in which there is a number of uniformly moving bodies, with different velocities, which are separate from one another through vacuum interspaces.

With regard to system K', we will call the vector of the electric force $\mathbf{E}'$, that of the magnetic force $\mathbf{H}'$, that of the dielectric shifting $\mathbf{D}'$ (now called electric displacement - Ed. note), that of the magnetic induction $\mathbf{B}'$, that of the electric current density $\mathbf{J}'$. Further, ρ' will denote the electric charge density. Let the Maxwell-Hertz equations be valid for the reference system K':

(1) curl $\mathbf{H}' = 1/c\ (\partial\mathbf{D}'/\partial t' + \mathbf{J}')$

(2) curl $\mathbf{E}' = -1/c\ (\partial\mathbf{B}'/\partial t')$

(3) div $\mathbf{D}' = \rho'$

(4) div $\mathbf{B}' = 0$.

We observe a second right-angled reference system K, whose axes are constantly parallel to those of K'. The starting point of K' must move with constant velocity in the positive direction of the X axis of K. Then, it is known that the following transformation equations are valid for a suitably chosen

----

* A. Minkowski, *Gottinger Nachr.* 1908

starting point of time according to the theory of relativity for each point occurrence[*]:

$$x' = \beta (x - v t)$$

$$y' = y$$

(5) $$z' = z$$ where $\beta = 1/\sqrt{(1-v^2/c^2)}$

$$t' = \beta (t - v x/c^2)$$

where x, y, z, t stand for the space-time coordinate in system K. If we carry out the transformations, then we will obtain the following equations:

(1a)   curl $\mathbf{H} = 1/c(\partial D/\partial t + \mathbf{J})$

(2a)   curl $\mathbf{E} = -1/c(\partial B/\partial t)$

(3a)   div $\mathbf{D} = \rho$

(4a)   div $\mathbf{B} = 0$

where it is set:

(6) $E_x = E'_x$

$E_y = \beta (E'_y + v/c\ B'_z)$

$E_z = \beta (E'_z - v/c\ B'_y)$

$D_x = D'_x$

$D_y = \beta (D'_y + v/c\ H'_z)$

$D_z = \beta (D'_z - v/c\ H'_y)$

(7) $H_x = H'_x$

$H_y = \beta (H'_y - v/c\ D'_z)$

$H_z = \beta (H'_z + v/c\ D'_y)$

$B_x = B'_x$

----
[*]A. Einstein, *Ann. d. Phys.*, 17, p.902, 1905. (Also in *Princ. of Relativity* by A. Einstein --Ed. note)

$$B_y = \beta \, (B'_y - v/c \; E'_z)$$

$$B_z = \beta \, (B'_z + v/c \; E'_y)$$

and

(8) $\qquad \rho = (\, \rho' + v/c \; J'_x\,)$

(9) $\qquad J_x = \beta \, (J'_x + v/c \; \rho'\,)$

$$J_y = J'_y$$

$$J_z = J'_z$$

If we want to have the terms for the crossed out quantities as function of the non-crossed out terms, then we have to exchange the crossed out and the non-crossed out quantities and replace v with -v.

The equations (1a) through (4a), which describe the electromagnetic processes in relation to system K, have the same form as equations (1) through (4). This is why we will name quantities **E**, **D**, **H**, **B**, ρ, **J** analogous, like the corresponding quantities in relation to system K'. **E**, **D**, **H**, **B**, ρ, **J** are then the electric force, the dielectric shifting, the magnetic force, the magnetic induction, the electric charge density, and the electric current density, respectively, in relation to K.

The transformation equations (6) and (7) are reduced, for the vacuum, to the previously found equations for electric and magnetic forces. It is clear that, through repeated use of such transformations, such as the ones just carried out, one always has to come to equations of the same form as the original (1) through (4), and that equations (6) through (9) are determinative for such transformations. Then, in the transformation carried out in formal relation, it was not made use of the fact that matter was at rest in relation to the original system K'.

We assume the validity of the transformed equations (1a) through (4a) also for the case in which the velocity of matter is spacially and temporally variable, which in a first approach, will be correct.

It is worth noting that the limiting conditions for vectors **E**, **D**, **H**, **B** are the same, just like for bodies at rest. This follows directly from equations (1a) through (4a).

Equations (1a) through (4a) are valid just like equations (1) through (4), in general for inhomogeneous and anisotropic bodies. Those same equations do not determine yet completely the electromagnetic processes. Rather, certain relations must be given which represent vectors **D**, **B**, and **J** as function of **E** and **H**. We want to indicate such equations now for the case in which matter is isotropic. Let us first observe once again the case in which all matter is at rest in relation to K'. In this case, the following equations are valid in relation to K':

(10) $\qquad \mathbf{D'} = \epsilon \, \mathbf{E'}$

(11) $\qquad \mathbf{B'} = \mu \, \mathbf{H'}$

(12) $\qquad \mathbf{J'} = \sigma \, \mathbf{E'}$

where ϵ = dielectric constant (now called permitivity--Ed. note), μ = permeability, σ = electric conductance are to be seen as known functions of x', y', z', t'. Through the transformation of (10) through (12) to K by means of the inversion of our transformation equation (6) through (9), we will obtain the following valid relations for system K:

(10a) $D_x = \epsilon \, E_x$

$D_y - v/c \, H_z = \epsilon \, (E_y - v/c \, B_z)$

$D_z + v/c \, H_y = \epsilon \, (E_z + v/c \, B_y)$

(11a) $B_x = \mu \, H_x$

$B_y + v/c \, E_z = \mu \, (H_y + v/c \, D_z)$

$B_z - v/c \, E_y = \mu \, (H_z - v/c \, D_y)$

(12a) $\beta \, (J_x - v/c \, \rho) = \sigma \, E_x$

$J_y = \sigma\beta \, (E_y - v/c \, B_z)$

$J_z = \sigma\beta \, (E_z + v/c \, B_y)$

If the velocity of matter is not parallel to the X axis, but rather, this velocity is determined by vector v, then we will obtain with equations (10a) through (12a) similar vectorial relations:

(13) $D + 1/c \, (vH) = \epsilon \, \{E + 1/c \, (vB)\}$

$B - 1/c \, (vE) = \mu \, \{H - 1/c \, (vD)\}$

$\beta \, (J_v - |v|\rho/c) = \sigma \, \{E + 1/c \, (vB)\}_v$

$J_y = \sigma\beta \, \{E + 1/c \, (vB)\}_y$

where index v means that the component is in the direction of v, and the index y means that y is in the direction perpendicular to v.

2. On the Electromagnetic Behavior of Moving Dielectric Media. Wilson's Experiment.

In the following section we want to see how, in a single special case, moving dielectric media behave according to the theory of relativity, and where the results differ from those supplied by Lorentz' theory.

Figure:

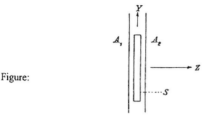

Let S be a prismatic strip, indicated in cross-section (see Figure), of an homogeneous, isotropic non-conductor, which extends itself, perpendicular to the paper level, in both directions to infinity, and which moves from the observer through the paper level with constant velocity v between the condenser plates A_1 and A_2. Let the expansion of strip S, perpendicular to plates A, be infinitely small in relation to that expansion parallel to the plates and to both expansions of plates A. In addition, let the space between S and plates A (called the "interspace" for short) be negligible, in relation to the thickness of S. We refer to observed system of bodies to a system of coordinates, at rest in relation to plates A, whose positive direction X falls in the direction of motion, and whose axes Y and Z are parallel and perpendicular to plates A respectively. We want to observe the electromagnetic behavior of that piece of strip which is found between plates A, in the case in which the electromagnetic state is stationary.

Let us imagine an enclosed area, which includes, precisely, the effective part of the condenser plates together with that of the piece of strip lying in-between. Because within this area, neither moving true charges nor electric conduction currents are to be found, the following equations are valid (compare (1a) through (4a)):   curl $H = 0$ and   curl $E = 0$.

Within this area, both the electric and the magnetic force are derivable from a potential. So, we can know immediately the division of vectors E and H, in case the division of the free electric or magnetic density is known. We limit ourselves to the observation of the case in which the magnetic force H is parallel to the Y axis, and the electric E is parallel to the Z axis. At the same time, on condition that the fields to be taken into consideration within the strip and also within the interspace be homogeneous, the above-mentioned conditions for quantity ordering for the measurements of the observed system justify us. In the same way, we conclude that the magnetic masses which are found at the end of the strip's cross-section supply only a vanishingly small contribution to the magnetic field.* The equations (13) give then, for the interior of the strip, the following relations:

$$D_z + v/c \, H_y = \epsilon \, (E_z + v/c \, B_y)$$

$$B_y + v/c \, E_z = \mu \, (H_y + v/c \, D_z)$$

----

*This is also elucidated by the fact that, without substantial modification of the proportions, we could give to the condensor plates and the strip circular form (like Wilson, *Pro. Royal Soc. London A*, 89, 99, 1913- Ed. note), in which case free magnetic masses would not be able to occur at all due to symmetry considerations.

These equations can also be written in the following form:

(1) $\quad (1 - \epsilon\mu v^2/c^2) B_y = v/c\, (\epsilon\mu - 1)\, E_z + \mu(1 - v^2/c^2)\, H_y$

$\quad (1 - \epsilon\mu v^2/c^2)\, D_z = \epsilon\, (1 - v^2/c^2)\, E_z + v/c\, (\epsilon\mu - 1)\, H_y$

To interpret (1) let us observe the following: On the surface of the strip, the dielectric shifting D_z experiences no jump, so D_z is the charge of the condenser plates (more exactly of plate A_1) per unit of area. Further, $E_z \times \delta$ is equal to the potential difference between the condenser plates A_1 and A_2, where δ indicates the distance between the plates, then we imagine the strip separated through an infinitely narrow space running parallel to plane XZ, then E is, according to the boundary conditions valid for this vector, equal to the electric force in the space.

Next we observe the case in which one magnetic field induced from the outside is not available, i.e. according to the above-mentioned, that in the observed area, the magnetic field intensity H_y completely disappears. Then equations (1) have the following form:

$\quad (1 - \epsilon\mu v^2/c^2)\, B_y = v/c\, (\epsilon\mu - 1)\, E_z$

$\quad (1 - \epsilon\mu v^2/c^2)\, D_z = \epsilon\, (1 - v^2/c^2)\, E_z$

Because $v < c$, then the coefficients of E_z are positive in both of last equations, where $(\epsilon\mu - 1) > 0$. The coefficients of B_y and D_z are, on the contrary, greater, equal or smaller than zero, depending if the strip velocity is smaller, equal or greater than $c/\sqrt{\epsilon\mu}$, i.e., than the velocity of electromagnetic waves in the strip medium. If E_z has a certain value, i.e., if we put a certain tension (now called voltage--Ed. note) on the condenser plates and if we vary the velocity of the strip from smaller to greater values, then both the charge of the condenser plates proportional to vector D and the magnetic induction B in the strip grow. When v reaches the value $c/\sqrt{\epsilon\mu}$, then both the charge of the condenser and the magnetic induction become infinitely great. In this case, a destruction of the strip through any small applied potential difference would take place. For all $v > c/\sqrt{\epsilon\mu}$ results a negative value for D and B. In this last case, a tension put on the condenser plates would cause a charge of the condenser in the sense opposite to the difference of potential.

We now observe the case, in which there is a magnetic field H_y induced from the outside. Then we will obtain the following equation:

$\quad (1 - \epsilon\mu v^2/c^2)\, D_z = \epsilon\, (1 - v^2/c^2)\, E_z + v/c\, (\epsilon\mu - 1)\, H_y$

which, given H_y, gives a relation between E_z and D_z. If we limit ourselves only to magnitudes of the first order in v/c, then we have:

(2) $\quad D_z = \epsilon E_z + v/c\, (\epsilon\mu - 1)\, H_y$

while Lorentz' theory leads to the following expression:

(3) $D_z = \epsilon E_z + v/c \, (\epsilon - 1) \, \mu \, H_y$

The last equation* was experimentally investigated by H. A. Wilson (the "Wilson effect"). We see that (2) and (3) are differentiated in terms of the first order. If we had a dielectric body of considerable permeability, we would be able to find an experimental distinction between equations (2) and (3).

If we connect plates A_1 and A_2 through a conductor, then a charge of magnitude D_z per unit area appears on the condenser plates; we obtain it from equation (2), if we take into consideration that, in connected condenser plates, $E_z = 0$. This results in the equation:

$$D_z = v/c \, (\epsilon\mu - 1) \, H_y$$

If we connect condenser plates A_1 and A_2 with an electrometer of infinitely small capacity, then $D_z = 0$, and we obtain for the tension ($E_z \times \delta$) the following equation:

$$0 = \epsilon E_z + v/c \, (\epsilon\mu - 1) \, H_y$$

Bern, 29. April 1908.

----

*Equation (3) can be called "Einstein's equation" for insulators which also may have magnetic properties, e.g. a magnetic dielectric --Ed. Note

ON THE PONDEROMOTIVE FORCES EXERTED ON BODIES AT REST IN THE
ELECTROMAGNETIC FIELD

by A. Einstein and J. Laub
Annalen der Physik, V. 26, 1908, p. 541)
(translated from the German by Integrity Research Institute)

In a recently published treatise Mr. Minkowski[1] indicated an expression for the ponderomotive forces (term still used for particle separators with E or B fields - Ed. note) of electromagnetic origin at work on any moving body. If we specify Minkowski's expressions for homogeneous and isotropic bodies at rest, then we will obtain for the X component of the force at work on the unit of volume:

(1) $\qquad K_x = \rho E_x + J_y B_z - J_z B_y$

where ρ represents the electric charge density, J the electric conduction current, E the electric field strength, and B the magnetic induction. This expression seems to us not to be in accord with the theoretical electronic picture due to the following reasons: while namely an electric current (conduction current) flows through a body in the magnetic field, which suffers a force, this would not be the case according to equation (1), when the body located in the magnetic field is penetrated by a polarizing current ($\partial D/\partial t$) instead of a conduction current[2]. According to Minkowski there is here, then a difference in principle between a displacement current and a conduction current in such a way that a conductor cannot be looked at as a dielectric with an infinitely great dielectric constant.

In view of this situation, it seemed interesting to us to derive the ponderomotive forces for any magnetizable body in a theoretical, electronic manner. Next, we give such a derivation, but in which we restrict ourselves to bodies at rest.

1. Forces which are not dependent on the velocities of elementary particles

In the derivation, we place ourselves consistent with the standpoint of electronic theory[3]:

(2) $\qquad\qquad D = E + P$
(3) $\qquad\qquad B = H + M$

where P represents the electric polarization vector, M the magnetic polarization vector ("magnetization" in today's language - Ed. note). We imagine the electric or the magnetic polarization existing in spatial displacements of mass particles of electric or magnetic dipoles, bound
----
1) H. Minkowski, *Gott. Nachr.* 1908 p. 45
2) The time-varying flux of ϵE or D is presently called "displacement current" as Einstein indicates in the next sentence, which can be thought of as a "finite magnetomotive force" in the same way that there is a finite electromotive force associated with a time-varying flux of μH or B. (See *Electromagnetic Fields, Energy, and Waves* by Leonard Magid, 1972, p.26) - Ed. note
3) For the sake of a simpler presentation, we hold to a dual treatment of the electric and magnetic phenomena.

in positions of equilibrium. Besides, we assume the presence of moving electric particles (conduction electrons) not bound in dipoles. In the space between the mentioned particles, let Maxwell's equations be valid for the empty space, and consistent with Lorentz, let the interactions between matter and electromagnetic field be conditioned exclusively by these particles. We assume accordingly that the forces exerted by the electromagnetic field on the element of volume of matter are equal to the resultants of the ponderomotive forces, which are exerted by this field on all electric and magnetic elementary particles located in the element of volume in question. Under an element of volume of matter we always assume a space large enough to contain a great amount of electric and magnetic particles. Further, one must think always of the boundaries of a considered element of volume as taken in such a way, that the boundary surface does not intersect any electric or magnetic dipoles.

We calculate first the force at work on an electric dipole, which results from the fact that the field strength E is not the same in the places in which the elementary masses of the dipole are found. If we represent by p the vector of the dipole moment, then we obtain for the X component of the force, the following expression:

$$f_x = p_x \, \partial E_x / \partial x + p_y \, \partial E_x / \partial y + p_z \, \partial E_x / \partial z$$

If we imagine this expression formulated for and summed over all microscopic dipoles in the unit of volume, then we obtain in view of the relation,

$$\sum p = P$$

the equation:

(4) $$F_{1x} = P_x \, \partial E_x / \partial x + P_y \, \partial E_x / \partial y + P_z \, \partial E_x / \partial z$$

If the algebraic sum of the positive and negative conduction electrons does not disappear, then another term arrives for the expression (4) which we want to calculate now. The X component of the ponderomotive force at work on a conduction electron of electric mass e is eE_x. If we sum over all conduction electrons of unit volume, then we obtain:

(5) $$F_{2x} = E_x \sum e$$

If we imagine the observed existing matter in a unit of volume, surrounded by a surface which does not dissect any dipoles, then we obtain, according to Gauss' theorem and the definition of the vector of displacement D:

$$\sum e = \operatorname{div} D$$

so that,

(5a) $$F_{2x} = E_x \operatorname{div} D$$

The X component of the force at work on the unit volume of matter of the electric field strength is then equal to:

$$(6) \qquad F_{ex} = F_{1x} + F_{2x} = P_x\, \partial E_x/\partial x + P_y\, \partial E_x/\partial y + P_z\, \partial E_x/\partial z + E_x\, \text{div}\, \mathbf{D}$$

In an analogous way, we obtain, in view of the relation div $\mathbf{B} = 0$, the X component of the delivered force of the magnetic field strength:

$$(7) \qquad F_{mx} = M_x\, \partial H_x/\partial x + M_y\, \partial H_x/\partial y + M_z\, \partial H_x/\partial z$$

It is to be noticed that, for the derivation of the expressions (6) and (7), no assumption should be made about the relations which connect field strengths E and H with polarization vectors P and M.

If we have to deal with anisotropic bodies, then the electric or the magnetic field strengths produce not only one force, but also couples of forces, which transfer themselves to matter. The angular momentum L is easily produced by the individual dipoles and summation over all electric and magnetic dipoles in the unit of volume. We obtain (with a "×", presuming an intended cross product, added to each [ ] from now on. Compare L with total energy density, $u = \mathbf{E}\cdot\mathbf{D} + \mathbf{B}\cdot\mathbf{H}$ - Ed. note):

$$(8) \qquad \mathbf{L} = [\mathbf{P}\times\mathbf{E}] + [\mathbf{M}\times\mathbf{H}]$$

Formula (6) produces the ponderomotive forces, which play a role in electrostatic problems. We want to transform this equation for the case in which we have to deal with isotropic bodies, so that it allows a comparison with that expression for the ponderomotive forces, as indicated in electrostatics. Let us set $\mathbf{P} = (\epsilon-1)\,\mathbf{E}$, then equation (6) becomes:

$$F_{ex} = E_x\, \text{div}\, \mathbf{D} - \tfrac{1}{2} E^2\, \partial\epsilon/\partial x + \tfrac{1}{2}\partial/\partial x\, (\epsilon-1)E^2$$

The two first terms of this expression are identical with the ones known from electrostatics. The third term is, as we see, derivable from a potential. If we are dealing with forces which work on a body in a vacuum, then the term yields no contribution over the body, by integration (since $\epsilon = \epsilon_0$ in a vacuum - Ed. note). If we are dealing however, with the ponderomotive effect on liquids, then the portion of the force corresponding to the third term is compensated, in equilibrium by a pressure distribution in the liquid.

2. Forces which are dependent on the velocities of elementary particles

We go now to that portion of the ponderomotive force, which is derived from the velocities of motion of the elementary charges.

We start from Biot-Savart's law. On an element of volume traversed by current, which is in a magnetic field, the force $1/c\,[\mathbf{J}\times\mathbf{H}]$ is at work, according to experience, per unit of volume, in case the observed matter, traversed by current, is not magnetically polarizable. As far as we know, for the interior of magnetically polarizable bodies, that force was set equal*, up until now, to $1/c\,[\mathbf{J}\times\mathbf{B}]$

----

* Compare for example, also M. Abraham, *Theory of Electricity 2*, 1905, p. 319

where **B** represents the magnetic induction. We want to show now that also in the case in which the material traversed by current *is magnetically polarizable*, the force at work on the element of volume, traversed by current, is obtained when we add to the force expressed through equation (7), the force of volume (compare with **J·E**, <u>work</u> done per unit time per unit volume by E/M fields - Ed. note):

(9) $F_B = 1/c \, [\mathbf{J} \times \mathbf{H}]$

We want to make this clear by a simple example:

Figure: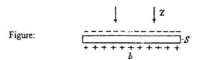

Let the infinitely thin strip S, drawn in cross-section, extend to infinity, on both sides, perpendicularly to the paper plane. Let it be formed of <u>magnetically polarizable</u> material and let it be found in an homogeneous magetic field H_a, whose direction is indicated by the arrows (see Figure). We want to find out about the force at work on the material strip, in case the same is traversed by a current i.

Experience teaches that this force is independent of the magnetic permeability μ of the conductive material, and we infer from there that it must not be field strength H but rather magnetic induction B_i which is decisive for the ponderomotive force, because in the interior of the strip magnetic induction B_i is equal to force H_a working on the exterior of the strip, independently from the value of the permeability of the strip, while force H_i dominant in the interior of the strip depends on μ in a given external field. This conclusion is not, however, sound because the contemplated ponderomotive force is not the only one which works on our material strip. The external field H_a induces, namely on the upper and underside of the material strip, magnetic coatings of density:

$$M_i = B_i - H_i = H_a (1 - 1/\mu)$$

and in fact, a negative covering on the upper side and a positive covering on the underside. On each of the coatings works a force generated by the traversing current in the strip, of strength i/2b per unit of length of the strip*, which magnetic force is differently directed on the upper and underside. The resulting ponderomotive forces are added, so that we obtain the ponderomotive force $(1-1/\mu)iH_a$. This force does not seem to have been taken into account until now.

The force exerted on the unit of length of our strip on the whole is now equal to the sum of the just calculated force R, exerted on the elements of volume of the strip as a result of the passage of current in the magnetic field. As experience shows, because the whole ponderomotive force exerted on the unit of length is equal to iH_a , then the following equation holds:

----

* Instead of these forces exerted on the coatings, we would have to introduce, strictly speaking, forces of unit volume according to the results of the previous paragraph. This is however, of no importance.

or
$$(1 - 1/\mu)\, iH_a + R = iH_a$$

$$R = iH_a/\mu = iH_i$$

We see then that for the calculation of ponderomotive force R, which is exerted on elements of volume traversed by current, field strength H_i is decisive, not induction B_i.

To put aside every doubt, we still want to try an example, from which we can conclude that the principle of equality of action and reaction demands the formulation chosen by us.

Let us imagine a cylindrical conductor, surrounded by vacuum and traversed by current J, which stretches along the X axis of a coordinate system, on both sides, to infinity. The material constants of the conductor and the field vectors, appearing subsequently, are to be independent of x, but should be functions of y and z. Let the conductor be a magnetically hard body and let it possess a magnetization perpendicular to the X axis. We assume that an external field has no effect on the conductor and so that a magnetic force H disappears at great distances from the conductor.

It is clear that no ponderomotive force is exerted on the conductor as a whole, because to this action, there would be no reaction which could be estimated. We want to show now that, by chosing our formulation, that force indeed disappears. The whole force acting on a unit length of our conductor in the direction of the Z axis lets itself be represented according to equations (7) and (9), in the form:

(10) $$R = \int (M_y\, \partial H_z/\partial y + M_z\, \partial H_z/\partial z)\, ds + 1/c \int J_x H_y\, ds$$

where ds represents an element of area in the plane YZ. We assume that all quantities to be considered on the surface of the conductor are constant. Initially we will handle the first integral of equation (10). It is:

$$M_y\, \partial H_z/\partial y + M_z\, \partial H_z/\partial z = \partial M_y H_z/\partial y + \partial M_z H_z/\partial z - H_z\,(\partial M_y/\partial y + \partial M_z/\partial z)$$

If we substitute the right side of this equation into our integral, the the first two terms disappear in the integration over plane YZ, because the forces disappear at infinity. The third term can be transformed in view of div $B = 0$ so that our integral assumes the form:

$$\int H_z\,(\partial H_y/\partial y + \partial H_z/\partial z)\, ds$$

which now becomes:

$$H_z\,(\partial H_y/\partial y + \partial H_z/\partial z) = \partial H_y H_z/\partial y + \tfrac{1}{2}\, \partial H_z{}^2/\partial z - H_y\, \partial H_z/\partial y$$

But in the integration, the first two terms $\partial H_y H_z/\partial y + \tfrac{1}{2}\partial H_z{}^2/\partial z$ disappear. The last term, $H_y\, \partial H_z/\partial y$ is transformed by means of Maxwell's equations into:

$$-1/c\, H_y\,(J_x + \partial H_y/\partial z)$$

so that finally we can write equation (10) as:

$$R = -1/c \int H_y \ (J_x + \partial H_y/\partial z) \ ds \ + \ 1/c \int J_x \ H_y \ ds$$

$$= -1/c \int H_y \ \partial H_y/\partial z \ ds \ = \ -1/(2c) \int \partial H_y{}^2/\partial z \ ds$$

The last integral is zero, because the forces disappear at infinity.

After we have so determined the force which is at work on matter traversed by a conduction current, then we obtain the force which works on a body penetrated by a polarization current, if we take into consideration that the polarization current and conduction current must be completely equivalent in relation to the electrodynamic action from the standpoint of the electronic theory.

If we take into consideration the <u>duality of magnetic and electric phenomena</u>, then we also obtain the force which is exerted on a body in an electric field penetrated by a magnetic polarizing current. As a general expression for those forces which are dependent from the velocity of the elementary particles, we will obtain the following equations (substituting A' for $\partial A/\partial t$ - Ed. note):

(11) $\qquad F_a = 1/c \ [J \times H] + 1/c \ [P' \times H] + 1/c \ [E \times M']$

3. Equality of action and reaction.

If we add equations (6), (7) and (11) then we obtain the total expression for the X component of the ponderomotive force acting per unit volume of matter in the following form:

$$\begin{aligned}
F_x \ &= \ E_x \ \text{div} \ D + P_x \ \partial E_x/\partial x + P_y \ \partial E_x/\partial y + P_z \ \partial E_x/\partial z \\
&+ M_x \ \partial H_x/\partial x + M_y \ \partial H_x/\partial y + M_z \ \partial H_x/\partial z \\
&+ 1/c \ [J \times H]_x + 1/c \ [P' \times H]_x + 1/c \ [E \times M']_x
\end{aligned}$$

We can also write the equation like this:

$$\begin{aligned}
F_x \ &= \ E_x \ \text{div} \ E \ + \ 1/c \ [J \times H]_x \ + 1/c \ [D' \times H]_x + H_x \ \text{div} \ H \ + 1/c \ [E \times B']_x \\
&+ \ \partial P_x E_x/\partial x \ + \ \partial P_y E_x/\partial y \ + \ \partial P_z E_x/\partial z \\
&\quad \partial M_x H_x/\partial x \ + \ \partial M_y H_x/\partial y \ + \ \partial M_z H_x/\partial z \ - \ 1/c \ \partial/\partial t[\ E \times H\ ]_x
\end{aligned}$$

If we substitute $1/c \ (\sigma + D')$ and $1/c \ (B')$ by means of Maxwell's equations with curl H or with curl E, then we will use a simple transformation:

(12) $\qquad F_x \ = \ \partial X_x/\partial x + \partial X_y/\partial y + \partial X_z/\partial z \ - 1/c^2 \ \partial S_x/\partial t$

to obtain, where it is set*:

$$\begin{aligned}
&X_x \ = -\ \tfrac{1}{2} (E^2 + H^2) + \ E_x D_x \ + H_x B_x \\
(13) \quad &X_y \ = \qquad\quad E_x D_y \ + H_x B_y \\
&X_z \ = \qquad\quad E_x D_z \ + H_x B_z \\
&S_x \ = \qquad\quad c \ [\ E \times H\ ]_x
\end{aligned}$$

*Note: Privy councillor Wien was so kind as to call our attention to the fact that H.A. Lorentz had already indicated the ponderomotive forces for non-magnetizable bodies in the following form. *Enc. of Math.* V.5, p. 247.

Corresponding equations are valid for both of the other components of the ponderomotive force. If we integrate (12) over infinite space then we will obtain (in case the field vectors disappear at infinity) the following equation:

(14) $\qquad \int F_x \, d\tau = -1/c^2 \int d\tau \, dS_x/dt$

It affirms that our ponderomotive forces, by the introduction of an electromagnetic quantity of motion, satisfy the principle of the equality of action and reaction.

May 7, 1908

Editor's Afterword

To show the relevance of these two articles to the homopolar generator, we quote John T. Tate (*Bull. Nat. Res. Council*, V. 4, Part 6, 1922, p.75-95) who writes:

"It is interesting to inquire in how far (the) view of the motion of the lines of induction is verified by experiment. As pointed out above, the experiments of Kennard, Barnett, and Pegram indicated that the lines of induction did not partake of the rotation of the magnet as a whole. Is there any experiment in which, to account for the results, one must take account of the motion of translation of the elementary magnets composing the magnet? Clearly such an experiment would have to be one in which the rotating magnet is a non-conductor for, as pointed out above, if the magnet is a conductor the field due to the fictitious polarization produced by the individual translatory motions of the elementary magnets is completely cancelled out both at points inside and at points outside the magnet. In the case of the conducting magnet, therefore, the hypothesis of the stationary lines of induction will yield correct results. But this would no longer be the case if the magnet were a non-conductor.

"The importance of doing an experiment of this kind on a non-conducting magnet was first pointed out by Einstein and Laub (*Ann. d. Phys.*, 26, 532, 1908). These authors showed from relativity considerations that if in the Wilson experiment, in which a cylindrical dielectric is rotated in a magnetic field parallel to its axis, the dielectric were at the same time magnetic the effect observed (for instance, thhe potential difference between the inner and outer coating of the dielectric) should involve the factor $(\epsilon\mu-1)/\epsilon$ instead of of the factor $\mu(\epsilon-1)/\epsilon$ which they ascribed to the theory of Lorentz...An experiment of the kind here discussed has been performed by M. Wilson and H.A. Wilson (*Proc. Roy. Soc. London A*, 89, 99, 1913) using an artificially prepared magnetic dielectric composed of steel balls imbedded in paraffin. Their results were decisively in favor of the relation given by Einstein and Laub and are in complete agreement with the present theory..."

Tate concludes with these words: "A theory which postulates that the lines of induction stand still while the magnetic system rotates through them will yield correct results if the magnetic system is a conductor but incorrect results, in general, if it is a dielectric." (emphasis added - Ed.).

Einstein and Laub's first article (on p. 122) reminds us of Roentgen's work (see p. 4) and H. A. Wilson's experiment (Fig. 3) as well as Eichenwald's experiment. Roentgen's experiment (rotating a flat dielectric between flat metal disks) is equivalent to Einstein's figure (p. 126) in as much as the rotating homopolar generator is equivalent to the linear case of a conductor moving in a magnetic field. Roentgen's experiment is often cited as a followup to the historical "Rowland effect." Rowland (1876) simply rotated an electrically charged metal wheel and measured a resulting magnetic field. However, as Sommerfeld [20] pointed out, the question naturally arises whether also the so-called "free charge," which occurs at the surface of a homogeneous dielectric in an electric field, is magnetically active when a dielectric is set into motion. Roentgen's experiment proved just that affirmatively. In his text, Sommerfeld proves that the *Roentgen current* is simply equal to vP where v is the velocity of the dielectric and P is the polarization. He calls it a "pure surface current" with the same direction as the Rowland current.

Then in 1904, Wilson's experiment of Fig. 3 with a cylindrical dielectric advanced the science of rotating static charge into the homopolar arena, in effect rotating the "magnet" and the "disk" (dielectric in an axial magnetic field) with the "brushes" (cylindrical capacitor) extracting the electricity. Furthering this work, Eichenwald's experiment (A. Eichenwald, *Ann. Physik*, Vol. 11, pgs. 1 and 241, 1903) showed that rotating the cylindrical capacitor and the cylindrical dielectric together as a unit also gives rise to a residual magnetic field which he said is independent of the material of the dielectric. Wilson's 1913 experiment testing Einstein, with magnets imbedded in a rotating dielectric, then carried the rotating dielectric into the murky realm of the moving lines of magnetic induction. As Tate indicates, this was a decisive experiment to show that such an arrangement has to involve the motion of the magnetic field with the rotation of the magnets.

Einstein and Laub's second article (p. 129), from the same issue, is referred to in *Nature* (V. 285, 5/15/80, p. 154) in a seminal article entitled, "Observation of Static Electromagnetic Angular Momentum *in vacuo* by Graham and Lahoz. The authors are the first to prove that "the vacuum is the seat of something in motion whenever static fields are set up with (a) non-vanishing Poynting vector, as Maxwell and Poynting foresaw." (The Poynting vector is simply $S = E \times H$ where the electric and magnetic fields must be in different directions to be non-vanshing. S is equal to the power per unit area and S/c^2 is the momentum density, per unit volume, of the field.) Their experiment is similar to Feynman's disk paradox (see p. 6) but involves a cylindrical capacitor is suspended by a torsion oscillator in a vacuum surrounded by a superconducting magnetic field uniform to 2%. The torque caused by the field alone is verified. The authors note that Einstein and Laub call for the time derivative of the Poynting vector to be integrated over all space to preserve Newton's third law. Furthermore, they say that Einstein's eq. 14 (p. 135) "also represents a real reaction force even with induction fields" and that S is "azimuthal inside the vacuum gap of the capacitor." Their conclusion is simply amazing: "permanent magnets and electrets can be used to build a flywheel of electromagnetic energy steadily flowing in circles in the vacuum gap of a capacitor as if Maxwell's medium were endowed with a property corresponding to superfluidity." This conclusion may also be regarded as a suggestion to combine both into a magnetic dielectric, as the Paulsen report seems to suggest (see Preface). The figure to the right illustrates how such a disk with for example, oppositely polarized magnets as on p. 67, will then create an time-varying magnetic flux and a toroidal electric field. With Dr. Corson's insight (p. 51), perhaps a homopolar design can aid a dielectric flywheel to accumulate charge. If the distinction also involves circulating currents (without a radial component) then the current accumulator of Sir William Thomson (see p. 172 of this book) cited by Tesla, may be finally pinpointed. As to rotating charges or currents, the intrguing article "Conducting Spiral as an 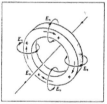 Acyclic or Unipolar Machine" (*Am. J. Phys.*, V. 38, No. 11, 1970, p. 1273) brings into focus the circumferential currents in a disk, as does the Sears patent (p. 2 and 168 of this book) which also is exploited by Tesla (p. 77 of this book). It is also worthwhile to mention "The Radial Magnetic Field Homopolar Motor" (*AJP*, V. 56, No. 9, 1988, p. 858-9). Here Eagleton and Kaplan suggest unbalanced forces at work.

Finally, there is an indication that such experiments have relevance to the Searl effect which involves the use of non-conductive rings, since an even number of alternatively oriented homopolar permanent magnets are attached to the non-conductive rings. The original Searl design of the 1950's was substantially simpler than recently reported and allowed each non-conductive ring to slide on freely turning ball-race bearings. Extraordinary voltages were developed in this manner, which impacted the physical vacuum, affecting gravity.

442   from SUNBURST, Return of the Ancients by Norman Paulsen
copyright 1980 (reproduced with permission of the author)

would be followed by blue, and violet. At this point we would vanish from this dimension in a bright flash of light as brilliant as any sun."

"Yes, I understand this. You have demonstrated this phenomena to me in the past."

During the course of this conversation we had been descending in an elevator, finally arriving at the level which contained the ship's propulsion drive units. This level was gigantic and spanned the entire diameter of the ship's hull. Standing on a walkway, we looked down on the drive systems which filled the whole immense area.

"My Son, the propulsion system which drives our mother Mu is patterned after the perfect design of The Great Central SüN-SöN. The application of vortexes by Divine Spirit on its infinite body of life force, as you know, generated the first ignition of Light. The visible expanding sphere of creation and all forces and images existing in it were projected outward from the center of The Great Central SüN-SöN. A spinning, centripetal vortex projected into Spirit's infinite body of life-energy, produced a whirlpool. This thought-produced whirlpool began drawing Spirit's life-energy particles towards its center. Spirit's life-energy particles moving towards this center created directional lines of force for the pulling effects of magnetic attraction to operate on. This created a perpetual flow of life-energy particles into the vortex from the Eternal Sea of Life Energy. The accumulation of masses of life energy particles at this center of vortex, under tremendous pressure and friction, produced light and images. The masses of life energy particles were now shaped by Divine Consciousness into the images and forces Spirit wanted to see.

"The propulsion unit on this ship operates upon the same divine principles. To create a vortex which would operate in this physical dimension in a similar manner, we must spin a physical object which is, or can be, magnetized. Spinning a magnetized object, we would create a vortex which would induce the energy in space to move towards its center. As the energy particles in space are drawn into the vortex by magnetic attraction, they would take orbital positions around the center of the magnetic core. The accumulation of energy particles around the spinning magnetic center would generate a high density magnetic field. With this condition we can create two poles, one at the center of the magnetic core, and one on the perimeter of the magnetic field. Here we can perpetually draw off energy in the form of positive and negative electrical currents. This is the principle on which our propulsion units operate.

"Any type of physical material which has been magnetized will generate electrical current if the object is rotated. The rotation of permanent magnets will, therefore, generate electrical current. The higher the velocity of rotation, the greater the flow of energy. Our propulsion unit consists of two gigantic rotating discs. Facing each other, one disc will spin clockwise while the other spins counterclockwise. By rotating our two discs we have created two spinning vortexes.

The outside perimeter of each disc carries twelve magnets. The simultaneous clockwise and counterclockwise rotation of these two discs creates two spinning magnetic fields. Here we can draw off electrical current from the central hubs on which they spin and the rapidly rotating outside perimeter. The generation of a perpetual flow of electrical energy from each disc will continue as long as the discs rotate. The space between the two discs is the area in which both spinning vortexes contact each other. It is here that the two spinning magnetic fields create a gyroscopic effect on each other. The magnetic fields generated by the two discs are so intense that any other gravitational or magnetic lines of force are bent around this force field. Therefore, the object which contains the generators of this magnetic and gyroscopic effect creates its own gravity. The object, or in this case, the spaceship, generates its own force field which becomes so intense that the ship's hull exists in an anti-gravity space all its own.

"You have now seen much of our mother Mu, my Son, and your memory, I am sure, is refreshed. The basic design I have given you of this ship's power and drive systems, gives you the keys to many doors. Sometime in the future you could construct one half of the ship's drive systems and have an unlimited supply of electrical energy. This system would require no out-

444   *Sunburst*

side sources of energy to run it, such as fossil fuels or atomic power. That generator would be self-perpetuating as it would produce more energy than it would take to run it. You would. therefore, have an unlimited supply of totally free energy. The Earth as it exists today is not ready for this Divine Truth! The Evil Ones would use it in an unlimited variety of weapons!"

My elder brother then went on to describe the entire design of the ship to me in detail. As I listened, I realized that this was knowledge that I had already recorded deep within. After the tour of the entire ship we returned to the guidance and communications center. Standing in front of the viewscreen I looked at the massive image of Jupiter which was filling up the heavens in front of us.

Two figures emerged and descended the stairs

19

E: JULY 11, 1979

3JECT: SPACE-ENERGY GENERATOR; COSMOGONIC, WITH TWELVE (OR ANY NUMBER) PERMANENT
3GNETS ROTATING ABOUT A CENTRAL AXIS, THE MAGNETS CONSISTING OF HORSESHOE SHAPES OR
IE HALF SECTIONS OF CIRCULAR MAGNET, ORIENTED MAGNETICALLY TO HAVE NORTH-SOUTH POLES AT
EIR ENDS. THIS DESIGN FIRST SET DOWN JULY 8, 1979.   Chrys. Bernard July 11, 1979

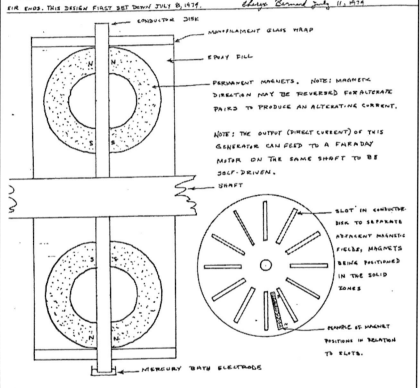

CONDUCTOR DISK

MONOFILAMENT GLASS WRAP

EPOXY FILL

PERMANENT MAGNETS. NOTE: MAGNETIC
DIRECTION MAY BE REVERSED FOR ALTERNATE
PAIRS TO PRODUCE AN ALTERATING CURRENT.

NOTE: THE OUTPUT (DIRECT CURRENT) OF THIS
GENERATOR CAN FEED TO A FARADAY
MOTOR ON THE SAME SHAFT TO BE
SELF-DRIVEN.

SHAFT

SLOT IN CONDUCTOR-
DISK TO SEPARATE
ADJACENT MAGNETIC
FIELDS; MAGNETS
BEING POSITIONED
IN THE SOLID
ZONES

EXAMPLE OF MAGNET
POSITIONS IN RELATION
TO SLOTS.

MERCURY BATH ELECTRODE

Chrys. Bernard. July 11, 1979 14,000 Calle Real. Route 1, Goleta, California 93017

ESS: Mary A. Paulsen   DATE: July 12, 1979
DRESS: 14,000 Calle Real Rt. 1
       Goleta, CA. 93017

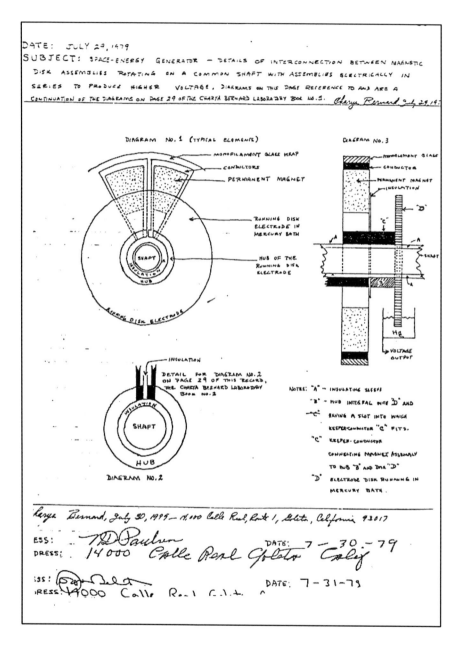

APPENDIX VI

DePalma Material

B-2   Santa Barbara, Calif. News-Press, Sunday, Aug. 31, 1976

Machine gathers energy from space, physicist claims

By Michael Gershberg

Physicist Bruce De Palma claims to have invented an energy machine whose output ranges from 10 to 100 times more than its input.

He says it doesn't defy the law of conservation of energy, which says that energy can neither be created nor destroyed. Instead, he says, the N-machine gathers energy fluid from space.

(When asked about De Palma's claims, several physicists on the UCSB faculty either rejected them or said that too little was known of De Palma's theories to comment. None wanted their names used in responding to the claims for the energy machine.)

The Montecito resident demonstrated his machine for the News-Press.

"What we do in our demonstrations is put a cylindrical collection of eight 2 7/8-inch diameter ceramic magnets which we got from some old five-inch loudspeakers together with a 3/8-inch bolt in the center, into a drill press and spin it at 1,500 revolutions per minute. We put two electrical contacts onto it, one at the 'center still point' and the other at the edge of the metal disk which is glued into the middle array of magnets, and we extract the electricity," he said.

That's the demonstration model. The actual N-machine is made of a copper or bronze conducting shaft and disc and four ferrite ring magnets. Two magnets are epoxy-cemented on either side of the conducting disc so that the shaft passes through two magnets, a conducting disc and two more magnets in that order.

There is energy in space that flows through everything and gives objects mass and inertia, De Palma said. With this concept, he interpreted the rotation of objects in a new way.

"Here is a piece of metal that flows in the energy fluid. When I spin it I can create a condition of polarization in it, meaning that the outside of this object is moving but the center is not moving. It is what I call the still point. The condition of polarization that occurs is called 'male' on the outside and 'female' in the center. In elec-

trical terms, the center becomes positive and the outside becomes negative. When the energy fluid of space flows through this piece of metal it becomes male, or negatively charged in contact with the outer moving edge and becomes female or positively charged in the center.

"So the basic discovery is simply that a rotating disc in a magnetic field produces electricity which can be simply taken from a contact at the center and one at the outside moving edge," De Palma said.

If large amounts of energy from space can be gathered with this machine, he said, then the electric output from the machine can be used to drive a small electric motor on the same shaft. This combination could keep going and would produce much more energy than is needed to run the motor, he believes.

Such a combination was built in conjunction with Sunburst Farms in Tajiguas.

"It's based on the fact that you might be able to liberate say 15 or 20 horsepower from a machine weighing about 200 pounds," he said. "It takes only about one horsepower to turn the rotor shaft against the friction of wind, bearings and brushes, so you end up with 19 horsepower left over to run your house, car, community or hospital."

But the machine at Sunburst is capable of putting out 40 times as much electricity as is put in, De Palma said.

The N-machine can be made self-sustaining, De Palma said. "Once started, it will keep going until the magnets lose their strength or the bearings wear out. And it makes no noise . . . People can make these N-machines in their basement or garage once they get the idea of how it works and how simple they really are to put together."

The machine has potential for large-scale applications, he said, such as supplying power for a city. A single home unit would be about the size of a one-ton air conditioner, he added.

De Palma graduated from Massachusetts Institute of Technology and then returned to Cambridge, Mass., in 1961 for

BRUCE De PALMA shows a section of his energy machine, explaining it in terms of a gyroscope.

News-Press photo by Lon Wood

graduate work on applied physics at Harvard University.

After experimenting with the rotation of gyroscopes, ball bearings and pendulums, De Palma said he discovered that, "simply stated, you can drop a rotating object and find that it falls faster and consequently hits harder . . . than a non-rotating object . . . And you can collide a rotating object and find it collides harder. These collisions and droppings are taking energy out of space in some way that at that time we didn't understand."

This information was the basis for his work with the N-machine.

De Palma tried to send his experimental results to the Physical Review, a leading scientific journal. He received a letter saying his work was not understandable and further submissions would be useless.

He said he regrets that experiments that were done in the 1800s and early 1900s were put into the form of equations and formulas which are not taken to be gospel.

De Palma's work is principally funded by the Tanners, a Mormon family. "I am not into public relations or money-raising or any of those things," he said. "I am interested only in providing a new source of energy so that we can liberate ourselves from outside sources of energy in order to learn how to handle this kind of free energy . . . If we are going to survive on this planet we have to get over the idea of burning fuel, because we are burning up a substance which is very valuable as a source of rubber, fertilizer, medicine, plastics and lubricants."

He said that the social problems of the 1960s prompted him

to find a way to help by applying himself scientifically.

"My feeling throughout the whole situation was that unless we developed some new source of energy and a new way to help people get around, and some new form of transportation that was cheaper, quieter and non-polluting, we would never have peace in the world . . .

"As long as we were completely preoccupied with how to get this energy and how to divide up the remaining resources, we'd always be contending with each other and we'd never achieve peace. So my interest was to find something that I as a scientist could do that could help the situation which I had perceived arising from a basic shortage of energy."

(Michael Gershberg is a student in the UCSB Environmental Studies Program and an intern at the News-Press.)

DE PALMA INSTITUTE

Santa Barbara, California

11 October 1985

Critique of the N-machine constructed by Trombly and Kahn by:

Bruce DePalma

Recently the International Patent Application of Trombly and Kahn, (assigned to Acme Energy Co., of San Rafael, California), has become public property under the PCT (Patent Cooperation Treaty) and can be obtained from the International Bureau of the World Intellectual Property Organization. A copy of this patent application is attached. The difference between international patents and the U.S. patent system is that in the U.S. the material of the patent is secret until the patent is granted, while overseas the application itself is the basis of the patent; which stands until challenged by a third party.

Thus although Adam Trombly, the senior designer of the machine, has received two written gag orders from the pentagon D.O.D., forbidding him to reveal details of the machine -- upon threat of ten years imprisonment for violating security relating to homopolar generator design; -- through the very nature of life itself by a totally automatic process, the attached document falls into the public domain.

The attached patent application and drawings represent the result of the expenditure of $290,000.- in two phases. The DOD imposed secrecy has prevented any recompense whatever from acruing to the men who performed this work. What is described is a machine, an electrical generator whose output exceeds the input by a factor of 4.92.

Summary of Machine Parameters:

rotor O.D.   14.0 inches
rotor length   9.25   "
internal rotor diameter   6 inches
shaft diameter (at widest point) 2   "
speed   7,200 r.p.m.
field   15,000 gauss   @ 150 watts field input

voltage output   2.9 volts d.c.   @ 15,000 amperes

load   drive motor (d.c.) input: 1.8 - 1.9 Hp. (1340 - 1470 watts)
                                              windage & friction
aded   drive motor input: 10.8 Kw., 14.5 Hp.

DE PALMA INSTITUTE

Santa Barbara, California

11 October 1985

Critique of the N-machine constructed by Trombly and Kahn by:

Bruce DePalma

Recently the International Patent Application of Trombly and Kahn, (assigned to Acme Energy Co., of San Rafael, California), has become public property under the PCT (Patent Cooperation Treaty) and can be obtained from the International Bureau of the World Intellectual Property Organization. A copy of this patent application is attached. The difference between international patents and the U.S. patent system is that in the U.S. the material of the patent is secret until the patent is granted, while overseas the application itself is the basis of the patent; which stands until challanged by a third party.

Thus although Adam Trombly, the senior designer of the machine, has received two written gag orders from the pentagon D.O.D., forbidding him to reveal details of the machine -- upon threat of ten years imprisonment for violating security relating to homopolar generator design; -- through the very nature of life itself by a totally automatic process, the attached document falls into the public domain.

The attached patent application and drawings represent the result of the expenditure of $290,000.- in two phases. The DOD imposed secrecy has prevented any recompense whatever from acruing to the men who performed this work. What is described is a machine, an electrical generator whose output exceeds the input by a factor of 4.92.

Summary of Machine Parameters:

rotor O.D.	14.0 inches	
rotor length	9.25 "	
internal rotor diameter	6 inches	
shaft diameter (at widest point)	2 "	
speed	7,200 r.p.m.	
field	15,000 gauss	@ 150 watts field input
voltage output	2.9 volts d.c.	@ 15,000 amperes

load   drive motor (d.c.) input: 1.8 - 1.9 Hp. (1340 - 1470 watts)
windage & friction

aded   drive motor input: 10.8 Kw., 14.5 Hp.

DePalma - Trombly N-machine

The solution described by Trombly seems to have been simultaneously invented by him, DePalma, and the DOD. Without necessarily having to add specific detail it should be obvious how to enlarge the structure to handle more current. The liquid metal could be circulated to provide additional cooling. Different metals could be used, i.e. mercury. I estimate the Trombly machine should be able to produce 100,000 amperes without difficulty.

Conversion of the low voltage d.c. output to the standard 110 and 220 volt a.c. 60 cps. requires innovative engineering. The easiest way is to run a Faraday Disc motor at the low voltage and drive a conventional electrical generator to produce whatever voltage and current required. Conversion could also be attempted by interrupting the low voltage high current with some sort of liquid metal commutator and transforming the voltage directly with a transformer. These ideas are treated by Tesla in his patents for the design of liquid metal commutators and interrupters. The voltage could be transformed electronically but this is beyond the state of the art of low voltage high current transistors at the present time.

A larger diameter machine could be built. Voltage goes as the square of the machine radius.

The low internal resistance, 6 - 10 micro-ohms, reported for the Trombly-Kahn machine speaks to quality of the liquid metal sliding contacts obtained with the construction method described. Low internal resistance is crucial to obtaining high power output and avoiding excessive internal heating.

The Trombly-Kahn machine represents what bright young minds can accomplish given the right circumstances and support. The attempted suppression of this work only points up the feeblemindedness of the gerontocracy which rules science in the U.S.A.

Building a useful N-machine is a high-technology accomplishment. Intelligent designers and craftmen can take this information and scale it to appropriate needs. The wish is to cause this technology to flourish on Earth.

Bruce DePalma

DePalma Institute

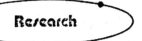

Re/earch

RESEARCHERS SEE LONG-LIFE SATELLITE POWER
SYSTEMS IN 19TH CENTURY EXPERIMENT

Experiments based on a neglected finding by 19th century physicist Michael Faraday hold the hope of doubling or tripling the lifetime of today's satellite power systems. Two researchers are experimenting on an unusual high-energy, "homopolar" generator. Another scientist says the device might eventually weigh as little as 10 kilos and generate 30 kw of power. Washington area engineers said it could last for 20-25 years if a solid state device incorporating the principle can be built.

The work of former MIT engineering instructor Bruce DePalma has attracted the attention of Dr. Edgar Mitchell, the former astronaut, and his research associates. Mitchell told SATELLITE NEWS he is interested enough to try to secure large-scale corporate funding for DePalma's work.

DePalma has devised a rotating magnetic generator using large cylindrical magnets. The machine generates huge amounts of electrical current—generating about 28 times the power needed to run it.

Dr. George Ainsworth-Land, until recently the chief of AT&T's strategic planning, believes DePalma's energy principle can be used to create a solid state device that would not only weigh less, but be more compact and potentially power a satellite with an output of 30 kw. Engineering consultants tell us such a device could have a life of 20-25 years if it were shielded from radiation.

Western satellites are currently powered by photovoltaic cells. These cells tend to wear out, however, in 7-10 years. Their life span is shortened by radiation, small meteorites and chemical changes in the cells themselves.

Ainsworth-Land told us he is "pretty sure the Japanese already have something" in the way of a solid state machine that generates energy like the DePalma machine does mechanically. A solid state device of this type could be developed in about 2 years with an R&D budget of $10-$15 million, according to Ainsworth-Land. He said a Japanese researcher, Dr. Shinici Seike, has developed an early prototype using magnetic "mobius strips tied together with a particular kind of transistor." Seike's technology, according to Ainsworth-Land, may offer a way to get energy effects similar to those DePalma's machine produces without the drawback of moving parts.

We interviewed DePalma at his workplace in the Santa Barbara foothills and witnessed a demonstration of the homopolar generator he calls the "N-machine." The device is based on the rediscovery of an electromagnetic principle first uncovered by Michael Faraday in 1831. Faraday discovered electrical current can be extracted from a rotating conducting disc when it is rotated between the poles of a magnet.

Nearly 150 years later DePalma repeated the experiment except that he rotated magnets and conducting discs together as a one-piece (or homopolar) generator. It generates an astounding amount of electrical current. AT 6000 rpm the 13-inch-diameter rotor puts out 7200 amperes at 1.5 volts, equivalent to 7560 watts or about 10 hp. Most important, there is almost no drag on the machine when an electrical load is put on it.

The discovery has caused a stir in the scientific world because it seems to defy principles of inertial mass set down by Einstein. For instance, University of Colorado physicist Adam Trombley started work on his own version of an N-machine after visiting DePalma. Trombley and his associates have formed Acme Energy Corp. in San Rafael, California. Acme is about a year away from completing a commercial prototype generator capable of producing about 50 kw of AC electrical power, according to Trombley. That is enough to power 5 or 6 households.

The power-in/power-out ratio for the Acme generator is not as high as the DePalma machine, but it still puts out about 3 to 4 times more electrical power than it takes to run the device.

DePalma is building a bigger N-machine—a 250 kw version with a 2-ft.-diameter rotor. There are a number of science graduate students assisting DePalma with his research, both in California and around the country. (Bruce DePalma, 702 Parklane, Montecito, CA 93108, 805/969-7057; Dr. George Ainsworth-Land, Wilson Learning Corp., 6950 Washington Ave., S. Eden Prairie, MN 55344, 612/944-2880; Dr. Adam Trombley, Acme Energy Corp., 25 Mitchell Blvd., San Rafael, CA 94903, Suite #6, 415/499-1460.)

p. 5

from *Satellite News*, June 15, 1981, Phillips Pub., Washington, DC

edgar d. mitchell

February 27, 1981

Mr. Carl Massopust
Group Vice President
Dart Industries, Inc.
Box 3157, Terminal Annex
Los Angeles, California 90051

Subject: Letter Revision to Mitchell/Ainsworth-Land Proposal

Dear M·. Massopust:

As a result of our numerous telephone conversations, our
February 2nd meeting in Los Angeles, the Santa Barbara meeting
with DePalma and White on February 23rd, and the Buffalo meeting between Howard Tracey and Ainsworth-Land on February 24th,
Dr. Ainsworth-Land and I are proposing certain revisions to
our previous proposal. Our purpose is to (a) quickly satisfy
the need for consistent and verifiable data on the "N" generator
experiment, (b) maintain and increase any lead time we may have
in the development of this new field, and (c) provide for
rapid execution of follow-on phases of this project, assuming
successful completion of further verifying the basic principles
of the "N" generator.

This proposal makes the following assumptions:

1. The Faraday-DePalma experiment, if properly verified,
    indeed offers the potential of a totally unique method of
    generating electrical energy. (For those of us who have
    studied this process for many months, the Faraday-DePalma
    principle has been sufficiently verified, but the quality
    of the data currently existing is inadequate to determine
    the parameters for cost-effective and marketable reduction
    to practice.) Thus the steps necessary to convince
    Dr. White, or anyone else, of the validity of the principle
    should also serve, if possible, to obtain usable data for
    subsequent design improvements.

2. The theoretical implications (i.e., apparent violations of
    the conservation of energy principle) will not be dealt with
    quickly. Both the DePalma and the Ainsworth-Land theories
    of operation of this class of devices will be the subject
    of much controversy for a number of years – BUT it is not
    necessary to have acceptance and complete understanding of
    the theory in order to produce useful devices. (The
    Ainsworth-Land theory is pre-publication, and thus, privi-
    leged information.)

Excerpts from Dr. White's Report of 3-9-81

by Dr. D.C. White
M.I.T. Energy Lab

Massopust
2/27/81
Page 2.

3. Verification of the Faraday-DePalma principle by Dr. White will be a highly visible, open invitation to the scientific community for research and debate, and to the business community to engage in a race for exploitation.

4. Dart Industries, Inc. is prepared to pursue this project to the point of establishing validity for this class of devices, and, if valid, to some further point where a proper business judgment regarding their economic and business potential can be made.

5. The previous Mitchell/Ainsworth-Land proposal, being primarily oriented toward data-gathering on state-of-the art devices did not propose at this early stage an in-depth legal foundation by way of extensive patent and literature searches. With the entry of prestigious representation like M.I.T. and the instant visibility this will provide to the project if validity is achieved, such in-depth legal work now seems vital.

6. Prof. D. C. White of the M.I.T. Energy Laboratory will be a major consultant to Dart Industries at least through the verification phase.

7. Mitchell and Ainsworth-Land will serve as project directors in conjunction with, and in response to, the representative from Dart Industries, Inc., appointed to this project.

In view of the foregoing, the following alternative tasks should be considered for implementation over the next 90 days.

I. Proceed with obtaining "clean" data to validate the Faraday-DePalma principle.

(a) Contract with DePalma to bring his small generator (demo of Feb. 23rd) to a configuration for obtaining proper data using a protocol devised by Dr. D. C. White.

Time: 2-1/2 months

Estimated Cost:		
DePalma		$25,000
Supervision:		
Mitchell		4,000
White, et al.		8,000
Travel		4,500
	Total	$41,500

Electromechanical Dynamics, Part I, Herbert H. Woodson and James R. Melcher, published by John Wiley and Sons 1968

(b)   Contract with DePalma to construct an improved
       device to do the same as (a), but incorporating
       state-of-the-art improvements which he considers
       proprietary. This is DePalma's preference, but it
       would necessitate a continuation agreement with him
       if successful.

   Time: 2-1/2 months

   Estimated Cost:
      Same as (a) – $41,500

   Alternative (b) is a higher risk path than (a) since
   inventors tend to be overly optimistic about how much
   they can achieve in a given time and within a budget.)

(c)   Complete the Ainsworth-Land device to validate the
       principle and to gather parametric data for future
       design.

   Time: 2-1/2 months

   Estimated Cost:
      Tom Valone (A-L Assistant) $10,000
      Materials   12,000
      Test Instrumentation   15,000
                                   Total $37,000

(d)   Contract with D. C. White to construct devices and
       perform validation at M.I.T.

   Time: ?

   Estimated Cost: ?

(e)   Contract with Berkeley group for demo.

   Time: ?

   Estimated Cost: ?

II.   State-of-the-Art Patent Search: The patents issued in
      this century on unusual electric generating devices
      which have not developed commercially is quite large.
      In particular, the work of Steinmetz and Tesla may relate
      closely to the Faraday-DePalma work. These patents

Massopust
2/27/81
Page 4.

probably number in the several hundreds, if not more.
These could yield ideas for design improvement as well
as being necessary for providing the legal foundation for
our own patents. Such a search would be carried out in
Dart Industry facilities assisted by Dr. Mitchell and
such additional energy generation consultants as necessary
to complete the screening task during this phase.

Time: 2-1/2 months

Estimated Costs:
Ed Mitchell	$20,000
Office and Staff Assistance	9,500
Three Consultants @ 3,000/month	22,500
Travel Expense	5,000
Total	$57,000

III. State-of-the-Art Literature Search and Theory Correlation:
Ainsworth-Land has in the last several weeks uncovered a
number of papers presented by the NASA and in the general
physics literature which describe effects relating to our
concepts of energy generation. Additional search is
producing an expanding group of papers, while seemingly
unrelated by classical theory, do have a significant
relationship when viewed from the perspective of Ainsworth-
Land transformation theory. This search and correlation
with transformation theory will have significant impact
as we proceed to the phase of designing and testing new
configurations.

Time: 2-1/2 months

Estimated Costs:

G. Ainsworth-Land	$20,000
Staff and Secretarial Support	12,000
Consultants (physicists)	15,000
Travel	6,000
Computer time purchase	5,000
Total	$58,000

IV. Development of Detailed Phase II Business Plan: Assuming
the continuing success of Phase I, Phase II detailed planning will begin in the second month of Phase I. This
planning will require decisions on setting up in-house vs.

Massopust
2/27/81
Page 5.

contracted work, which models and configurations of
energy devices to concentrate on, which inventors and
inventions to pursue, if any, which existing patents and
research papers are important to Phases II and III, etc.
Finally, detailed time tables and budget estimates for
Phase II will be developed. This effort will be a cooper-
ative effort of Dart Industries personnel, E. Mitchell and
G. Ainsworth-Land.

Time: 1-1/2 months

Estimated Costs:

E. Mitchell	$ 5,000
Ainsworth-Land	5,000
Staff and Secretarial Support	6,000
Outside Consultants	15,000
Travel Expense	5,000
Total	$36,000

V. Development of Preliminary Phase III Plan: Preliminary
Phase III planning will begin concurrently with the detailed
Phase II plan. Long lead time instrumentation and materials
relative to Phase II effort should be ordered upon Phase II
commitment - estimated laboratory instrumentation: approximately $100,000.

The foregoing tasks and costing are based upon known fees,
salaries and overhead costs, plus estimates of travel and
consultant time requirements. If the task statements are
approved, a 10% contingency should be added to the total for
Phase I. No allowance has been made for Dart Industries, Inc.
internal cost estimates.

It is suggested that at least two, and possibly three, of the
data verification tasks be done concurrently, i.e., one of
DePalma's - I(a) or I(b) - plus Ainsworth-Land's, plus, perhaps,
White's (if the legal implications are not too sticky.) Using
the Berkeley group as a data source is probably remote.

Sincerely,

EDGAR D. MITCHELL

EDM/jg

Excerpts from Dr. White's Report of 3-9-81

by Dr. D.C. White
M.I.T. Energy Lab

The invention of Bruce De Palma has been discussed in Section 6.3.1, page 284 of the book Electromechanical Dynamics*, including the example 6.3.1, page 286. The key issue is the definition of the magnetic field quantities **B**, **H** and **M** when there is relative motion of the magnetic material. In developing the constituent relation for magnetic field systems for relative motion in Section 6.3.1 the authors obtained the result summarized in the last paragraph on page 285:

> "Although the constituent relation as expressed by (6.3.8) or (6.3.9) was written for stationary material, the transformations of (6.1.35), (6.1.37), and (6.1.39) show that in a quasi-static magnetic field system **B**, **H**, and **M** are unaffected by relative motion. Consequently, (6.3.8) and (6.3.9) hold also when the material is moving with respect to the coordinate system in which the electromagnetic quantities are to be measured."

For the De Palma invention this means that the magnetic field seen in the stationary reference frame (the bench on which the homopolar generator and drive motor are mounted) is the same whether the magnets are stationary or rotating. The only thing that counts is whether the conducting disk is moving (rotating) in the magnetic field. De Palma admits to a normal homopolar machine - stationary magnets, rotating disk. Because of the invariance of the magnetic field under motion (rotation), his machine (rotating magnets) is identical to one with stationary magnets.

Thus the De Palma invention is a conventional homopolar machine, and such a machine driven by a mechanical source (electric motor, steam turbine, etc.) will generate d.c. electric power. Homopolar generators are typically low voltage, high current sources and all have problems of current collection at the brushes. Such machines do not violate the first law since the electric power produced is obtained from the mechanical shaft, just as in any generator whether a.c. or d.c.

De Palma's problem stems from his very sloppy measurement of power into the drive motor. Careful instrumentation would show that the input drive power goes up when current is drawn from the homopolar machine. You will recall that I noticed in his film that the ammeter in the drive motor circuit jumped (increased) when he drew power from the homopolar generator. There was no way to fully verify that result at the time of the visit.

The final issue involves the observed measurements by Faraday of a voltage produced by rotating magnets and a rotating conducting disk. The result is correct, as is De Palma's, and both are part of the physical measurements that verify the conclusion that the magnetic field is independent of the motion of the magnetic material. That is the mathematical formulation which includes constituent relations, Maxwell's equations, etc. which comes from physical measurements and not vice versa.

One caveat in the case of rotating magnets as used by De Palma is that one needs a rotationally symmetric magnetic field so that other effects do not come into play. For example, a space rate of change of B produced by rotating a non-uniform magnetic field complicates the effects but does not change any of the above conclusions. De Palma uses a rotationally symmetric magnetic field so the case of greater complexity does not have to be treated.

---

*Electromechanical Dynamics, Part I, Herbert H. Woodson and James R. Melcher, published by John Wiley and Sons 1968

Interview With A Physicist

Recently Beverly Dittrich spoke with an physicist in Washington state who is actively searching for an alternate source of energy. He asked to remain anonymous because he isn't concerned with being recognized for his work; as he put it, "We've got to stop worrying about egos and just save the planet!" We will keep in touch with this source, and as he gets closer to perfecting an alternate energy machine we will keep you updated.

Bev: Could you fill me in on how you got involved in researching this energy machine?

Physicist: We knew that we were going to have to find some sort of alternate energy, and it was not going to be solar because there's not enough sun here in the winter. Ramtha said the wind is going to blow, so put up your windmills. Well, we don't have enough wind around here to blow a windmill in the wintertime. We have it in the summertime, when we also have plenty of sun, but not in the winter. At one of the seminars he said, "Some of you are going to figure out how to put a rod in the earth and bring out energy."

Bev: I remember him saying that. (Denver, May 1986: "There will come a day very shortly in your time where only that which is called a lightning rod will be placed in a precise precinct where you live and it will begin to harness the magnetic energy of your northern regions and of your southern regions, and what you will experience will be no plug-in at all, but the availability of something that allows you to be even more sovereign.")

Physicist: My background was one of experimental physics. I had spent ten years at IBM and had a Ph.D. in electrical engineering, so I reasoned that I ought to have a lot of the necessary tools. But none of my tools applied to what Ramtha said. So I went back to check out Tesla, to read about his work.

How do you stick a rod in the earth or in the air and get energy? It turns out it's not totally preposterous! The earth is a giant capacitor, and there are discharges in the capacitor called lightning in the earth's center and in its atmosphere. Also, the shell of the earth itself acts as a conductor, and there is a resonance frequency associated with that--it starts at about eight cycles and has harmonics that go up eight, sixteen, twenty-four. So I did a little thinking about how we could tap into those frequencies, see what was going on there. And I thought about all the radiation that comes pouring down onto the earth and gets trapped here. Not only sunlight, but all kinds of particles come streaming in from the sun. There's a natural potential--you can find it in all the books--I think it's about 200 volts every ten feet as you go away from the surface of the earth; there's a field that can be measured, and we've never been able to tap it.

So I began digging into all these different groups. Perhaps right now the most famous is Joseph Newman and his followers. There's also Adam Trombly's work. Adam has designed a great machine. It's tough to build one of those things! I was all set to make one of Adam's devices; it was going to be the device that I centered on, and it may yet be the solution if we can figure out the contact problems. It turns out that Tesla had published some contact solutions, because he had worked on a device very similar to Adam's.

Bev: But Trombly's device is not available yet, and we're interested in locating one that is!

Physicist: Well, as far as I know there aren't any available yet. There are claims that there are some machines that will work, and people are hot trying to find them and get them going. The one big problem is the Patent Office. I made a radical proposal at a recent meeting; I said as far as I'm concerned the Patent Office ought to just issue a decree that they're not going to issue a patent on any energy device! It takes about two years to get a patent, and we don't have two years to waste!

There are several kinds of machines available that may be over-efficient. By that I mean you get more energy out than you put in. Trombly's homo-polar generator may be one of them. I say "may be" because there is a large group of people still trying to figure out if there was enough scientific rigor used in the measurements to justify classifying it as an over-efficient device. You've got to be very careful in the measurements.

That is where Newman comes under great attack, even by all the people in the "underground" physics group. It is very, very difficult to measure the amount of the power going in and the power coming out of the Newman device, especially the power coming out. It has to do with the fact that you can measure current and you can measure voltage, but you have to be very careful and measure the phase between the two in order to actually measure the true power. People slip up on that a lot. And I don't know if Newman has done that properly or not. I have not pursued Newman's device very much, so I don't really know.

There is a review, a collection of all the information that is readily available; Tom Valone has put it together. People who want to know what has been done so far should get hold of that review.

The homo-polar generator, Adam Trombly's device, looks like a great one, but it's not going to be available for a while. Quite a while! One of the reasons is because the government uses a device very similar to this in the railgun, a device that can shoot pellets through two tanks standing in a row. They use homo-polar generators to get the power to do that. It's written up in *Time* magazine (December 1, 1980, page 60) and it's included in that Tom Valone collection.

Bev: Exactly what are the technical problems with the homo-polar generator?

Physicist: For it to be successful, you have to have contacts to the spinning disk that will carry high current and have a very, very low resistance. The best technology to do that is classified, because of the railgun, so we're not going to have access to the best technology. One of the reasons that I wanted to give this interview is because I want people to know that although there's not a product there now, there *will* be a product if we all help create it. Whether you make a physical contribution in terms of going out and building one, or whether you create one in your head so that you know it's going to be there when you need it and you'll be able to buy one or barter for one. There are also contributions to be made in the technology. One of them is to design contacts that will carry these high currents at low voltages.

Bev: Is there someone working on this?

Physicist: Other than the government? Well, there are some things being developed that may be applicable, but not directly. First of all, in Texas there's a group that is under government contract to work on homo-polar generators. I think that there is in fact a homo-polar generator available that you can buy, but it operates in pulse mode rather than continuous mode, so they use it in welding and things like that, but you can't use it to power a home.

Bev: It can't be converted?

Physicist: No, because in order to get continuous use you have this disk that's spinning. What they do is get the disk spinning very fast and then they make contact with it by clamping onto it and stopping it and pulling out all the energy. That's not a good technology for continuous use.

No one that I'm aware of, other than the Texas group, has mounted a research effort to figure out the contact problem. Tom Valone was using a liquid metal which has a low melting temperature. Other people are using mercury. There has to be a solution! There are three people working on alternate energy forms that I know of who have gotten clues and input from extraterrestrials!

What I do with "strange" physics is collect the information, take it in, and don't make judgments on it. I keep taking it in and taking it in and finally some of the pieces start to fit together and I'm able to project from the information that I have into new areas. I'm still collecting as much information as I can. I just went to the Planetary Society for Clean Energy Conference in Canada in May thinking we're going to build a homo-polar generator and that will be it. But at the conference I found out so many exciting things that need to get out to the people.

Bev: I'd like to hear about some of these things that were discussed at the conference, but can you first tell me about the information that has been received from the extraterrestrials?

Physicist: Dr. Shinici Seike in Japan is doing some marvelous, different kinds of things in terms of alternate energy. He talked to Tom Valone and led him to believe that he had help from extraterrestrials.

There is a book by Norman Paulsen called *Christ Consciousness*. It describes an experience the author had with extraterrestrials. They took him on their ship and let him see the power plant of their vehicle. It consisted of two rotating rings with magnets in it. The extraterrestrials said to him "Some day you will take one-half of this system and get all of the energy you need." In other words, one ring. (*Editor's note:* The actual quotation from Paulsen's book is "The basic design I have given you of this ship's power and drive systems gives you the keys to many doors. Sometime in the future you could construct one half of the ship's drive systems and have an unlimited supply of electrical energy. This system would require no outside sources of energy to run it, such as fossil fuels or atomic power. That generator would be self-perpetuating as it would produce more energy than it would take to run it. You would, therefore, have an unlimited supply of totally free energy." *Christ Consciousness* by Norman Paulsen, Builders Publishing Company, 1980, pp. 443-444.)

Valone got very excited about this and thought that by pursuing the homo-polar generator he was doing what they said. After he had done his work, he had an interview with the guy in the book and he found out that actually it wasn't the same generator. No one to my knowledge has been working on this type of generator. It is an insulating disk with twelve magnets in it, spinning around in a circle with another ring around the outside. The magnets were oriented radially. In the homo-polar generator you have a conducting disk, not an insulating one, spinning around in one direction while the magnetic field goes in the other direction.

The third piece of information is from a man in England named Searle. He produced what is called the Searle disk, which is based on rotating magnets. You get the magnets rotating and it takes off! But no one pays attention to the guy, because he presents an appearance of being cracked up. Well, not "no one" because there are a few people who are very interested in this technology called the Searle disk. It may in fact be the same kind of disk that this extraterrestrial talked about. The thing that is totally fascinating about Searle and his disk is that he doesn't admit to any extraterrestrial contact at all. Let me say that my information about Searle is third-hand. I heard it from another scientist named Paul Brown, who is active in this area.

Anyway, Searle's magnets were analyzed by a university in England and were found to contain neodymium, which is an element that burns in air and was not commercially available when Searle put his disk together. Searle claimed that he made his magnets by pressing together a commercially available powder, but if he had done that the magnets probably would have burned up or exploded. So the real puzzle is where did he get his neodymium from? The conjecture is that he got it from an extraterrestrial.

Searle didn't like the way he was received in society. He was powering his house with some kind of apparatus and no one was paying attention to him so he took a chainsaw and cut down the power pole. Then he was

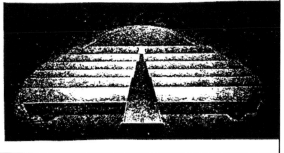

thrown in jail and his device was seized and his wife divorced him, so he changed his name and now he's in hiding. Again, this is all rumor!

Paul Brown is working on a battery that will run for 25 years on a single charge. The technology will be available next year, but it will take five years to get it to the marketplace. The licensing problem has to do with the fact that it's a nuclear battery and there are all sorts of safeguards you have to worry about. These batteries will be used in space vehicles because the licensing is greatly reduced for that. Then they will probably go to farm machinery, industrial use, and then home use. It's about a five-year period.

We have nuclear devices now in our homes called smoke detectors! You can take a smoke detector and make a nuclear battery. It won't be very powerful, but you can do it. The concept is there. Brown has designed this battery in a clean way—there's no waste. The only safety problem would be if you ingested the material. There won't be any radiation problems. The devices work, they continue to produce energy, they're very efficient. There will be a device available for about $20,000 that will power five homes for 25 years. If he doesn't hit any major snags in terms of licensing, it should be available in five years.

Bev: Where are we in terms of other devices?

Physicist: There's a whole class of devices, and Newman's is one of them, that take energy from a battery and feed back a high-voltage spike into the battery. They claim these devices are over-efficient, and they may be. But to my knowledge people aren't running these things for more than the battery's lifetime.

There is another class of generators called variable-reactance generators that are reported to be over-efficient sometimes, but not always. What may be happening is that our thoughts are interacting with the energy sources somehow, and if we get a delicate energy source, an unstable mechanism, it could be affected by just a little wave of thought. That may be what is happening with some of these.

Certainly I know that we're all connected; I've done measurements to show that. There is a mental energy that is real, that is detectable by biological devices. It may be that we can generate scaler waves from our brains, and that those waves interact in a system either with each other or with other scalar waves to produce anomalous effects. The fascinating thing is that the world and the universe is much greater than what we think it is. There's much more going on than just the grass growing under our feet. Getting to the bottom of it is fun and challenging and sometimes very frustrating. Ramtha was right when he said there is no mathematics to describe it.

Bev: Are there other conferences? Is this one in Canada a yearly thing?

Physicist: They're thinking about having another one next year. There have been some *great* conferences! If I had just started this a few years earlier, I would be way ahead of where I am now. There is a conference in Colorado Springs every year in memory of Tesla. There was a conference in Europe just recently where Tuari and Seike and Paul Brown spoke.

The Planetary Society is a good place to keep posted on what is going on. If people want to be updated as much as possible, then they probably ought to join that. It's a Canadian society and they put out a publication with names, addresses, and phone numbers, so you can contact people. I've used many of the names and addresses I've got from there; I think it's an excellent resource.

Just one example of how the Planetary Society can save you time is in the field of patents. There is a whole list of patents that have been granted on over-efficient devices or alternate energy machines. If you want a copy of this list or of a specific patent application, you can write to the government and get a copy for 50 cents. You don't have to figure out who has a patent library and go xerox the patent. It took me a long time to figure that out! I finally got this government address from a back issue of the Planetary Society. It's a good society to belong to. They'll tell you about upcoming meetings, too.

The purpose of the society is to be a clearing house, nothing else. If you're interested in a specific piece of information, you can write them and ask them if they have it. For the price of xeroxing, you'll get it if they have it in their files. The guy that runs it is collecting information all over the place. He's a searcher, also.

Bev: What else did you learn at the conference in Canada?

Physicist: The first speaker gave a talk on measurements of over-efficient devices. His purpose was to teach people to measure carefully so that their measurements would stand up to other engineers and scientists so that when they tried to get funding, when the consultants were called in, they wouldn't be embarrassed.

The next talk was given by the head of the Planetary Society. He gave a talk on extra-low frequency and its effects on us. Since 1976, the North American continent has been enveloped in a microwave network that's coming from Russia; when you demodulate the microwave, it gives a sound like a woodpecker pecking on rocks, so we call it the *woodpecker effect*. That is about six-cycle resonance and tends to pull down all of our natural resonances, which are around eight cycles. The effect this has on us is it tends to make us more depressed, it causes more illness, things like that.

Bev: Is this a purposeful, knowing thing that the Russians are doing?

Physicist: It's purposeful. It's knowing. We just don't know exactly what their purpose or knowing is! There's a lot of speculation on what's going on.

Bev: Is it coming from a ground device or from the atmosphere?

Physicist: It's directed at us from very specific stations in Russia. The signal stopped when Chernobyl went up, so they think at least one of the power sources is Chernobyl. It leads us to a whole new area which is trying to explain an alternate energy form that has to do with scalar waves. The interesting thing about scalar waves is you set up one source here and one source here, and if the sources are exactly of the right kind, you can transmit energy between them and not detect it on its way over. It's only when the two waves interact with each other that there's a detectable signal. We normally don't have devices that detect scalar waves. All our devices detect electromagnetic waves, "regular" waves.

To propagate information, like radio information, without radio electromagnetic waves is . . . well, if you said something like that to a meeting of the Electrical Engineering Society or the IEEE, you'd be thrown out of the room! And yet, it looks like that's the direction we're headed. It looks like there's something there, in these invisible waves that interact and cause strange effects. They can be transmitted to remote locations for useful purposes—pumping water—or for purposes of destroying tanks—or putting shields around people and environments.

There is a concern that the Russians may be far ahead of us in this area. That doesn't really concern me; what I'm concerned with is how to take the information and make a device that's going to work.

Some people have developed a watch that emits a signal to counteract the extra-low frequency signal. If you wear one of these watches, it's supposed to counteract the negative effects. The watches reportedly produce a scalar wave. You can't measure it, but if you were to take one apart you'd find an extra chip scotch-taped in the back and wired up to the electronics.

Bev: Do you feel a difference since you've been wearing one?

Physicist: I don't, but my wife does. My wife feels an enormous amount of difference. She has to take the watch off to go to sleep because she has so much energy! I normally have a lot of energy anyway and don't go into depressions, so I haven't noticed a big change myself.

Bev: What were some other topics at the conference?

Physicist: There's been some work done on allergies that is phenomenal. The book is by Cyril Smith and it's called *The Body Electromagnetic*. Smith says you can analyze a person's skin response, and you will get peaks and valleys which correspond to certain allergies. This is all in the low frequency range—zero to 30 cycles. If you take water and superimpose the signal that corresponds to the peaks, then give that water to the person with the allergies, he'll have relief from the allergies for a few days. Wild stuff!

Then there was a young fellow who talked about water sources, large water sources producing lots and lots of water. His concept was essentially to condense the water from the air using conventional technology. He was talking about collecting water and using it for places with little fresh water. The plant he was talking about would cost about a quarter of a million dollars.

Tom Valone gave a talk about his work, his attempts to build an over-efficient device.

Apparently there is also a guy in California who has a device that powers his home. We're going to try to find him. We're willing to license the building of a device for

anybody—we want to build a device, whatever the device is! The first one we come across.

Everybody thinks when they get a patent they're going to get rich. The people who get rich are those who have a good marketing team—and a good product! More money and time is wasted on patents; by the time you get a patent you don't have any money to market the thing.

Bev: Why can't you market it without a patent?

Physicist: You can! People are afraid that if they show their device to anyone, the idea will be stolen and someone else will patent it first. But they don't realize that if you put the information in the public domain—publish it or hold a meeting or just tell a bunch of people—*no one* can get a patent. No one will keep you from making your device.

In my opinion, the thing to do if you want to make money is to get a hot device and a good marketing team, and you're going to sell it. When you are the leader of the pack, you're going to make money. You're not going to make money forever, because the big guys are probably going to come in and capitalize on it, ultimately, but that's what you want anyway—to get the device out to the people.

Right now there's a market for over-efficient energy devices that is totally undefined. I venture to say that if you came out with a device that cost a million dollars, you would probably find buyers for it. If you designed a device that cost $100,000 you'd find buyers for it. If you designed a device that cost $3000 you'd find buyers for it. The market is there, it's just a question of getting the devices and selling them.

Bev: There are a lot of us out here who just want an energy machine. We don't care who's got it, who built it, why, where, all we want is the machine!

Physicist: I'm with you!

For more information:

"The One-Piece Farraday Generator: Theory and Experiment" by Thomas Valone is available from Integrity Electronics and Research, 558 Breckenridge Street, Buffalo, NY 14222 (716-886-6985). This is the collection of research mentioned in the interview.

For a subscription to the newspaper published by the Planetary Association for Clean Energy, Inc., send $22.50 to the Editorial Headquarters at 100 Bronson Avenue, Suite 1001, Ottawa, Ontario K1R 6G8 Canada or call 613-236-6265.

A free catalog is available from Tesla Book Company, 1580 Magnolia Avenue, Millsboro, CA 94030.

Another source for information on Tesla is *Inventions, Researches, and Writings of Nikola Tesla* by T.C. Martin, which is available from Health Research, P.O. Box 70, Mokelumne, CA 95245 for $15 plus $1.70 postage.

The Paulsen book, *Christ Consciousness*, is available from Windwords for $10.95. See page 27 for ordering information.

The extra-low frequency (ELF) watch is available from Wilma Harrell for approximately $100, depending on the style you choose. Contact her at P.O. Box 1238, Snohomish, WA 98290 or call (206) 771-3777.

MIND OF FARADAY REVEALED TO WORLD

N.Y. TIMES 1931

Scientist's Diary, Detailing Famous Electrical Experiments, Read at Ithaca Meeting.

ANESTHESIA IS ANALYZED

Unconsciousness From Anesthetics, Blow, Narcotics, Heat, Traced to Same Cause.

From a Staff Correspondent of The New York Times.

ITHACA, June 20.—The thoughts and emotions of Faraday as he worked on his inventions, which brought into being the modern era of electricity, were revealed for the first time this afternoon before an audience of 400 physicists and chemists gathered at Cornell University. Sir William Bragg, British scientist and Nobel Prize winner, read to them extracts from Faraday's diary, which has never been published.

The reading was before a joint meeting of the members of the American Physical Society and the Eighth Colloid Symposium of the Combined National Research Council and the American Chemical Society, here for two separate three-day conventions, which began yesterday.

Sir William revealed at the opening that Aug. 29, 1931, a hundred years from the date entered by Faraday in his diary reporting his first successful experiment on the relation of electricity and magnetism, which was in effect the first dynamo, is to be celebrated as the centenary of the dynamo. He said that on that date the diary would be published in full in six volumes.

"The diary which Faraday kept day by day," said Sir William, "contained his ideas as to the progress of his experiments, what he thought of them, and what he expected to do next. Its interest lies in the revelation of the thoughts of the man who changed the complexion of our entire civilization. We see him feel his way slowly toward an idea we now expect an elementary student to know.

Found Universe Interrelated.

"But Faraday was not guiding his way by accident. To him the whole universe was so connected that you could not try it in one place without finding some connection with the other. So he set out trying to find out two by two what this connection was.

"He felt there must be some connection between electricity and chemistry, electricity and magnetism and light, and he spent his time drawing the loose threads together. He knew the world was composed of a scheme which it was the business of man to explore. He had a complete vision of the universe and he widened our horizons by showing us that the study of nature was necessary before we could understand ourselves, that man is not an absolute thing, but related to the world around him, and to know himself he must first know the world. He gave us a new vision of what science means and what it stands for.

"He was so far in advance of his time that many of his ideas are still the field for speculation of some of our greatest minds. He thought, for example, that gravity must be connected with light, heat and electricity. He experimented to prove it and failed.

"It was not until Einstein proved that a ray of light was bent when it came into the gravitational field of the sun that this vision of Faraday was realized as a fact. All through his diary we find passages in which he states his ideas that there must be

an interrelation between gravitation, electro-dynamics and other forms of energy. That is the very thing Einstein is now working to prove."

Shows Pages of Diary.

At this point Sir William showed on the screen the pages of the diary telling of the first dynamo. It was dated Aug. 29, 1831, and he added "experiments on the production of electricity from magnetism, &c., &c." It reads as follows:

"Have had an iron ring made (soft iron) round and seven-eighth inches thick and ring six inches in external diameter. Wound many coils of copper wire round, one half the coils being separated by twine and calico. There were three lengths of wire, each about 24 feet long, and they could be connected as one length or used as separate lengths. * * * Will call this side of the ring, 'A.'

"On the other side, but separated by an interval, was wound wire in two pieces, together amounting to about 60 feet in length, the direction being as with the former coils. This side call 'B.'

"When all was ready the moment the battery was communicated with both ends of wire at 'A' side the Helix strongly attracted the needle; after a few vibrations it came to a state of rest in its original and natural position, and then on breaking the battery connection the needle was as strongly repelled, and after a few oscillations came to rest in the same place as before.

"Hence effect indirect but transient, but its recurrence on breaking the connections shows an equilibrium somewhere that must be capable of being rendered more distinct.

"May not these transient effects be connected with causes of difference between power of metals in rest and in motion in Aragos experiments?"

Tells of Aragos Experiment.

A later entry tells of his carrying out his idea. It reads:

"Made Aragos experiment with earth magnet only. No magnet used, but the plate put horizontal and rotated. The effect at the needle was slight but very distinct and could be accumulated upon the needle by reversion and reiteration of motion, &c. When plate revolved as marked, the marked end of the needle went east. No iron used here, wires not more than eighteen inches long and only bell wire. If had used thick wire in galvanometer and for conductors probably much more effect."

"The 'bell wire,'" interposed Sir William amidst laughter, "is not what we understand by 'bell wire,' but the wire that pulled the bells."

"Hence," the diary goes on, "Aragos plate a new electrical machine.

"On putting the apparatus over the

Continued from Page 1, Column 7.

pole of a bar magnet then it was easy to effect the galvanometer. As the disc revolved one way the electricity was from the centre to the circumference; as it revolved the other way from the circumference to the centre. This shows that so long as the wheel moves electricity is evolved, and as the radii are here not passing the pole as a whole but are always in the same relation to it, it shows that it is not mere vicinity but motion which evolves the electricity. Must consider this more presently. Probably build a machine up this way."

"This machine," interposed Sir William, "is of course the dynamo." Of particular interest to the physics of today is the entry of Aug. 25, 1849. It reads:

"I have been arranging certain experiments in reference to the notion that gravity itself may be practically and directly related by experiment to the other powers of matter and this morning proceeded to make them.

Saw Sublime Possibilities.

"It was almost with a feeling of awe that I went to work—for if the hope should prove well founded, how great and mighty and sublime in its hitherto unchangeable character is the force I am trying to deal with, and how large may the new domain of knowledge that may be opened up to the mind of man."

"If any effect is either electric or calorific—then consider the infinity of action in nature," reads another passage. "A planet or a comet when nearer or further from the sun, Dr. Winslow's observations on earthquakes, a falling river or cascade, the falls of Niagara, evaporation vapor rising, rain falling, hail, negative state of the upper regions, conditions of the inner and deeper parts of the earth, their heat, a falling stone or orolite heated, a volcano and the volcanic lightning, smoke in a chimney, perhaps goes out electrified."

"It took him days and weeks of experiments to find the action, if any, of magnetism on light," Sir William said. "Page after page we find him writing 'No result,' 'No experiment.'" The diary then continues:

"A piece of heavy glass was experimented with. It gave no effect when the same magnetic poles or the contrary poles were on opposite sides (as respects the course of the polarized ray)—nor when the same poles were on the same side either with the constant or intermitting current—but when contrary magnetic poles were on the same side there was an effect produced on the polarized ray, and thus magnetic force and light were proved to have relation to each other. This fact will most likely prove exceedingly fertile and of great value in the investigation of conditions of natural force."

"The mutual relation of electricity, magnetism and motion," reads another extract, "may be represented by three lines at right angles to each other, any one of which may represent any one of three points and the other two lines the other points. Then if electricity be determined in one line, and motion in another,

magnetism will be developed in the third, or, if electricity be determined in one line and magnetism in another, motion will occur in the third; or, if magnetism be determined first, then motion will produce electricity or electricity motion; or, if motion be the first point determined, magnetism will evolve electricity, or electricity magnetism.

"Tried experiments on effects of terrestrial magnetism in evolving electricity. Obtained beautiful results."

"Each leaf of a tree," Sir William read, "is subject to electric currents —each has its cisode and exode, the latter in the roots." * * *

"Gravity—Surely this force must be capable of an experimental relation to electricity, magnetism and the other forces, so as to bind it up with them in reciprocal action and equivalent effect. Consider for a moment how to set about touching this matter by facts and trial. * * *

Thought Gravity Convertible.

"Atmospheric phenomena favor the idea of the convertibility of gravitating force into electricity and back again probably (or perhaps then into heat).

"Matter is continually falling and rising in the air. The difference and the change of place of the bodies subject to gravity would perhaps give a predominant electric state above as the negative, but also an occasional charge of the other side, the positive. If there be this supposed relation of gravity and electricity, and the above space be chiefly or generally negative, then we might expect that as matter rises from the earth or moves against gravity it becomes negative.

"Then we might expect a wonderful opening out of electrical phenomena.

"So to say, even the changed force of gravity, as electricity, might travel above the earth surface, changing its place and then becoming the equivalent of gravity.

"Perhaps heat is the related condition of the forces when change of gravity occurs.

"Hence," he concluded in another part, "chemical action is merely electrical action and electrical action merely chemical."

One of the last entries is dated Nov. 11, 1851, and it tells of his famous experiment with iron filings on the distribution of lines of force.

"It is," concluded Sir William, "a priceless treasure, which scientific people will love to have by them."

Anaesthesia's Effects Discussed.

Special to The New York Times.

ITHACA, N. Y., June 20.—An explanation of what takes place in the human body under the influence of anesthesia, drugs and other stimulants was given here today by Dr. G. H. Richter, National Research Council Fellow at Cornell, before a gathering of 200 nationally prominent chemists attending the three-day Colloidal Symposium at Cornell University, in a paper on "The Chemistry of Anesthesia."

While the effects of the drugs have

been known, Dr. Richter said, so far there has been no adequate theory of narcosis, no adequate explanation of what takes place in the body under their influence. So he started to find out just what chemical and physical reactions take place.

"After a number of experiments," he said, "we have come to believe that back of all the different types of narcosis, whether they come from a blow on the head by a thug's blackjack, a knockout blow in the ring, the anesthesia administered in the operating room or the drug taken by the drug addict, there is one and the same cause. They are all due to a reversible coagulation of the cells."

Found Two Types.

"There are two types of coagulation of the cells. In the one case the coagulation is permanent, in the other the cell goes back to its normal state after the cause of coagulation is removed. The first is known as reversible and the second as irreversible coagulation.

"By coagulation," said Dr. Richter, "we mean formation of larger particles by the agglomeration of the smaller particles in the cell. When the cell is in a state of coagulation it is narcotized. When the drug is removed the colloidal material is again peptized, going back to its normal state.

"In order to prove that coagulation did take place we examined a number of small organisms we could get under the ultra-microscope. We put the small organisms under an ultra-microscopic instrument powerful enough to make us see colloidal particles actually in movement within the living cells and when the narcotic was added we could actually see the colloids come together and coagulate.

"When the narcotic was removed we could see the colloids peptized again and go back to their normal state.

"If the colloidal theory of reversible coagulation is right, then any coagulation should lead to a state of narcosis. If you coagulate material in cells by heat, for example, when the room is hot, you go to sleep. That is due probably to the coagulation of the colloidal particles in the body, probably the nerves."

Egyptians Used Mallet.

"Surgeons among the early Egyptians produced anesthesia when operating by fitting a wooden block on the patients head and hitting him on top of it with a mallet. The art consisted in making the blow neither too hard so that it would kill the patient, nor too mild so that it would not make him unconscious.

"What actually happened was that they produced a state of narcosis by bringing about a reversible coagulation of the cells. A prize fighter in the ring, administering a knockout blow, produces the same result."

Professor Wilder B. Bancroft of Cornell, one of the leading physical chemists in the country, hailed the discovery as being of far-reaching importance to medicine, especially in the treatment and cure of drug addicts.

Roller Magnet Experiments

In 1991, Brian DeMetz and myself performed some experiments on roller magnets. Some of these experiments were described in *ESJ* #1, 2, and 3. Anyone wishing to investigate "roller motors" further should review those notes carefully.

The rollers behaved and performed very much in the fashion as those described by Searl for his Levity Disk.

The following reports are from my 1991 experiments, which were not detailed at the time. The setup of the roller magnet motor and generator was as diagrammed in Fig. 5.

Experiment I: If the roller magnet is placed directly on the 1/8-inch thick flat steel plate and pushed manually in the direction shown, it rolls with a "sticky" resistance as though the magnet wants to hold itself in place on the steel. When it reaches the hole in the steel plate, it sluggishly wants to bounce backward. If pushed hard enough to cross the hole, the roller will zip around the far edge and roll on the underside since the neodymium magnets cling tenaciously.

Experiment II: Aluminum rails, 1/16-inch thick, are placed on each edge of the steel plate. The roller now rolls freely; the sticky resistance is gone. However, the attraction to the steel plate is still strong. Given a push in the direction shown, and as done in Experiment I, the roller bounces back vigorously from the hole, like an elastic rubber ball. If pushed vigorously to the plate edge, it zips around the edge easily.

Experiment III: A piece of Mylar tape is placed on top of the aluminum rails as an insulating barrier. The roller now rolls with the same sticky resistance, and to the same degree as it did in Experiment I.

For the apparatus to work in the fashion described, the roller magnet must be constructed so as to have opposing fields at its center: N-S:S-N. (A traditional single directional N-S polarization will not work.) I was first told about this opposing field roller motor design in 1962. It is assumed that the Searl rollers use opposing field design.

The opposing-field roller magnet, which is encased in a conductive material, has the following properties:

1. If an electric current is passed through the conductor sleeve to cross the roller central field, it will cause the conductor to rotate. This will happen whether the conductor is attached to the magnets or not. Only the conductor will rotate if it is not attached to the magnets.

2. If the roller magnet assembly is rotated about its axis, a voltage differential will develop in the conductive outer sleeve on each side of the opposing magnetic poles. This is, in effect, a homopolar generator configuration.

3. The rollers, placed on the outer periphery of a pair of steel rings, with an aluminum track layer, can be made to motor vigorously around with a battery terminal attached to the top and bottom rings. Basically, the flat track of Fig. 5 is wrapped into a closed ring shape. The apparatus can also perform as a generator if the rollers are forced around.

These experiments (from early 1991) involve many characteristics of Searl's roller, and that is why they are mentioned. Perhaps this will help experimenters who want to look further into this matter.

For more information on John R. R. Searl and his Levity Disk, or to order any of his books on the subject, contact John A. Thomas, Jr., 373 Rock Beach Road, Rochester, New York 14617-1316 USA. ▼

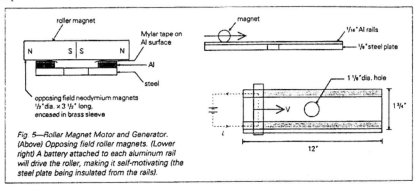

Fig. 5—Roller Magnet Motor and Generator. (Above) Opposing field roller magnets. (Lower right) A battery attached to each aluminum rail will drive the roller, making it self-motivating (the steel plate being insulated from the rails).

A New Homopolar Generator Design

By Thomas Valone, PhD

Recurring interest in the Searl device, as pictured on the cover of Antigravity, the biography of Searl by John Thomas, should also center on the homopolar generator (HPG). Preliminary analysis reveals that there are actually two separate HPG phenomena occurring simultaneously, one which can be called the "revolution" effect (#1) and the second that could be called the "rolling" effect (#2). The first effect can be visualized as magnetized segments of an imaginary solid ring revolving around a common center. As suggested by drawings in my Homopolar Handbook (HH), p.141-2, there are precedent designs that allow for segmenting an HPG rotor.

With this model in mind, the #1 effect can be calculated, for 1 Tesla strength magnets, magnetized axially, adjacent to a single ring 1 meter in diameter, to produce more than 2 volts emf across each roller, (E field directed radially from outer diameter of rollers to outer diameter of the adjacent ring) with say, 500 RPM. Note that this #1 effect is independent of any rolling of the magnet. The magnetic field in an HPG is tied to space and not to the magnet so rolling will not affect this large scale homopolar generator's Lorentz force effect (HH, p.10).

The #2 effect, located within each roller magnet, is the one noted in Electric Spacecraft Journal, Issue 12, 1994, (HH, p.160) where each roller, is a small homopolar generator. This effect is found to be somewhat weaker as it generates electricity from the center of each roller to its periphery. This design is like Tesla's HPG (HH, p.81) where a rolling belt is contacting the outer edge of a circular magnet. With rollers in the vicinity of a tenth of a meter in diameter rolling, without slipping, around a 1 meter ring, approximately a half of a volt will be generated. The Searl design of ring magnetic material will normally strengthen the roller's B field.

It is important to realize at this point that the principle of superposition applies to these two effects. The #1 effect is a uniform E field across the diameter of the roller. The #2 effect is a radial effect as stated above (see HH, p.6-8). However, only the emf in the section of a roller between the two contacts, say at the center of the roller and its edge which contacts the ring, will actually cause current flow in any external circuit. This realization means that the effective voltage from the #1 effect will be half of the available emf, or a little more than 1 volt, which is still about double of the #2 effect. Upon applying superposition in the limited region indicated, we also find that the two effects oppose each other and the two emfs must be subtracted.

The result of this analysis is that approximately one half of a volt of regulated emf will be present to generate electricity from a single set of rollers and one ring about 1 meter in diameter. As current is drawn, a Ball Bearing Motor effect will also take place (HH, p.54) that actually pushes the rollers along, assuming the roller magnets have a reasonable conductivity.*

In a related work, (Tech. Phys. Lett., V. 26, #12, 2000, p.1105-07), Roshchin and Godin have published experimental results of their one-ring device, called a Magnetic Energy Converter, with rolling magnets on bearings. Though my above analysis does not depend upon the ring being made of magnetic material, Roshchin and Godin did so. Their

---

* Thanks to Dr. Paul LaViolette for this reminder.

findings are encouraging enough for researchers to find renewed interest in this type of magnetic motor.

SPACE

POWER

Editor's Note: Paramahamsa Tewari received his B.Sc. Engineering (Electrical) degree from Ganaras Engineering College, Banaras Hindu Univeristy, India, in 1958.

After working initially in Bhilai Steel Project on electrical installations, he joined Department of Atomic Energy and worked at Plutonium Plant of electrical works. For one year he was deputed to Douglas Point Nuclear Generating Station (1964-65) for training in field engineering and installation of electrical equipment in Nuclear Power Projects. He worked as Erection Superintendent (Electrical) at Rajasthan Atomic Power Project; Deputy Chief Engineer at Narora Atomic Power Project; Chief of Transmission in National Thermal Power Corporation, India, and ' then to Head of Quality Assurance, 500 MWe Group, Nuclear Power Board, Department of ATomic Energy.

He has authored works on electron structure with space dynamics.

For the presentation of Space Power Generation and lecture on the new principles of space vortex theory he was awarded first prize at The International Congress of Gravity Field Energy held at Hannover, West Germany in March 1987.

G E N E R A T I O N

BY P. Tewari
Chief Project Engineer
Kaiga Project
Kaiga-581 400
Karnataka
India

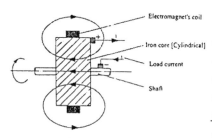

FIGURE 1
DEPALMA'S N-MACHINE

It *has been elsewhere discussed that a rotating electromagnet with its coil mounted rigidly around a cylindrical iron core and in rotation with the core (figure1) develops DC voltage between the core's periphery and the axis of rotation when DC excitaiton is given to the coil. Also, conclusive experimental results have revealed that the passage of the load current across the longitudinal magnetic field in the core, does not create torque in opposition ot the prime mover's torque, which is unlike the case of a conventional homopolar generator.*

MAGNETS

August, 1988

(The basic difference between a conventional homopolar generator and a space power generator (SPG) is in the mounting of the electromagnet's coil. While in the homopolar generator there is relative

disc rotate together (figure 3B) voltage is induced similar to the case shown in figure 3A. From above it is evident that for the electromagnetic induction to take place with a steady flux in the conducting disc, rotation of the conductor (disc) is essential.

All the known effects of voltage generation due to magnetic induction in DC/AC generators and also transformers take place due to "flux changes" in circuits. In the absence of "flux changes" in the rotating disc conductor, the generatio of EMF is pinpointed due to the rotation of interatomic space as discussed in earlier articles1 describing the phenomenon of space power generation. The electron and other material particles including atoms and molecules are considered as "space vorticles" as per Space Vortex Theory2 and it follows that in the rotating disc conductor referred above, along with the space vortices of the atoms and electrons, the inter-atomic space

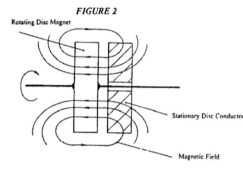

FIGURE 2

Rotating Disc Magnet

Stationary Disc Conductor

Magnetic Field

motion between the coil and the core's conductor, in SPG such a relative motion is non existent). It can thus be inferred that in SPG, due to the co-rotation of the coil and the core, the magnetic field produced by the coil and the magnetic field of the load current, have no relative motion and that should precisely be the basic reason for the absence of torque in opposition to the prime mover's torque when the machine is loaded. Regarding generation of voltage in SPG, the "N-effect" discovered by Bruce DePalma is in accordance with the results of experiments carried out in 1831 by Faraday as discussed below:

Refer to Figure 2. A rotating magnet does not induce voltage in a stationary conducting disc, though there is relative motion between the magnet and conductor. If the disc is rotated and the magnet is kept stationary (figure 3A) voltage is induced despite the fact that in both the above cases, there is no "flux changes: through the conducting disc. Again, when the magnet and the

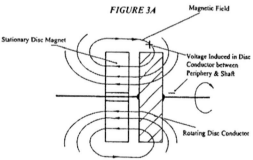

FIGURE 3A

Magnetic Field

Stationary Disc Magnet

Voltage Induced in Disc Conductor between Periphery & Shaft

Rotating Disc Conductor

also rotates. The release of orbital electrons, due to interatomic space rotation and further interaction with magnetic field that deflects the electrons and thus forms the electrical polarities and thus forms the electrical polarties have been analysed before1. In the following pages, experimental findings on different

FIGURE 3B

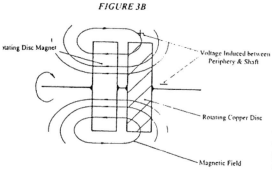

Rotating Disc Magnet

Voltage Induced between Periphery & Shaft

Rotating Copper Disc

Magnetic Field

very high and was most accurately measured3 as 760%. In figure 4, basic design of a homopolar generator developed by Adam Trombly[4] is shown. The magnetic field's path through air is across a narrow gap and this reduces the ampereturns to a large extent, however, the disadvantages of this system revealed through the experiments by the writer is in the generation of high torque in opposition to the prime mover within the airgap through which the load current passes through and hence, the advantage of free power generation in the core is substantially lost.

types of SPGs that provide positive proof on the generation of power from space at efficiency much higher than unity are reported.

DEVEOPMENT OF SPACE POWER GENERATORS:

A rotating electromagnet (figure 1) with the coil rigidly mounted around the core, was first discovered by Bruce DePalma who named it as "N-Generator". The air return path for the magnetic field being large, the machine requires much higher ampere-turns compared to other designs discussed below, however, the efficiency of power generation of "N-Generator" is

Figure 5 shows basic features of SPG, in which the loss of power in the airgap-1 as mentioned above is partly gained in the airgap-2 since the direction of load current in the airgap-2 is reversed while the magnetic field direction in both the airgaps remain the sam. The machine abbreviated as SPGM is in fact a combination of SPG and Space Power Motor (SPM). Efficiency as high as 400% at load current of 3000 A DC and generated voltage 3V DC, at 3000 rpm have been repeatedly measured from different designs of SPGMs.

Fig. 6 shows another design of sPG where major portion of the magnetic path is static and thus reduces the rotating mass of the SPG. the advantage of this system is that the load current does not pass through an air gap, and the magnetic field is totally confined within the rotating and stationary iron paths. Initial tests showed that the passage of load current through the shaft interacts, through its magnetic field, with the magnetic field in the stationary verticla iron path and thereby reduces the efficiency. A larger opening in the verticla iron path around the rotating shaft does provide solutio partly to the above loss of power. However, further detailed tests indicate that the static iron paths on either side of the

FIGURE 4
TROMBLY'S HOMOPOLAR GENERATOR

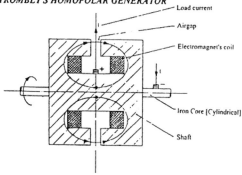

Load current

Airgap

Electromagnet's coil

Iron Core [Cylindrical]

Shaft

FIGURE 5
SPACE POWER GENERATOR

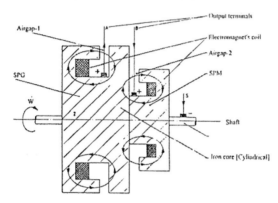

Airgap-1

SPG

W

Note: Terminal 'A' is more positive than terminal 'B'

Output terminals

Electromagnet's coil

Airgap-2

SPM

Shaft

Iron core [Cylindrical]

field in the core. Motor action takes place only in the airgap-2 of the SPM unit (figure 5). Whereas in the conventional motor unit (figure 7) the magnetic circuit being different (in the sense that there exists a relativ motion between the magnetic field and the rotating disc conductor), motor torque is produced on the entire surface on the rotating disc, whenever it is cut by the flux.

VOLTAGE DISTRIBUTION IN SPGM:

Refer to figure 8. If the radius of the central core of SPG is rg, Bg is the magnetic field there and W is the angular velocity, the voltage developed in SPG,

$$V_g = (^1/_2)w\, B_g r_g$$

Similarly, the voltage developed in the central core of SPM,

$$V_m = (^1/_2)w\, B_m r_m$$

If the magnetic field in the outer flux returns paths for SPG and SPM are B'g and B'm respectively. the corresponding voltages induced in the outer paths will be,

$$V'_g = (^1/_2)w\, B'_g (r_g\, -r^2_g)$$

and

$$V'_m = (^1/_2)w\, B'_m (r_m\, -r^2_m)$$

The voltages measured between terminals A, S, and B, S, are V_g and V_m respectively.

Though the leads A and B to the respective output brushes do cut the flux in the airgap-1 and airgap-2, no voltage is induced in the leads due to these flux

rotating electromagnet, hold the magnetic field stationary. The efficiency of power generation in the rotating iron core falls down thereby indicating that the rotaiton of the magnetic field within the core and along with the core conductor is obstructed due to the stationary paths external to the rotating iron core.

Figure 7 shows a SPG coupled to a SPM where SPM's design is based on conventional motor design. The design of the SPG is similar to the one described in figure 5, except for the SPM part. The efficiency of this set is about 300%. The advantage of this motor over SPM shown in Figure 5, is in fact that in SPM, there is a disadvantage in the load current being pushed against the voltage developed within the core and yet there is no torque due to the absence of relative motion between the core conductor and the magnetic changes. This is in accordance with Faraday's experiment (figure 2) that a rotating disc magnet does not induce voltage on a stationary conducting disc. If, however instead of stationary lead A, a nonmagnetic ring is welded at the inner core of the SPG as shown in figure 9 due to which the ring is now rotating with the core, the voltage induced between the output brush and the shaft will be $(V_s - V'_s)$.

The voltages between points C, D and S at shaft are also quite close to $(V_s - V'_s)$ and $(V_m - V'_m)$ respectively.

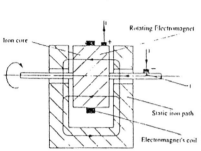

FIGURE 6

Labels: Rotating Electromagnet; Iron core; Static iron path; Electromagnet's coil

TORQUE DEVELOPED IN SPM:

The load current from SPG (figure 5) is fed to sPM through a shunt connected between the terminals A and B. The output/input terminals of SPG/SPM are non-magnetic aluminium rings tipped with heavy copper/graphite brushes that can carry three to four kilo-ampheres current. The stationary aluminium ring with brushes in the airgap-2 feeding power to SPM has no induced voltage in the airgap as stated before. However, there is positive torque developed in airgap-2. Here is a case of generation of torque in the airgap of SPM without any back EMF in the air gap. The current flows in the central core of SPM against the induced voltage V_m, resulting in some loss of generated voltage V_s, but producing no torque within the core since the cirrent and the magnetic field there have no relative motion.

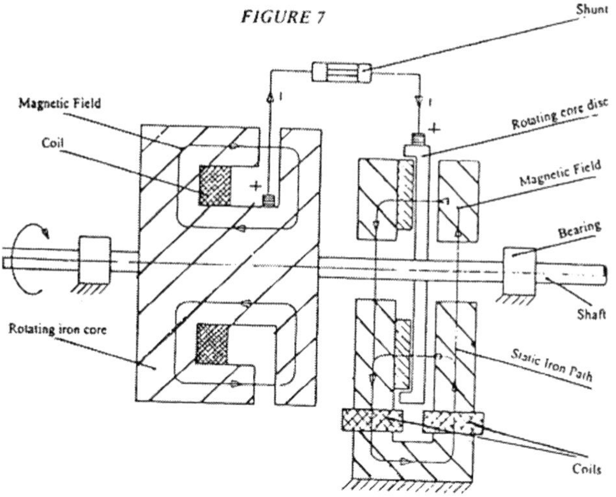

ROTATION OF MAGNETIC FIELD

Refer to Figure 8. In the airgap-1 the output current flows through the stationary brushes. For the production of torque (in opposition to DM's torque for rotation) the magnetic

FIGURE 7

Labels: Magnetic Field; Coil; Rotating iron core; Shunt; Rotating core disc; Magnetic Field; Bearing; Shaft; Static Iron Path; Coils

FIGURE 8
SPACE POWER GENERATOR

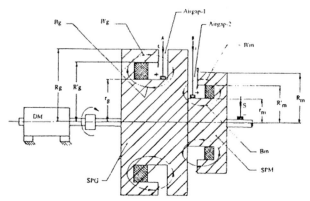

Note: Terminal 'A' is more positive then terminal 'B'

field interacting with the stationary brushes in the airgap must be rotating. Therefore, it is concluded that if the entire path of the magnetic fields (B_g, B'_g) is through the magnetic iron which is co-rotating with the coil that produced the fields, then the magnetic field will rotate not only along with the iron core as stated above, but also in the intervening airgap. Whereas, in case of figure 6, where only part of the magnetic path is though stationary iron, the magnetic field behaves as if it is held stationary not only in the stationary iron paths but also within the rotating electromagnet's core despite the co-rotation of the coil and the ironcore. In figure 9, the non-magnetic metal ring welded to the iron core rotates with it, and since the magntic field in the airgap also rotates, no torque can be developed there. free power can thus be drawn between the terminals A and S, but for teh fact that the voltage between a and S is reduced to (V_a - V'_a). which has a low value.

ELECTRICAL OUTPUT GREATER THAN MECHANICAL INPUT

The test results of a SPG are shown in Table-1, The

open circuit characteristic curves for SPG and SPM are shown in figure 10. BAsed on the results in Table-1, input/output power curves against speed of rotation are shown in figure 11. It is seen that around 2500 rpm, electrical output I^2R) form the SPG exceeds the

FIGURE 9

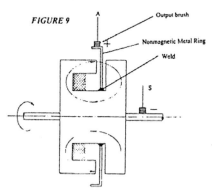

mechanical input to SPG given to rotate it.

As discussed before, there is loss of power of SPG in the core of the SPM where current is forced against the back eMF developed there, without generation of equivalent torque to aid the DM. If this power, termed here as "electromagnetic power" is also added to I²R power, total output power curve becomes much steeper as shown in figure 11. A comparison between the curves A and D shows that the rise in mechanical input to sPG when loaded at varying speed is slower than the generatio of the corresponding I²R power, which, however, is never the case in conventional electrical generation.

The above tests are only the very few of the numerous tests performed to discover the source of generation of electrical power that exceeds the input mechanical power and therby violates the law of conservation of energy and also the law of conservation of charge. The only recourse to save these laws is to recognize that the absolute vacuum rather than being an extension of nothingness, is the fundamental and universal substratum of basic reality.

FIGURE 10
OPEN CIRCUIT CHARACTERISTICS (O.C.C.) CURVE

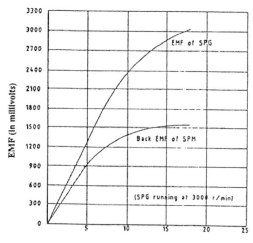

Excitation Current (Amps)

SPG's electromagnet: 2.5 ohms
Turns: 399
14 SWG
Iron core dia: 230 mm

SPM's electromagnet: 1.25 Ohms
Turns: 350
145 SWG
Iron core dia: 140 mm

MAGNETS

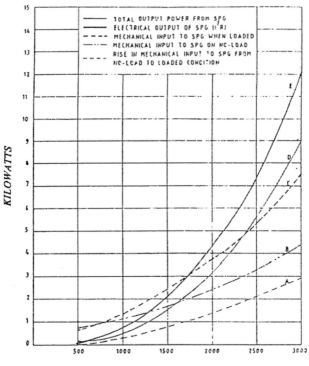

FIGURE 11
INPUT/OUTPUT
POWER V/S SPEED
OF POWER
GENERATOR

Legend (in figure):
— TOTAL OUTPUT POWER FROM SPG
— ELECTRICAL OUTPUT OF SPG (I^2R)
- - - MECHANICAL INPUT TO SPG WHEN LOADED
-·-·- MECHANICAL INPUT TO SPG ON NC-LOAD
— — RISE IN MECHANICAL INPUT TO SPG FROM
NO-LOAD TO LOADED CONDITION

KILOWATTS (vertical axis): 0–15

SPEED - RPM (horizontal axis): 500, 1000, 1500, 2000, 2500, 3000

I)	SPG's E.M.F. - VOLT (dc)	0.305	1.013	1.523	2.022	2.537	3.010
II)	SPM's BACK E.M.F. - (dc)	0.298	0.517	0.776	1.023	1.294	1.548
III)	DM's TERMINAL VOLTAGE - VOLT (dc)	90	170	240	315	385	440
IV)	DM's NO-LOAD CURRENT - AMPS (dc)	7.6	8.75	9	9.6	10	11.75
V)	DM's ON-LOAD CURRENT - AMPS (dc)	8.25	10	13	14.75	17	18.75
VI)	INPUT (MECHANICAL) TO SPG WITH DM's EFFICIENCY AS 82% ON NO-LOAD - WATTS (III) x (IV) 0.82	560.8	1219.7	1771.2	2479.6	3157	4432
VII)	INPUT (MECHANICAL) TO SPG ON-LOAD WITH DM's EFFICIENCY AS 82% (III) x (V) 0.82	608.8	1394	2358.4	3909.9	5346.9	7449.7
VIII)	RISE IN MECHANICAL INPUT TO SPG WHEN LOADED - WATTS	48	174.2	587.2	1330.7	2709.9	3312.7
IX)	LOAD CURRENT OF SPG - AMPS	200	520	1120	1613.3	2213.3	2494.6
X)	ELECTRICAL OUTPUT (I^2R) OF SPG - WATTS (I) x (IX)	101	526.7	1705.7	3263.7	5559.8	9049.3
XI)	ELECTROMAGNETIC POWER DELIVERED TO SPM AND NOT CONVERTED TO MECHANICAL POWER - WATTS (II) x (IX)	59.6	268.8	871.3	1645.5	2866.4	4622.7
XII)	TOTAL POWER FROM SPG - WATTS (X) + (XI)	137.6	795.5	2577	4924.2	8426.2	13672.5
XIII)	SPEED - R.P.M.	600	1002	1508	2002	2512	3000
XIV)	MAGNETIC EXCITATION AMPS (dc)	18	18	18	18	18	18

TABLE 1
SPACE POWER
GENERATOR - MOTOR
(SPGM) TEST RESULTS

SPG: SPACE POWER GENERATOR
SPM: SPACE POWER MOTOR
DM: DRIVE MOTOR
SPG'S ELECTROMAGNET: 2.5 Ohms.
SPM'S ELECTROMAGNET: 1.25 Ohms.

MAGNETS

Integrity Research Institute
1377 K Street NW, Suite 204
Washington, DC 20005
202-452-7674, 1-800-295-7674

Dr. Beverly Rubik   6-7-94
Center for Frontier Sciences
Temple University
Philadelphia, PA

Dear Bev,

Thank you for inviting me to supply a short statement debating the claims of N-machine researchers. I will attempt to be brief and summarize my opinions.

You may be aware of my book on the subject, *The Homopolar Handbook: A Definitive Guide to Faraday Disk and N-Machine Technologies*, due to be reprinted in paperback this summer, which includes my Master's Thesis and provides the basis for much of my argument.

My critique starts with Paramahansa Tewari's 1993 ISNE paper, which upon the invitation of Toby Grotz, I wrote a two-page "Tewari Report" analyzing his mistakes with the N-machine. Tewari believes that there is an absence of relative motion between the conductor and the magnetic field, which shows he has not done a literature search. He also proposes that such a low voltage, high current machine proves his Space Vortex Theory which generates "mass of electron from the mass-less medium of space". Experimentally, he fails to mention the power factor of the AC drive motor or the motor efficiency curve, both of which are vital to input power calculations. Tewari also uses I^2R for calculation of the output power of the homopolar generator instead of the more reliable $P = IV$. This doubles the error in the measurement of current, not mentioning the resistor error, which can be as high as 10%. Yet, when his machine shows a large, increasing back torque, or drag, Tewari still wants to claim 9 kW output from the machine with 7 kW input. It's basically an error in measurement.

Since you mention Inomata,* I will comment briefly on his latest paper from 1993 IECEC which is based upon only a 3 inch disc magnet with a 2.5" hole in it! The hole actually reverses the field through the conductor, as shown graphically in my paper on "Armature Reaction the the Homopolar Generator" published in the *1993 ISNE Proceedings* . This only begins the problems for Inomata for his current shunt is a milliohm shunt instead of a microhm shunt while his brush resistance varies radically up to 70 milliohms. With all of this resistance, it is not unusual that the input power to his drive motor goes as high as *300 watts* but his little N-machine only can put out *10 watts* at its peak (3% total efficiency!). He also admits that his back torque is "rather big" but because his homopolar generator output seems to increase with speed, he states that "we had confirmed the incremental over-unity or local violation of energy conservation law. We have concluded that the N-machine is one of different devices and machines which can elicit electrical energy from the vacuum." The basis for his conclusion should never include "incremental" efficiency for even a lightbulb will show over-unity efficiency incrementally.

Lastly, the originator of the term "N-machine", Mr. Bruce DePalma, is the subject of my 10-page article in the summer edition of *Extraordinary Science* entitled, "The Real Story of the N-Machine" which was suppressed by the 1994 ISNE Steering Committee. After fourteen years, I have finally described the details of the early 1980's when N-machine technology was at its peak. All of the critical photos and quotations are included for the public to reach an informed conclusion.

Sincerely,

Tom Valone

*Shiuji Inomata, Ph.D.
Japan Psychotronics Institute
2-2-2, Sekigawa-cho, Arai-shi
Niigata 944, Japan

256   THE ELECTRICAL ENGINEER.   [Sept. 2, 1891.

NOTES ON A UNIPOLAR DYNAMO.

BY

Nikola Tesla

It is characteristic of fundamental discoveries, of great achievements of intellect, that they retain an undiminished power upon the imagination of the thinker. The memorable experiment of Faraday with a disc rotating between the two poles of a magnet, which has borne such magnificent fruit, has long passed into every-day experience; yet there are certain features about this embryo of the present dynamos and motors which even to-day appear to us striking, and are worthy of the most careful study.

Consider, for instance, the case of a disc of iron or other metal revolving between the two opposite poles of a magnet, and the polar surfaces completely covering both sides of the disc, and assume the current to be taken off or conveyed to the same by contacts uniformly from all points of the periphery of the disc. Take first the case of a motor. In all ordinary motors the operation is dependent upon some shifting or change of the resultant of the magnetic attraction exerted upon the armature, this process being effected either by some mechanical contrivance on the motor or by the action of currents of the proper character. We may explain the operation of such a motor just as we can that of a water-wheel. But in the above example of the disc surrounded completely by the polar surfaces, there is no shifting of the magnetic action, no change whatever, as far as we know, and yet rotation ensues. Here, then, ordinary considerations do not apply ; we can not even give a superficial explanation, as in ordinary motors, and the operation will be clear to us only when we shall have recognized the very nature of the forces concerned and fathomed the mystery of the invisible connecting mechanism.

Considered as a dynamo machine, the disc is an equally interesting object of study. In addition to its peculiarity of giving currents of one direction without the employment of commutating devices, such a machine differs from ordinary dynamos in that there is no reaction between armature and field. The armature current tends to set up a magnetization at right angles to that of the field current, but since the current is taken off uniformly from all points of the periphery, and since, to be exact, the external circuit may also be arranged perfectly symmetrical to the field magnet, no reaction can occur. This, however, is true only as long as the magnets are weakly energized, for when the magnets are more or less saturated, both magnetizations at right angles seemingly interfere with each other.

For the above reason alone it would appear that the output of such a machine should, for the same weight, be much greater than that of any other machine in which the armature current tends to demagnetize the field. The extraordinary output of the Forbes unipolar dynamo and the experience of the writer confirm this view.

Again, the facility with which such a machine may be made to excite itself is striking, but this may be due—besides to the absence of armature reaction—to the perfect smoothness of the current and non-existence of self-induction.

If the poles do not cover the disc completely on both sides, then, of course, unless the disc be properly subdivided, the machine will be very inefficient. Again, in this case there are certain points worthy of notice. If the disc be rotated and the field current interrupted, the current through the armature will continue to flow and the field magnets will lose their strength comparatively slowly. The reason of this will at once appear when we consider the direction of the currents set up in the disc.

Referring to diagram in Fig. 1, *d* represents the disc with the sliding contacts B B' on the shaft and periphery.

x and s represent the two poles of a magnet. If the pole N be above, as indicated in the diagram, the disc being supposed to be in the plane of the paper, and rotating in the direction of the arrow D, the current set up in the disc will flow from the centre to the periphery, as indicated by the arrow A. Since the magnetic action is more or less confined to the space between the poles N s, the other portions of the disc may be considered inactive. The current set up will therefore not wholly pass through the external circuit F, but will close through the disc itself, and generally, if the disposition be in any way similar to the one illustrated, by far the greater portion of the current generated will not appear externally, as the circuit F is practically short circuited by the inactive portions of the disc. The direction of the resulting currents in the latter may be assumed to be as indicated by the dotted lines and arrows *m* and *n* ; and the direction of the energizing field current being indicated by the arrows *a b c d*, an inspection of the figure shows that one of the two branches of the eddy current, that is, A B' *m* B, will tend to demagnetize the field, while the other branch, that is, A B' *n* B, will have the opposite effect. Therefore the branch A B *m* B that is, the one which is *approaching* the field, will repel the lines of the same, while branch A B' *n* B, that is, the one *leaving* the field, will gather the lines of force upon itself.

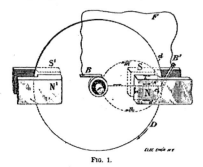

FIG. 1.

In consequence of this there will be a constant tendency to reduce the current flow in the path A B' *m* B, while on the other hand no such opposition will exist in path A B' *n* B, and the effect of the latter branch or path will be more or less preponderating over that of the former. The joint effect of both the assumed branch currents might be represented by that of one single current of the same direction as that energizing the field. In other words, the eddy currents circulating in the disc will energize the field magnet. Since as a result quite contrary to what we might be led to suppose at first, for we would naturally expect that the resulting effect of the armature currents would be such as to oppose the field current, as generally occurs when a primary and secondary conductor are placed in inductive relations to each other. But it must be remembered that this results from the peculiar disposition in this case, namely, two paths being afforded to the current, and the latter selecting that path which offers the least opposition to its flow. From this we see that the eddy currents flowing in the disc partly energize the field, and for this reason when the field current is interrupted the currents in the disc will continue to flow, and the field magnet will lose its strength with comparative slowness and may even retain a certain strength as long as the rotation of the disc is continued.

The result will, of course, largely depend on the resistance and geometrical dimensions of the path of the result-

172

ing eddy current and on the speed of rotation ; these elements, namely, determine the retardation of this current
and its position relative to the field. For a certain speed
there would be a maximum energizing action ; then at
higher speeds, it would gradually fall off to zero and finally
reverse, that is, the resultant eddy current effect would be
to weaken the field. The reaction would be best demonstrated experimentally by arranging the fields N s, N′ s,
freely movable on an axis concentric with the shaft of the
disc. If the latter were rotated as before in the direction
of the arrow D the field would be dragged in the same
direction with a torque, which, up to a certain point,

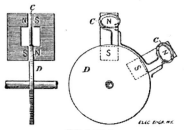

FIGS. 2 AND 3.

would go on increasing with the speed of rotation, then fall
off, and, passing through zero, finally become negative ;
that is, the field would begin to rotate in opposite direction
to the disc. In experiments with alternate current motors
in which the field was shifted by currents of differing
phase, this interesting result was observed. For very low
speeds of rotation of the field the motor would show
a torque of 900 lbs. or more, measured on a pulley 12
inches in diameter. When the speed of rotation of the
poles was increased the torque would diminish, would
finally go down to zero, become negative, and then the
armature would begin to rotate in opposite direction to the
field.

To return to the principal subject; assume the conditions
to be such that the eddy currents generated by the rotation of the disc strengthen the field, and suppose the latter
gradually removed while the disc is kept rotating at an
increased rate. The current, once started, may then be
sufficient to maintain itself and even increase in strength,
and then we have the case of Sir William Thomson's "current accumulator." But from the above considerations it
would seem that for the success of the experiment the employment of a disc not subdivided would be essential, for
if there would be a radial subdivision, the eddy currents
could not form and the self-exciting action would cease. If
such a radially subdivided disc were used it would be necessary to connect the spokes by a conducting rim or in any
proper manner so as to form a symmetrical system of closed
circuits.

The action of the eddy currents may be utilized to excite
a machine of any construction. For instance, in Figs. 2
and 3 an arrangement is shown by which a machine with
a disc armature might be excited. Here a number of magnets, N s, N s, are placed radially on each side of a metal
disc D carrying on its rim a set of insulated coils, c, c. The
magnets form two separate fields, an internal and external
one, the part of the disc rotating in the field nearest to the axis,
and the coils in the field further from it. Assume the
magnets slightly energized at the start ; they could be
strengthened by the action of the eddy currents in the solid
disc so as to afford a stronger field for the peripheral coils.
Although there is no doubt that under proper conditions a
machine might be excited in this or a similar manner, there
being sufficient experimental evidence to warrant such an
assertion, such a mode of exciting would be wasteful.

But a unipolar dynamo or motor, such as shown in Fig.
1, may be excited in an efficient manner by simply
properly subdividing the disc or cylinder in which the cur-

rents are set up, and it is practicable to do away with the
field coils which are usually employed. Such a plan is
illustrated in Fig. 4. The disc or cylinder D is supposed to
be arranged to rotate between the two poles N and s of a
magnet, which completely cover it on both sides, the contours of the disc and poles being represented by the circles
d and d′ respectively, the upper pole being omitted for the
sake of clearness. The cores of the magnet are supposed
to be hollow, the shaft c of the disc passing through them.
If the unmarked pole be below, and the disc be rotated
screw fashion, the current will be, as before, from the centre to the periphery and may be taken off by suitable sliding contacts, B B′, on the shaft and periphery respectively.
In this arrangement the current flowing through the disc
and external circuit will have no appreciable effect on the
field magnet.

But let us now suppose the disc to be subdivided spirally,
as indicated by the full or dotted lines, Fig. 4. The difference of potential between a point on the shaft and a
point on the periphery will remain unchanged, in sign as
well as in amount. The only difference will be that the
resistance of the disc will be augmented and that there will
be a greater fall of potential from a point on the shaft to a
point on the periphery when the same current is traversing
the external circuit. But since the current is forced to
follow the lines of subdivision, we see that it will tend either
to energize or de-energize the field, and this will depend,
other things being equal, upon the direction of the lines of
subdivision. If the subdivision be as indicated by the
full lines in Fig. 4, it is evident that if the current is of the
same direction as before, that is, from centre to periphery,
its effect will be to strengthen the field magnet; whereas,
if the sub-division be as indicated by the dotted lines, the
current generated will tend to weaken the magnets. In
the former case the machine will be capable of exciting itself
when the disc is rotated in the direction of arrow D; in the
latter case the direction of rotation must be reversed. Two

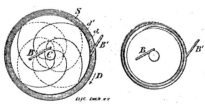

FIGS. 4 AND 5.

such discs may be combined, however, as indicated, the
two discs rotating in opposite fields, in the same or
opposite direction.

Similar dispositions may, of course, be made in a type
of machine in which, instead of a disc, a cylinder is rotated.
In such unipolar machines, in the manner indicated, the
usual field coils and poles may be omitted and the
machine may be made to consist only of a cylinder or of
two discs enveloped by a metal casting.

Instead of subdividing the disc or cylinder spirally, as
indicated in Fig. 4, it is more convenient to interpose one
or more turns between the disc and the contact ring on the
periphery, as illustrated in Fig. 5.

A Forbes dynamo may, for instance, be excited in such a
manner. In the experience of the writer it has been found
that instead of taking the current from two such discs by
sliding contacts, as usual, a flexible conducting belt may
be employed to advantage. The discs are in such case
provided with large flanges, affording a very great contact
surface. The belt should be made to bear on the flanges
with spring pressure to take up the expansion. Several
machines with belt contact were constructed by the writer
two years ago and worked satisfactorily, but for want of time
the work in that direction has been temporarily suspended.
A number of features pointed out above have also been
used by the writer in connection with some types of alternating current motors.

SELECTED LIST OF HOMOPOLAR (HPG) PATENTS		
338,169	Forbes	Dynamo cited by Tesla, iron core, single/dual coil (1886)
339,772	Hering	Unipolar Dynamo, multiple disk, field coil pairs
406,968	Tesla (1889)	Dynamo Electric Machine, 2-disk, conductive belt ☺
645,943	Dalen	Dynamo Electric Machine, 2-disk, opposite spin ☺
804,440	Steinmetz	Dynamo, "eliminates armature reaction", eddy currents☺
970,407	VonUgrimof	Electrical Sliding Contacts, liquid brush, radial force
970,827	Hubbard	Dynamo, radial laminations prevents backward spiral
1,919,139	Walton	Homopolar AC Generator, 2-disk, 2-transformer ☺
2,088,729	Taylor	Magnetic Reaction Motor, radial fins spray mercury ☹
2,408,080	Lloyd	Power Transmission Device, brush variations shown
3,185,877	Sears	Optimal spiral conductor path design strengthens field ☺
3,229,133	Sears	DC Homopolar Generators, spiral drum, spool designs
3,283,646	Havlicek	Photocathode Light, 2-disks, vacuum, no friction!
3,390,290	Kaplan	Statorless HPG Reaction Torque Generator
3,465,187	Breaux	Parallel Positioned Faraday Disks, pairs of disks ☺
3,469,137	Huhta-Koivi	Sodium Sulfate liquid brush, high speed, coolant
3,594,596	Eastham	Sectorially subdivided rotor, 2 magnetically separate
3,611,113	Cherry-RCA	Superconductive HPG, no moving parts, field moves! ☺
3,616,761	Valls	Homopolar Locomotive Railway, spiral conductor too
3,639,793	Appleton	Superconducting HPG Dynamoelectric Machines
3,646,394	Swartz (GE)	Vacuum Arc Commutator, energy pulses, multi-disk
3,736,450	Emaldi	Unipolar Double Inductor Dynamo, stops axial back flux
4,024,422	Gill	Homopolar Motor-Battery! Multi-disk and magnets ☺
4,034,248	Mole	Segmented Magnet HPG motor and generator
4,077,678	Studer	Energy Storage Apparatus (NASA)
4,097,758	Jenkins(GE)	Coaxial Disk Stack Acyclic Machine, multiple disks
4,105,963	Dobranis	Brushless Welding Generator
4,151,455	Janotik	Divided Housing, liquid metal expandable bellows (Ford)
4,185,216	Mole	Circumferentially Segmented HPG eliminates eddies
4,208,600	Hatch (GE)	Disk/Drum Acyclic Machine, plurality of disks
4,499,392	Giacoletto	HPG Alternator Power Conversion Machine
4,712,033	Hatch	Acyclic Generator - Liquid Metal Current Collectors
4,716,328	Shah	Magnetic Field Compensated Liquid Metal Collector
4,816,709	Weldon	Energy Density HPG, self-excited, electromagnetic
4,935,650	Hannan	MHD Turbomachine ferromagnetic rotors
5,032,748	Sakuraba	Superconducting DC Machine
5,144,179	Hilal	Superconducting Brushless HPG ☺
5,146,125	Kerlin	DC Machine Using Hall Effect Material
5,241,232	Reed	2-disk, belt, copied Tesla ☹, but inc. manufacturers info.
5,278,470	Neag	DC High Voltage Generator or Motor HPG
5,451,825	Strohm	Voltage Doubling HPG, co-rotating, cites Trombly ☺
5,530,309	Weldon	Homopolar Machine, solid brush lots of references
5,532,573	Brown	Reconfigurable Hybrid Power Generation System
5,587,618	Hathaway	DC HPG Machine, co-linear shafts cites Valone
5,723,925	Kambe	Superconductor Motor with Superconductor Shield ☺
5,821,659	Smith(USN)	Homopolar Transformer steps up voltage ☺
6,051,905	Clark	Homopolar – uses dielectric, magnet & conductor layers
6,822,361	Roschin	Orbiting Multi-Rotor Homopolar System , Searl generator
7,459,823	Kerlin	Resonant Unipolar Generator - AC high frequency

PCT

WORLD INTELLECTUAL PROPERTY ORGANIZATION
International Bureau

INTERNATIONAL APPLICATION PUBLISHED UNDER THE PATENT COOPERATION TREATY (PCT)

(51) International Patent Classification³ :		(11) International Publication Number:	WO 82/02126
H02K 31/00, 39/00	A1	(43) International Publication Date:	24 June 1982 (24.06.82)

(21) International Application Number: PCT/US81/01588

(22) International Filing Date: 1 December 1981 (01.12.81)

(31) Priority Application Number: 215,463

(32) Priority Date: 11 December 1980 (11.12.80)

(33) Priority Country: US

(71) Applicant: THE ACME ENERGY COMPANY [US/US]: 25 Mitchell Boulevard, San Rafael, CA 94903 (US).

(72) Inventors: TROMBLY, Adam, Douglass ; KAHN, Joseph, Mardell ; 25 Mitchell Boulevard, San Rafael, CA 94903 (US).

(74) Agent: SLONE, David, N.; Townsend and Townsend, One Market Plaza, Stewart Street Tower, San Francisco, CA 94105 (US).

(81) Designated States: AT (European patent), AU, BR, CH (European patent), DE, DE (European patent), DK, FI, FR (European patent), GB, GB (European patent), JP, NL (European patent), NO, SE (European patent), SU.

Published
With international search report.

I. CLASSIFICATION OF SUBJECT MATTER (if several classification symbols apply, indicate all)
According to International Patent Classification (IPC) or to both National Classification and IPC
B02K 31/00, 39/00
310 /178,219

II. FIELDS SEARCHED	
Minimum Documentation Searched⁴	
Classification System	Classification Symbols
U.S.	310/178,219,102R,102A,112-114

3,185,877	Sears	25 May 1965
3,736,450	Emaldi	29 May 1973
3,944,865	Jewitt	16 March 1976
2,408,080	Lloyd	24 Sept 1946
2,845,554	Schwab	29 July 1968
3,270,228	Rioui	30 Aug 1966
3,513,340	Appleton	19 May 1970

(54) Title: CLOSED PATH HOMOPOLAR MACHINE

(57) Abstract

A co-rotating homopolar generator has a rotor (12) comprising a disk conductor (30) and co-rotating coaxial electromagnets (32a and 32b) on either side, and achieves improved operation by utilizing a low reluctance magnetic return path for the magnetic flux that passes through the disk conductor (30). The low reluctance path permits the electromagnets (32a and 32b) to produce a high field with a relatively low value of coil excitation current. Thus overheating is avoided and the full potential of the homopolar generator is achieved. The low reluctance magnetic return path (220) is preferably provided by a relatively high permeability co-rotating enclosure having enclosure halves 32a and 37b) of sufficient radial and axial dimensions to enclose the electromagnets and disk conductor of the rotor. The disk conductor (30) is preferably constructed from a high permeability, low resistivity material such as iron, and can indeed be integral with the electromagnet cores (35a and 35b).

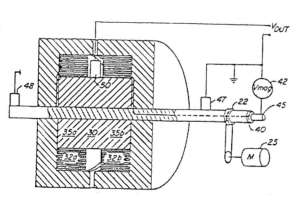

Adam Trombly's PTC Patent Application

日 本 意 識 工 学 会
JAPAN PSYCHOTRONICS INSTITUTE
2-2-2, Sekigawa-cho, Arai-shi, Niigata 944, Japan
Fax/Tel. 0255-72-0558
15 June 1998

Mr.Thomas Valone,President,
Integrity Research Institute,
1422 K Street NW, Suite 204,
Washington, D.C. 20005
U.S.A.

Dear Mr. Valone:

Thank you for your fax of 11, June. As there seems to be no
big room, I suggest the inclusion of my IECEC 1991 paper
entitled "New Paradigm And N-Machine" in the Appendix section.
At that time, I flew from Tokyo to New York and to Boston. And
we met at the conference.
The experiments as to the place of EMF of N-machine had indicated that it is in the copper disk and not in the conducting
wire from the brush. So, the relativity could not be applied for
the analysis. This was also asserted by Prof. Johnson from the
other experimental facts in the Forward in your book. Also, the
conservation laws of electrical charge and energy are violated
in N-machine. So, as Dr. Baily suggested, the N-machine
functioning is in conflict with the present,physiclaws. And we
need a new paradigm of science. Also, the interaction between
rotating magnetic field and current in the conducting wire causes
the back-toque. And the magnetic shielding conducting wire would
reduce it. Should you have any other inquiries, please fax me.

On the other hand,, I happened to talk with Mr. DePalma over
telephone several months before his passing. I asked "Will you be
back to CA". He answered "I won't, because, I had a lot of hard
time over there". It is sad that an America's towering scientific
genius passed away in exile and in despair in foreign land.
Your next book should be dedicated to the soul of Mr. DePalma.

Another sad thing is the suicide of Mr. Marinov. After fighting
the old paradigm scientic journals such as the Nature and etc.,
he staged a spectacular death diving from the top of the library
building of Gratz University, Austria, last summer. You should
comment it in the new book.
By the way, the Frontier Perspective of the Center For
Frontier sciences will publish my peer-reviewed article,
Consciousness(Ki) and New Science"in the upcomming issue.
In there, I treat Cold Fusion and N-machine problems in ⁻ more
broader perspectives. Also, we will have book exhibition and
sales place in the Nov.Symposium on Consciousness, New Medicine
and New Energy. Dr. Beverly Rubik isᴬUS agent of our conference.

With very best regards.   Sincerely yours
                                           Shiuji Inomata,phD
                                           Chairman of 2nd Sympo./
                                           President,JPI.

Prof. Inomata paper published in the Proceedings of the International Energy Conversion Engineering Conference (IECEC), 1991

IECEC

NEW PARADIGM AND N-MACHINE

Shiuji Inomata, ETL, MITI, Japan
1-1-4 Umezono, Tsukuba-shi, Ibaraki, Japan 305
Tel. 0298(58)5835

ABSTRACT

Relativistic EM fails to tell the exact place where an EMF appears in an N-machine. H.A. Lorentz's treatment in which stationary eather is assumed, gives the correct answer. Even in this case, the new-paradigm of science is necessary for the full understanding of the N-machine functioning.

INTRODUCTION

At the JPI monthly meeting held on 20 July 1990, in Tokyo, Mr. Toshiki Sugiyama of National/Panasonic presented an interesting paper entitled "Theory and Experiment of N-Machine"[1]. However, his treatment based on the relativistic EM has failed to tell the exact place where an EMF is created. Referring to his paper, this author thought the same problem by H.A. Lorentz's EM of absolutism, which presupposes the stationary eather. This treatment seems to give the result which conforms to the experimental reality. As the substance of the stationary eather, one might think a sea of neutrinos as elementary particles of consciousness-dimension and shadow physical parameters. As far as it expels the eather, the relativity is a materialistic doctrine. Nonetheless, in the sense that physical phenomena exist in the mind of an observer, it is an idealistic doctrine. This confuses the situation. Mathematical formulae are the same for both relativistic and absolutism treatments; the interpretations become different, however. The MKSA system will be used throughout.

THEORETICAL TREATMENTS

We designate an inertial system which is absolutely stationary as K(x,y,z,t). By K'(x', y',z',t'), we designate another inertial system which moves in the x direction, with velocity v. Fig. 1. We consider Lorentz's transformation as below[2].

$$x' = (x-c\beta t)/(1-\beta^2)^{\frac{1}{2}}$$

$$y' = y, \quad z' = z \qquad (1)$$

$$t' = [t-(1/c)\beta x]/(1-\beta^2)^{\frac{1}{2}}, \quad \beta = \frac{v}{c}$$

We think that, in the K system (absolutely stationary system), Maxwell equation is satisfied. That is, putting $\vec{x}=(x,y,z)$, as below.

$$\text{rot } \vec{H}(\vec{x},t) = \frac{\partial \vec{D}(\vec{x},t)}{\partial t} + \vec{i}_e(\vec{x},t)$$

$$\text{rot } \vec{E}(\vec{x},t) = -\frac{\partial \vec{B}(\vec{x},t)}{\partial t}$$

$$\text{div } \vec{D}(\vec{x},t) = \rho_e(\vec{x},t) \qquad (2)$$

$$\text{div } \vec{B}(\vec{x},t) = 0$$

In this case, the equations of the same forms are satisfied in the moving K' system. Those are as below.

$$\text{rot}' \vec{H}'(\vec{x}',t') = \frac{\partial \vec{D}'(\vec{x}',t')}{\partial t'} + \vec{i}'_e(\vec{x}',t')$$

$$\text{rot}' \vec{E}'(\vec{x}',t') = -\frac{\partial \vec{B}'(\vec{x}',t')}{\partial t'}$$

$$\text{div}' \vec{D}'(\vec{x}',t') = \rho'_e(\vec{x}',t')$$

$$\text{div}' \vec{B}'(\vec{x}',t') = 0 \qquad (3)$$

In this case, $\vec{D}$ and $\vec{H}$ are transformed as below.

$D'_x(\vec{x}',t') = D_x(\vec{x},t)$

$D'_y(\vec{x}',t') = [D_y(\vec{x},t)-(\beta/c)H_z(\vec{x},t)]/(1-\beta^2)^{\frac{1}{2}}$

$D'_z(\vec{x}',t') = [D_z(\vec{x},t)-(\beta/c)H_y(\vec{x},t)]/(1-\beta^2)^{\frac{1}{2}}$

$H'_x(\vec{x}',t') = H_x(\vec{x},t)$

$H'_y(\vec{x}',t') = [H_y(\vec{x},t)+vD_z(\vec{x},t)]/(1-\beta^2)^{\frac{1}{2}}$

$H'_z(\vec{x}',t') = [H_z(\vec{x},t)-vD_y(\vec{x},t)]/(1-\beta^2)^{\frac{1}{2}}$

$$--- (4)$$

On the other hand, current and charge densities are transformed as below.

$i'_x(\vec{x}',t') = [i_x(\vec{x},t)-c\beta\rho_e(\vec{x},t)]/(1-\beta^2)^{\frac{1}{2}}$

$i'_y(\vec{x}',t') = i_y(\vec{x},t)$

$i'_z(\vec{x}',t') = i_z(\vec{x},t)$

$\rho'_e(\vec{x}',t') = [\rho_e(\vec{x},t)-(1/c)\beta i_x(\vec{x},t)]/(1-\beta^2)^{\frac{1}{2}}$

$$--- (5)$$

Also, E and B are transformed as below.

$E'_x(\vec{x}',t') = E_x(\vec{x},t)$

$E'_y(\vec{x}',t') = [E_y(\vec{x},t)-vB_z(\vec{x},t)]/(1-\beta^2)^{\frac{1}{2}}$

$E'_z(\vec{x}',t') = [E_z(\vec{x},t)+vB_y(\vec{x},t)]/(1-\beta^2)^{\frac{1}{2}}$

$B'_x(\vec{x}',t') = B_x(\vec{x},t)$

$B'_y(\vec{x}',t') = [B_y(\vec{x},t)+(\beta/c)E_z(\vec{x},t)]/(1-\beta^2)^{\frac{1}{2}}$

$B'_z(\vec{x}',t') = [B_z(\vec{x},t)-(\beta/c)E_y(\vec{x},t)]/(1-\beta^2)^{\frac{1}{2}}$

$$--- (6)$$

In the equation (4), if we put $D_x(\vec{x},t)=D_y(\vec{x},t)=D_z(\vec{x},t)\equiv0$, we obtain the following.

$D'_x(\vec{x}',t) = 0$

$D'_y(\vec{x}',t) = [-(\beta/c)H_z(\vec{x},t)]/(1-\beta^2)^{\frac{1}{2}}$ $\quad\quad$ (7)

$D'_z(\vec{x}',t) = [(\beta/c)H_y(\vec{x},t)]/(1-\beta^2)^{\frac{1}{2}}$

The above equation (7) can be utilized for the analysis of the N-machine. In the general case where $\vec{v}=(v_x,v_y,v_z)$, the equation (7) can be extended to the form of a vector product. That is,

$$\vec{D}'(\vec{x}',t') = [1/(1-\beta^2)^{\frac{1}{2}}][(\vec{v}\times\vec{H}(\vec{x},t)]/c^2 \quad (8)$$

The above can be approximated as below.

$$\vec{D}'(\vec{x}',t') = (\vec{v}\times\vec{H}(\vec{x},t)]/c^2 \quad (9)$$

In the paradigm of relativistic EM, $\vec{D}'(\vec{x}',t')$ only exists in the mind of an observer of $(\vec{x},t)$ system. On the contrary, in the paradigm of the absolutism EM, $\vec{D}'(\vec{x}',t')$ is thought to be "real", irrespective of the existence of an observer.

As,

$$\left.\begin{aligned}\vec{x}' &= \vec{x}'(\vec{x},t)\\[1em] t' &= t'(\vec{x},t)\end{aligned}\right\} \quad (10)$$

The equation (9) can be rewritten as,

$$\left.\begin{aligned}\vec{D}'(\vec{x}',t') &= \vec{D}'[\vec{x}'(\vec{x},t),t'(\vec{x},t)]\\[1em] &= \vec{D}(\vec{x},t) = [\vec{v}\times\vec{H}(\vec{x},t)]/c^2\end{aligned}\right\} \quad (11)$$

Now, we will obtain the EMF of an N-machine shown in Fig. 2, by modifying Mr. Sugiyama's treatment from the Standpoint of the EM of absolutism. Concerning the cordinate system (x,y,z), which is absolutely stationary, we consider the revolving system $(r,\omega t)$ with z-cordinate as the axis. Fig. 3. And we identify the revolving system as the copper disk of the N-machine. On the other hand, from the equation (11), we obtain the following.

$$\left.\begin{aligned}D_x &= (v_yH_z)/c^2\\[1em] D_y &= -(v_xH_z)/c^2\\[1em] D_z &= 0\end{aligned}\right\} \quad (12)$$

As to the velocity of the revolving system which is attached to the copper disk, we consider the following two equations.

$$x = r \cos(\omega t)$$

$$y = r \sin(\omega t) \tag{13}$$

The velocities can be obtained as follows.

$$v_x = dx/dt = -r\omega \sin(\omega t) = -y\omega$$

$$v_y = dy/dt = r\omega\cos(\omega t) = x\omega \tag{14}$$

Inserting (14) into (12), we obtain,

$$D_x = (x\omega H_z)/c^2$$

$$D_y = (y\omega H_z)/c^2 \tag{15}$$

Real electrical charge which is created in the copper disk is, in terms of the stationary cordinate, is as follows.

$$\rho = \text{div } \vec{D} = \frac{\partial D_x}{\partial x} + \frac{\partial D_y}{\partial y} = (2\omega H_z)/c^2 > 0 \tag{16}$$

This positive charge is created uniformly in the copper disk. Fig. 4. If we think the uniform positive charge were concentrated in the center, the quantity will be as follows.

$$\rho' = \pi r^2 \rho \tag{17}$$

Inserting (16) into (17), we obtain,

$$\rho' = (2\pi r^2 \omega H_z)/c^2 \tag{18}$$

The electrical field E_r, which is at the distance r from the axis, can be obtained as,

$$E_r = \rho'/(2\pi\varepsilon_0 r) = (r\omega H_z)/(\varepsilon_0 c^2) \tag{19}$$

If we use $c^2 = 1/(\varepsilon_0\mu_0)$, in the above equation, we obtain,

$$E_r = r\omega\mu_0 H_z \tag{20}$$

On the other hand,

$$B_z = \mu_0 H_z \tag{21}$$

Inserting (21) into (20), we obtain the following.

$$E_r = r\omega B_z > 0 \tag{22}$$

This expression is the same as the Faraday generator. If the rotation is reversed, the equation (22) changes the sign.

The potential difference between the center and the periphery of a copper disk becomes as below. R is the radius of a copper disk.

$$V = \int_0^R E_r dr = \omega B_z \int_0^R r dr = (1/2)\omega B_z R^2 \tag{23}$$

Thus, the polarity and the quantity of the potential difference are equal to the case of Faraday generator. The exact place where EMF is created is in a copper disk, and is not in a conducting wire, as relativistic EM (Einstein theory) predicts. H.A. Lorentz's theory which presupposes the stationary eather can supply the correct answer. However, in this case, the creation of real electrical charge in a copper disk violates the conservation law of electrical charge in conventional physics.

On the other hand, in the case electrical current flows in the copper disk, "action-reaction" occurs between the copper disk and the disk of permanent magnet (internal force), resulting in no back-torque in N-machine configuration. We cannot but think that the excess energy is extracted from the vacuum. And the conservation law of energy should be extended. The N-phenomenon cannot be understood by the conventional physics, but by the new-paradigm science[3]. On the other side, in the trans-formation formulae of B'(x,t), if we put $B_x(x,t) = B_y(x,t) = B_z(x,t) \equiv 0$, we obtain the following.

$$\vec{B}'_x(\vec{x}',t') = 0$$

$$\vec{B}'_y(\vec{x}',t') = (\beta/c)E_z(\vec{x},t)/(1-\beta^2)^{\frac{1}{2}}$$

$$\vec{B}'_z(\vec{x}',t') = -(\beta/c)E_y(\vec{x},t)/(1-\beta^2)^{\frac{1}{2}} \tag{24}$$

The above equation can be extended in a form of vector product, as below.

$$\vec{B}'(\vec{x}',t') = [1/(1-\beta^2)^{\frac{1}{2}}][-\vec{v} \times \vec{E}(\vec{x},t)]/c^2 \tag{25}$$

From this, we can expect the existence of the electrical version of an N-machine. Fig. 5. This electrical N-machine creates the magnetic energy from the vacuum.

Now, we consider the condition that an N-machine and Faraday-motor pair could rotate, while feeding electrical energy outside. We designate by P_0 the energy for no-load rotation of an N-machine at a speed of rotation. And we designate by a ~0.1[4] the ratio of back torque at an output P_1 of the N-machine. Also, we designate by b the efficiency of the Faraday motor which drives the N-machine, P_2 being an input to the Faraday motor. Then we obtain the following.

$$P_0 + aP_1 = bP_2 \qquad (26)$$

$$P_2 = (P_0 + aP_1)/b \qquad (27)$$

$$P_1/P_2 = bP_1/(P_0 + aP_1) \geq 1 \qquad (28)$$

If the condition (28) should be met, the so-called over-unity operation becomes possible. From equation (28), we obtain,

$$bP_1 \geq P_0 + aP_1 \qquad (29)$$

$$(b-a)P_1 \geq P_0 \qquad (30)$$

$$P_1(b-1) + (1-a)P_1 \geq P_0 \qquad (31)$$

$$P_1(1-a) \geq P_0 + (1-b)P_1$$

$$\geq P_0 + (1-b)P_2 \qquad (32)$$

$$[\text{from equation (28)}]$$

The equation (32) indicates that the over-unity operation will be possible when the energy created from the vacuum is bigger than the energy needed for no-load rotation of the N-machine plus the loss in the Faraday motor. For this situation to happen, one has to use stronger magnets such as Nd magnet and super-conducting magnet. And also, it might be necessary to contain the motor-generator system into a vacuum chamber to reduce the wind-loss.

CONCLUSIONS

Although Mr. Sugiyama's representation at JPI monthly meeting was very interesting, it turned out that the relativistic EM failed to show the correct place where an EMF is created. This had driven this author to write this article.

Acknowledgements should be given to Mr. Sugiyama for referring to his paper in this article. Acknowledgements should also be given to Prof. Sunagawa for quoting the formulae from his book. The true scientific understanding of the N-phenomenon needs the new paradigm of science beyond conventional EM and conventional physics.

REFERENCES

[1] Toshiki Sugiyama, "Theory and Experiment of N-machine", JPI, 20 July, 1990, Tokyo.
[2] Shigenobu Sunagawa, "Theoretical EM", Kinokuniya Pub. Co. Tokyo.
[3] Shiuji Inomata, "Paradigm of New Science-Principia for the 21st Century", Gijutsu Shuppan Pub. Co. Tokyo.
[4] B. DePalma, "On the Possibility of Extraction of Electrical Energy Directly from Space", Autumn Edition, Speculations in Science and Technology, 1990.

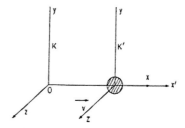

Fig. 1. A material body is in K' system.

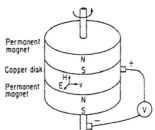

Fig. 2. N-machine

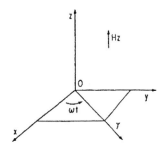

Fig. 3.
Stationary and revolving systems.

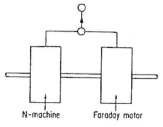

Fig. 6.
N-machine and Faraday motor.

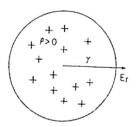

Fig. 4.
Real charge
in a copper disk.

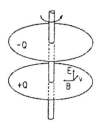

Fig. 5.
Electrical version
of N-machine.

The following homopolar articles by Pelligrini and Kelly both cite problems and conflicts with analyzing the rotating magnetic disk. Kelly also gives credit to this book "for the useful list of references on the subject." These are two-page samples and it is worthwhile to read the entire papers. - TV

Maxwell's equations in a rotating medium: Is there a problem?

Gerald N. Pellegrini
37 Granby Road, Worcester, Massachusetts 01604

Arthur R. Swift
Department of Physics and Astronomy, University of Massachusetts, Amherst, Massachusetts 01003

(Received 22 September 1994; accepted 23 February 95)

In 1908 Einstein and Laub used special relativity to predict that a moving magnetic dipole develops an electric dipole moment. The classic 1913 experiment of Wilson and Wilson on a polarizable, permeable medium rotating in an external magnetic field has long been cited as verifying this prediction. We argue that since the experiment involved rotation rather than uniform translation, it did not test special relativity. The analysis should properly be done in a rotating coordinate system. The field equations for a rotating object are well known and the analysis is straightforward, but the result disagrees with the Wilson experiment. After carefully examining all steps in the derivation, we conclude that either the experiment is wrong or the theoretical analysis must be modified. One possible resolution of the conflict is the hypothesis that the dielectric constant ϵ and permeability μ are well defined only in a frame in which the medium is at rest and time and space are orthogonal coordinates. © *1995 American Association of Physics Teachers.*

I. INTRODUCTION

In this day and age no one doubts the correctness and compatibility of special relativity and classical electrodynamics. However, there is an obscure corner of the subject that generates controversy even in the latter half of the 20th century. How does one extend relativistic electrodynamics to material media? A consensus has developed when the medium is in uniform motion.[1] There is a history of confusion when the medium is rotating.[2,3] This paper addresses one unresolved question. One of us has approached the same issue from a different viewpoint.[4] The equivalence principle and the principle of general covariance provide a definite prescription for extending Maxwell's equations to accelerated frames.[5] Although the choice of fundamental fields in a rotating coordinate system is ambiguous, there is no inconsistency in the vacuum formulation of electrodynamics.[6] Inside a material medium, it is necessary to deal with the polarization P and magnetization M. General covariance dictates the form of the field equations, as long as the origin of P and M is not specified. However, the constitutive equations $P = [(\epsilon - 1)/4\pi]E$ and $M = 1/4\pi(1 - 1/\mu)B$ are not valid in every frame. The physics of the medium becomes important.

Our interest in this subject was triggered by a reevaluation of a classic experiment[7] that provides an empirical founda-

tion for our faith in the correctness and compatibility of special relativity and electrodynamics. Although the experiment was done on a rotating medium, it was assumed that a rotating frame approximates a frame in uniform motion. We analyze the experiment as a test of physics in a rotating medium. Correctly done the theory predicts a result different from that obtained by assuming that special relativity can be used. Since the experiment verified the prediction of special relativity, we have a fundamental conflict between theory and experiment.

According to special relativity a moving magnetic dipole moment m develops an electric dipole moment $p = v/c \times m$. Einstein and Laub[8] proposed an experiment to test this prediction. If an insulating slab of material with dielectric constant ϵ and permeability μ moves through a magnetic field with uniform velocity, the resulting magnetization density should be accompanied by a polarization density. The electric field associated with the polarization contributes to the measurable potential between the opposite faces of the slab. It is difficult to create a uniformly moving slab of material in the laboratory. In 1913 M. Wilson and H. A. Wilson[7] published the results of an experiment in which a rotating medium was substituted for one in uniform motion. The assumption was that rotation is locally equivalent to uniform motion. The electric potential that they measured agreed with the prediction of special relativity.

back to the standard rotating coordinate system produces both magnetization and polarization. Equations (28) are replaced by

$$\nabla \times (\mathbf{B}') = 4\pi(\nabla \times \mathbf{M}'), \tag{56a}$$

$$\nabla \cdot [\mathbf{E}' + 4\pi(\mathbf{v} \times \mathbf{M}') - \mathbf{v} \times \mathbf{B}''] = 0. \tag{56b}$$

The magnetic field is $\mathbf{B}' = 4\pi \hat{\mathbf{e}}_z M'$. If $\nabla \cdot \mathbf{E}' = 0$ everywhere, the electric field is zero inside the cylinder as well as outside. In the laboratory frame there is an internal electric field $\mathbf{E} = -4\pi\rho\omega M' \hat{\mathbf{e}}_\rho$. This field is produced by the radial polarization density $\mathbf{P} = \rho\omega M' \hat{\mathbf{e}}_\rho$. Since $\nabla \cdot \mathbf{P} \neq 0$, there is a nonzero polarization charge density inside the rotating cylinder. However, the net charge is zero, and there is no external electric field in the laboratory frame.

There is a conceptual difficulty with the proposed modification of the field equations in the rotating coordinate system. As we saw in the analysis of a rotating permanent magnet with $\epsilon = 1$, there is a nonzero charge density in the rotating frame associated with $-\nabla \cdot \mathbf{P}' = -\nabla \cdot (\mathbf{v} \times \mathbf{M}'') \neq 0$. To order v/c the laboratory and rotating frame polarizations are the same. A magnet that is not rotating has no charge density; but a magnet that is rotating has a charge density in its local rest frame! Intuitively we would expect that a magnet should be locally neutral whatever its state of motion.

VI. CONCLUSIONS

A careful analysis of the electromagnetic fields associated with a rotating material object reveals an apparent conflict between theory and experiment. If the Wilson experiment is wrong, the standard analysis of electrodynamics in a rotating coordinate system survives. If the experiment is correct, we must modify our theoretical analysis of the phenomena involved. It is our opinion that the solution to the problem lies in a better understanding of the conditions under which the constitutive equations $\mathbf{P} = [(\epsilon - 1)/4\pi]\mathbf{E}$ and $\mathbf{M} = 1/4\pi(1 - 1/\mu)\mathbf{B}$ are valid. There is no ambiguity in an inertial frame, but the situation is more complicated in a rotating frame. It might be necessary to focus on the definition of the time coordinate and simultaneity. We definitely conclude that the conventional theory applied in the conventional way does not describe the results of existing experiments.

ACKNOWLEDGMENTS

We want to thank Barry Holstein for his continued skepticism and Bob Krotkov for always asking the penetrating question. One of us (G.N.P.) want to thank Hussein Yilmaz for his continued interest in and frequent conversations about this problem.

APPENDIX

The transformation between the laboratory frame and the rotating frame is accomplished by the set of equations

$$t' = t, \tag{A1a}$$

$$x' = x \cos \omega t + y \sin \omega t, \tag{A1b}$$

$$y' = -x \sin \omega t + y \cos \omega t, \tag{A1c}$$

$$z' = z. \tag{A1d}$$

Rotating coordinates carry the prime. According to the rules of general covariance a four-tensor defined in an inertial frame can be calculated in any other coordinate system by means of a tensor transformation. In particular contravariant four-vectors J^α, contravariant four-tensors $F^{\alpha\beta}$, and covariant four-tensors $F_{\alpha\beta}$ transform according to

$$J'^\alpha = \frac{\partial x'^\alpha}{\partial x^\gamma} J^\gamma, \tag{A2a}$$

$$F'^{\alpha\beta} = \frac{\partial x'^\alpha}{\partial x^\gamma} \frac{\partial x'^\beta}{\partial x^\delta} F^{\gamma\delta}, \tag{A2b}$$

$$F'_{\alpha\beta} = \frac{\partial x^\gamma}{\partial x'^\alpha} \frac{\partial x^\delta}{\partial x'^\beta} F_{\gamma\delta}. \tag{A2c}$$

If we define the matrices $N_{\gamma\alpha} \equiv \partial x^\gamma/\partial x'^\alpha$ and $N'_{\gamma\alpha} \equiv \partial x'^\gamma/\partial x^\alpha$, then $J' = N'J$, $F' = N'FN''$ (contravariant), $F' = N'FN$ (covariant). The matrices N' and N are

$$N' = \begin{pmatrix} 1 & 0 & 0 & 0 \\ \omega y' & \cos \omega t & \sin \omega t & 0 \\ -\omega x' & -\sin \omega t & \cos \omega t & 0 \\ 0 & 0 & 0 & 1 \end{pmatrix}, \tag{A3a}$$

$$N = \begin{pmatrix} 1 & 0 & 0 & 0 \\ -\omega y & \cos \omega t' & -\sin \omega t' & 0 \\ \omega x & \sin \omega t' & \cos \omega t' & 0 \\ 0 & 0 & 0 & 1 \end{pmatrix}. \tag{A3b}$$

Note that N and N' are simply related by changing the sign of ω and interchanging primed and unprimed coordinates. The transformation back to inertial coordinates is obtained by reversing the sign of ω. Using $J' = N'J$ and $F' = N'FN$, we find that

$$\rho' = \rho, \tag{A4a}$$

$$j'_x = \omega y' \rho + \cos \omega t j_x + \sin \omega t j_y, \tag{A4b}$$

$$j'_y = -\omega x' \rho - \sin \omega t j_x + \cos \omega t j_y, \tag{A4c}$$

$$j'_z = j_z, \tag{A4d}$$

and

$$E'_x = \cos \omega t E_x + \sin \omega t E_y + \omega x' B_z, \tag{A5a}$$

$$E'_y = -\sin \omega t E_x + \cos \omega t E_y + \omega y' B_z, \tag{A5b}$$

$$E'_z = E_z - \omega y B_y - \omega x B_x, \tag{A5c}$$

$$B'_x = \cos \omega t B_x + \sin \omega t B_y, \tag{A5d}$$

$$B'_y = -\sin \omega B_x + \cos \omega t B_y, \tag{A5e}$$

Physics Essays

volume 12, number 2, 1999

Experiments on Unipolar Induction

A.G. Kelly

Abstract

Novel experiments on the relative motion of conductors and magnets are described. In contrast with the currently accepted interpretation, it is shown that the field of a magnet rotates with the magnet about its north-south axis. Faraday's law is shown to be a particular case of a more general rule.

Key words: unipolar induction, magnetism and electricity, Faraday's law, relative motion, Faraday generator, magnetic field, lines of force

1. INTRODUCTION

This paper gives a description of a series of novel experiments on the relative motion of conductors and magnets.

Faraday[1] showed in 1832 that a current was generated in a conductor in each of the following cases:

(i) The pole of a magnet is moved laterally near a stationary conductor.

(ii) A conductor is moved laterally near the pole of a stationary magnet.

(iii) A conductor is rotated upon the north-south axis of a nearby stationary magnet.

But, he also showed the following:

(i) When a magnet and conductor are rotated in unison upon the north-south axis of the magnet, a current is generated in the conductor.

(ii) When a magnet is rotated about its north-south axis, no current is caused in a nearby stationary conductor.

He concluded[1] that "rotating the magnet causes no difference in the results; for a rotating and a stationary magnet produce the same effect upon the moving copper." In 1852 he said "No mere rotation of a bar magnet on its axis, produces any induction effect on circuits exterior to it" and "The system of power in a magnet must not be considered as revolving with the magnet."[1]

The following tests that reproduced Faraday's results have been identified: Lecher,[2] Barnett,[3] Fehrle,[4] Pegram,[5] Kennard,[6] Cramp and Norgrove,[7] Then,[8] and Das Gupta.[9]

The anomaly, where the rotation of a conductor and a magnet about the north-south axis of the magnet does not produce reciprocal results, has been the subject of much controversy over the intervening years. The present experiments were carried out to further investigate this phenomenon.

2. PRELIMINARY EXPERIMENTS

In this section is described a preliminary series of experiments, which reproduce the results of those earlier authors.

The apparatus (see Figs. 1 and 2) is composed of two concentric shafts. On one shaft is mounted an aluminum disc, which forms the conductor, and on the other shaft is mounted a magnet (for "magnet" read "solenoid" as appropriate). The magnet and the disc can be rotated independently or in unison. A galvanometer is connected between carbon brushes rubbing on the rim and the axis of the disc. The galvanometer sensitivity is 1.42 μV and 0.066 μA/mm.

A disc is equivalent to a single piece of conductor rotating about the axis; this has been confirmed by replacing the disc with a single radial conductor connected to an outer ring, from which the voltage is taken. This shows that no circulation of currents in the disc contributes to the results.

The apparatus using a permanent magnet is shown in Fig. 1, with the north-south axis of the magnet on the axis of the driving shaft. The magnet is on the left and the aluminum disc in the center foreground. The driving motor and the controller are behind the magnet. Two pairs of driving pulleys are on the right, and the belt can be changed from one pair to the other. By bolting the two pulleys together, the magnet and the disc can be rotated in unison. By twisting one of two driving belts, the magnet and the disc can be rotated in opposing directions. The galvanometer is, for the purpose of the photograph, placed in the back right corner; its normal position was at a distance of 1 m left of the magnet. The distance between the disc and the magnet can be adjusted. The magnet has a head-and-shoulders shape and is 35 mm in length; the dark central portion (22 mm long in the north-south direction) is of ceramic material, and the two bright side portions (each 8.5 mm long) of ferrous material. The diameter of the ceramic portion is 166 mm, and that of the ferrous parts 148.5 mm. The disc is 155 mm in diameter and 5 mm wide.

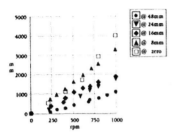

Figure 5. Variation of distance from disc to magnet.

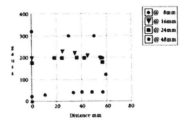

Figure 6. Field at magnet.

In Fig. 9 are shown two different arrangements of a circuit that is totally external to the magnet and which is cut (a net) twice by the lines. The apparatus is constructed so that the complete circuit back to the galvanometer (but not the galvanometer itself, which is situated on the axis of the magnet and at a distance of 1 m) can be rotated. The connections to and from the galvanometer are via two slip-rings on the end of the driving shaft, which are on the extreme left of the driving shaft in Fig. 1. In this way, connections to the disc rim and to the shaft can be brought out to the galvanometer as the apparatus is rotated. The connection from the rim of the disc is made via an insulated wire threaded through the core of the driving shaft and thence out to one of the slip-rings on the left-hand end of the shaft; this connection cannot be seen in Fig. 1. Similarly, connections can be brought from the rim of the magnet; this latter connection is to be seen in Fig. 1.

In Table I are shown the test results. The tests are described in the order in which they appear in the table. First, consider a circuit which is totally external to the magnet, as in Fig. 9. No voltage is generated in the following cases:

(a) The circuit alone is rotated; this is the total circuit composed of the disc and the leads to and from the galvanometer. The circuit concerned cuts the stationary lines twice and therefore there is no resulting voltage. Note that this is different from the earlier experiments where rotation of the disc alone yielded a voltage; the difference between the two cases will be later explained.

(b) The magnet alone is rotated; this gives the same result as in the earlier tests. The moving lines cut the stationary circuit twice, and therefore there is no resulting voltage.

(c) Both the magnet and the whole circuit are rotated in unison. There is no relative motion between the lines

and the circuit and therefore there can be no resulting voltage. Again, this result is different from the earlier case, where only the magnet and the disc (but not the rest of the circuit, composed of the leads to and from the galvanometer) were rotated in unison; the difference will be explained below.

Test (c) does not seem to have been repeated since it was done by Faraday. These results are all in conformity with the proposal that the lines rotate with the magnet.

In Fig. 10, the lines cut the circuit but once (net). This is the Faraday generator. The body of the magnet forms part of the conducting circuit. The circuit is G-B-[through the body of the conducting magnet]-A-G. The spinning disc used in the earlier experiments is replaced by the spinning conducting magnet body. The same effect could be obtained by attaching the disc to the face of the magnet and rotating the two together, as in the earlier tests using a rotating disc; the voltage would be measured from the rim of the disc to the axle. In Fig. 10, the nearer the connection A is to the middle of the magnet, the greater the effect.

Tests (d), (e), and (f) in Table I are on the Faraday generator. The standard explanation of this phenomenon has been that the magnet cuts its own lines as it rotates. It is a phenomenon that has heretofore never been satisfactorily explained. In case (d) spinning the magnet generates a voltage in the lead A-G from the rim of the magnet to the galvanometer, because the rotating lines cut that lead mainly once (Fig. 10). In case (e) spinning the leads alone produces the same result, because the lead A-G cuts the stationary lines once. Faraday commented that the conductor crossed the lines once in this test, but did not continue with this distinction in his other tests. Rotating both in unison (case (f)) gives a zero result, because there is no relative motion between the magnet and the leads; this test does not seem to have been done before. These results are also in conformity with the proposal that the lines rotate with the magnet.

INDEX

A

B

C

G

H

Lowes, F.   4

M

S

T

U

V

W

Z